SOCIAL THEORY AND CRITICAL UNDERSTANDING

G. Llewellyn Watson

UNIVERSITY
PRESS OF
AMERICA

Library of Congress Cataloging in Publication Data

Watson, G. Llewellyn.
  Social theory and critical understanding.

  Bibliography: p.
  Includes indexes.
  1. Sociology--Philosophy. 2. Sociology--Canada.
3. Polemics. 4. Sociology of knowledge. 5. Pluralism
(Social sciences) I. Title.
HM24.W286 1982   301'.01   82-45010
ISBN 0-8191-2590-3
ISBN 0-8191-2591-1 (pbk.)

To the Memory of My PARENTS

ACKNOWLEDGMENTS

I wish to thank the Editors of The Canadian Journal of Sociology and of Human Mosaic for permission to reuse, with minor revisions, material previously published in those journals. I also thank International Publishers of New York for permission to reprint passages from Karl Marx, The Economic and Philosophical Manuscripts of 1844; from Karl Marx, Capital, Volume 1; and from Karl Marx and Friedrich Engels, The German Ideology.

In addition, I would particularly like to thank Judi MacKinnon, our department secretary, for having patiently and skillfully transformed my ragged manuscript into decent typescript for publication; and my wife, Barbara, for her encouragement, relentless scrutiny, and all-round support. Finally, I thank Helen Hudson and James Lyons of University Press of America for the patient understanding, cooperation and professional assistance which they accorded me during the different stages of writing this book.

TABLE OF CONTENTS

It is the political task of the social scientist -
as of any liberal educator - continually to translate
personal troubles into public issues, and public issues
into the terms of their human meaning for a variety of
individuals. It is his task to display in his work
this kind of sociological imagination.

C. Wright Mills, <u>The Sociological Imagination</u>

INTRODUCTION

This book is written on the basis of several intellectual concerns, two of which stand out above the others: one, that there is an overwhelming necessity for a social theory which is unashamedly <u>critical</u> of modern society at all its levels of organization and operations; and two, that there is a need to develop and refine the polemical dimension of intellectual life to a level where free and vigorous discussion of sociological issues can be pursued. These concerns are certainly not original. The tradition of constructive polemics is firmly entrenched and highly respected elsewhere, notably in European intellectual circles (as in the works of Georges Gurvitch in France, and Karl Popper in England); and the critical spirit is also well-developed in Europe. To a lesser extent that spirit can be located in scattered cases in North America, but the polemical challenge presented in the United States in the 1950s by scholars such as C. Wright Mills, was quickly overruled by a sociology intent on rinsing itself of politics, ideology, values and humanism. By a curious type of cultural osmosis, Canada has often been a recipient of traditions established elsewhere; critical sociology and intellectual polemics in sociology do seem, however, to have suffered some blockage.

Both of these concerns animate the pages of this book. But this is not a position or style for which we want to apologize. There are two very important reasons why this posture is crucial. <u>First</u>, there is an important sense in which good critique is almost bound to be polemical, that is to say argumentative and disputatious, for in order to unsettle old ideas, it is often necessary to vigorously dispute their putative authenticity and "law-like" naturalness. The nature of social facts are such that they can never be assumed to be settled, once and for all, like the law of gravity. Too often the theories of modern society casually attribute the source of crises and problems to any-thing but the system itself. A critical viewpoint has the potential of getting to the societal roots of problems generated in society. In the end, this is what it means to be radical.

A <u>second</u> reason for adopting a contentious approach is very much related to the first. It is the fact that good polemics have the potential of poking out of hiding many latent value assumptions and hidden premises that might otherwise remain obscure, yet operative, in intellectual discourse and thought process.

Both of the above positions can offer intellectual enrichment. But, unfortunately, Canadian social scientists tend to shy away from debates or topics that promise to become even mildly polemical. And students, in turn, experience extreme discomfort when it is suggested to them that academic discussions and analyses can be argumentative, yet probing, respectable and explanatory. If anything, we would like to keep alive that tradition so well hoisted by C. Wright Mills, a sociologist who succeeded as Miliband puts it, in proving to a new generation of students what most of their teachers had managed to conceal from them: that social analysis could be probing, tough-minded, critical, relevant, and scholarly; that ideas need not be handled as undertakers handle bodies, with care but without passion; that commitment need not be dogmatic; and that radicalism need not be a substitute for hard thinking.[1] The need to be critical of modern society is often camouflaged by cliches and meaningless phrases such as "rule of law," "the free world," or "human nature"; and uncritical social science never manages to penetrate these well-worn phrases in an effort to enhance our understanding of some of the deep structural problems that these same phrases belie. This book seeks to sharpen our image of some of the problems - theoretical and pragmatic - and themes relevant to a fuller understanding of modern industrial and cosmopolitan societies.

Many of the issues which are debated in the following pages stem, essentially, from my several years of effort to present a social theory which could assume the definition of a critical reflection upon modern society. I have chosen to explore and pursue the particular themes found in this book because of their relative de-emphasis in conventional books on "sociological theory." My hope is that the articulation of these themes will spark some new and necessary debate, even connect with ongoing reflections, research and dialogue, likely to be especially rewarding to students who find it difficult to move from the highly formal and abstract level of much of sociological theory, to the more reflective level of insight.

Anyone who has participated in social science discourse and teaching at the University level in the last two decades, and who has even a mildly critical perspective, can readily recognize the lacunae that exists in the theories that purport to explain industrial society and the lived experiences in such societies. And while it would be presumptuous for this author to suggest that this book will provide sufficient ideas to fill the hiatus, there is the expectation nevertheless that the presentation of the selected ideas will point, once more, to the potential of sociological theory as a critique of society.

The book is intended for undergraduate as well as graduate students, but it is not written as a "text-book," in the conventional sense of that term. Consequently, it is expected that the educated and informed laypersons who are interested in debating some of the received ways of looking at contemporary society, will be amongst its readers. Regular readers of radical journals such as Telos, New Left Review, Science and Society, New German Critique, Politics and Society, Dialectical Anthropology, among others, might perhaps find this presentation somewhat unchallenging, since many of the ideas and concerns expressed here are frequently aired in these journals. Such readers, however, can participate in the debate by helping to translate some of the dense prose of critical theory into meaningful (yet not oversimplified) language by which students can understand the dynamics of modern society. Students typically shy away from the writings of theorists such as Habermas, or Adorno or Marcuse, not because they (students) are lazy, but because the rococo convolutions and the cultivated obscurity of these writers demand heroic stamina which many (especially undergraduates) simply do not have to devote to one area.[2] Yet what the theorists of the critical tradition have to say is penetrating and highly significant. Some of their style, too, eventually terminate in some of the above-mentioned journals, and this fact has provided another justification for airing social theory in a style that is, hopefully, digestible to the busy undergraduate, and the graduate student who searches for some fresh light on old problems.

Specifically, this book seeks to situate social theory in its philosophical (ontological and epistemological) ambiance, from which, of course, the cultural interpretation of human society cannot reasonably be divorced. Generally speaking, the principal questions of ontology have to do with the fundamental nature of the world; while those of epistemology, at least since Descartes, concern the nature and scope of understanding and the very foundation on which our knowledge claims rest. Both these categories, and theoretical sociology, are inextricably intertwined, so much so that one might well insist that an adequate epistemology must itself be a social theory. Indeed, it is difficult to see how social inquiry can be pursued oblivious of epistemology. Even after the impressive developments in science and other modes of knowing in the twentieth century, it is still legitimate to pose the troublesome epistemological question of two centuries ago: what do we, and what can we, know for certain? Once posed in these terms, the question of what constitutes well-grounded knowledge becomes distinctly perplexing, at least for some social inquirers, who recognize that such questions, tied as they are to the very meaning of what it entails to construct social reality, do not always terminate in final truths. In this book, a major aim is to initiate a level of theoretical clarity sufficient to stimulate the reader to rethink or conceive certain social issues in a different light, specifically, from the vantage point of social critique. The idea of a critical social theory as a necessary searchlight of modern complex (and mystifying) society, runs as a permanent descant throughout these essays, and provides the obvious prolegomena to the author's teaching and scholarly pursuits. But this disposition also seeks to broaden the understanding of social systems so as to accurately reflect the temper of our time. Understanding comes not from making good the oversight of others, nor indeed from merely noting what others had not. In theoretical analysis, these ends are often achieved. What is more important, however, and what this book aims for, is to go even further, by disclosing that which is systematically concealed by the apparent facts, and by the form believed to be real.

Chapters 1 and 2 consist of an introduction to the many interlocking elements of social theory: to the ideological, political and humanistic assumptions that inform it. These elements recur throughout the entire text, serving all along to remind the reader of the essentially composite nature of our explanations of social life, and of the role of critical philosophy in social theory. A critical philosophy, like a critical sociology, has the prime task of expositing that all idea-systems, including social theory itself, as well as science, incubate in social structure and must be approached on this premise. Chapter one, in particular, is purposefully discursive, in such a way that even if critique is not produced in it, it evokes the question of the historical contexts of, and the potential ideology in, systems of thought, including sociology. Social theory cannot avoid these sorts of queries.

Chapter 3 is the "oldest" essay in this book. It was first written in the Spring of 1974 for the Eighth World Congress of Sociology held that Summer in Toronto, but it was never formally presented at the Congress. In its draft stage, it elicited near-hysterical, chauvinistic, reader-reaction, and was withdrawn from the Congress' program. It was subsequently published in the Canadian Journal of Sociology the following year. It is presented here essentially as it appeared in the journal, with only minor revisions, but with a postscript indicating that whilst much important work has been done in Canadian sociology since this essay first appeared, the thrust of the main criticisms articulated earlier, is still valid. Some evidence for this position can be found in the frequency with which this critique is being cited in on-going Canadian sociology. Certain anxieties which are central to this programmatic essay are worth commenting upon, very briefly. Whilst I have not altered the primary thesis of this early essay, I am now a lot less optimistic than I was earlier, about the viability of a close collaboration - for collaboration's sake - between sociology and other disciplines, as that which would ignite the fuse of a Kuhnian social scientific "revolution" which would solve the many social puzzles that confront us. In the professional angst of the mid 1970s, it was imperative to define a renewal in social theory, and to encourage and anticipate some interdisciplinary accord. However, what is now being experienced can best be described as a deep sense of privation, even a dilemma, in that one senses that once-dominant paradigms are dead; yet the new will not be born. In the meantime, it has become quite clear that the fragility of collaboration - indeed, the reason for discontinuity - has a lot to do with the absence, in social science, of a common definition of humankind. The doubts and the anxiety now entertained are, apparently, familiar experiences

xvii

in science. Evidence that "normal science' is incessantly plagued by uncertainties, has been provided by Kuhn in his path-breaking analysis of scientific development.[3] On reflection, it seems that what Kuhn identified as anomalies in normal science, is what is being experienced as a prenatal vacuum. And, apparently, there can be benefits from this experience, for in the effort to fill the vacuum, it is possible that practitioners (in any given science) will be stimulated to engage in novel thinking and to reconsider the largely implicit assumptions of old paradigms. In congruence with Kuhn's contention, the conscious attention paid to previously taken-for-granted details necessitates an increased interest in philosophical problems and analysis. This seems to have held true for this author, as will be recognized if chapter 3 is read in its proper historical and projective contexts.

Chapter 4 centres on the idea of dialectics and its relation to social science thinking. We have argued that the dialectical tradition raises some of the most incisive questions about human society, and that contrary to the generalized idea that the method of the dialectic is a bottomless quagmire, it is in fact a fundamental mirror of human self-activity and philosophical snares. The reason why the dialectical method is so critical for social science is because it involves and overlaps with, both ontology and epistemology. The important issue of reification which this chapter explores continues into chapter 5 where the ideas of Max Weber concerning formal rationality are confronted and critically evaluated. Reification, regardless of its content, emphasizes the permanence and seemingly "natural" shape of the present social arrangements, thereby occluding and/or limiting alternative conceptions of social reality and eventually contributing to the destruction of subjectivity. It amounts to the loss of historical memory. Of this tendency in modern society we offer some constructive criticisms. Chapters 6 through 8 focus on how we may sharpen our understanding of certain aspects of Canadian society.

Throughout, we have attempted to offer concrete, illustrative examples of lived experiences where social theory can intervene to provide sharp understanding of historical situations. Among the selected topics opened for discussion is that of socio-cultural pluralism, a thesis which has not received the attention that it deserves in Canadian sociology, not least, one suspects, because there are some points of serious conceptual confusion in current discussions of this subject. Such confusion, no doubt, serves to discourage students from a closer examination of pluralism. It is suggested that the sociology of knowledge (chapter 8) is an area that is potentially significant for unmasking the interests and biases which perhaps, unconsciously, influence the structure of all ideas, including those on pluralism. The sociology of knowledge requires, above all, that the sociologist's own thinking about a distorted reality should itself be constantly questioned, for the thinking of the sociologist is not immune to the prevailing social conditions that shape human consciousness. The book ends with a brief sketch of what it means to speak of a critical theory, what its assumptions and aims are and what kinds of limitations it confronts in the context of modern-day realities. This final chapter also discusses some of the persistent dilemmas and contradictions of modern social theory and highlights the contested nature of sociological theory as that theory is welded to philosophy, history and claims to scientificity.

Constructive criticism is that which tests and revitalizes scholarship. Therefore, any bombardment of criticism which this book might evoke will have to be regarded as a significant test case in social theory, in that, we have given the impression throughout that sociologists should be willing to put up for public judgment and assessment, their own peevishness, if they think others might benefit therefrom. In a word, we have insisted that sociological self-images are an important datum of social theory. With the full awareness that positivistic sociology is the dominant posture in North America, and with the understanding that that posture is at best distrustful of, and some-times hostile to, the humanistic perspective of the sort portrayed in this book, we have nevertheless striven to present social perceptions and hints having the potential for creative thought and practice. Hope-fully, some will find enough stimulation and encouragement within these pages to pursue further some specific issues that would otherwise have evaporated, were they not brought under discussion in this particular context.

In short, this book seeks to open dialogue and

discussion on a series of themes and issues where communication seems to have been frozen, and in the process it will, hopefully, widen our horizon and sharpen our grasp of the growingly complex world around us. Unlike the standard books in the area of social theory, this book exhorts students to think critically about what they are being asked to imbibe, and to grasp the macro importance of the ideas that happen to be in currency. This approach holds the best chance of reaching understanding, as opposed to unreflective, visceral recitation of the virtues of modern society. Finally, while the book focuses specifically on Canadian themes and issues, its theoretical orbit is sufficiently broad to be applicable to other contexts that are premised on the liberal democratic model of industrial society. It harbors no pretence in being comprehensive. Indeed, its objectives are very modest: to introduce the student of social and political theory to a structure of ideas with which he/she can begin to sketch a critique and a deeper understanding of the contemporary social and political order. The social critique which is pursued is one which should not only identify the many contradictions in our understanding of the world, but should locate their very roots in the internality of society.

One final word must be said about the style followed in this book. The many references to "man" in contexts clearly involving men and women, and to "him" or "his" when what is meant is his/her, etc., are made simply for convenience and efficiency of expression. They are not meant to carry a sexist bias, for the reference is always to humankind in general.

CHAPTER I

TOWARD A SOCIAL THEORY FOR OUR TIMES

The Ideological Aspect of Theory

Anyone bold enough nowadays to write a book or even an article on the topic of social theory runs the risk of being taken less than seriously by the liberal academic community as a whole, for there is a persistent point of view today that we have not discovered anything new since the great masters - Marx, Durkheim, Weber, Simmel, and others - propounded their theories up to a century ago. There is also the point of view that, as one sociologist succintly put it, "perhaps we have enough social theory," therefore what we need now are simply fresh insights into already existing situations so that we can interpret anew our own historical period.[1] There is an air of plausibility surrounding these observations. Yet they do not go far enough in the diagonstic sense, for it should also be added that one of the major problems of contemporary social theory is that sociologists and other social scientists are unwilling to face up to the important fact that a social theory is closer to a belief system[2] or an ideology than it is to some ideal conception of science in the positivistic sense. If Althusser is right in his contention that there is a constant struggle to free science from ideology and that ideology occupies science, haunts it and lie in wait for it,[3] then it is difficult to see how social scientists in their various quests for scientificity and purity can completely avoid the ideological fact. That would be no more possible than, in C. Wright Mills' excellent phrase, "pretending to study the process of birth but ignoring motherhood."

This chapter, then, sketches, albeit in a hesitant and tentative way, some of the ideological aspects of social theory. Social theory, as used in this book, is to be understood as a critical reflection upon society as social arrangements. A perfectly logical place to begin this discussion is to reflect on what has been given as <u>sociological theory</u> and what they omit, dismiss or deny. Here, it is important to note that many of the standard "Readers," that is to say, collections of essays in Sociological Theories, and some of the well-known, and recent books on theory, simply do not incorporate ideas from this perspective

1

into their overall presentation.[4] The sociology of knowledge, for all its unmasking potential, lives on the periphery of accepted knowledge, from whence it can easily be pushed completely outside the domain of what is accepted as knowledge. This situation was recently demonstrated by the sad fact that in the transition from the third to the fourth edition of Lewis Coser and B. Rosenberg's Sociological Theory, 1976, the chapter on "The Sociology of Knowledge" was dropped. This factor can only serve to focus attention away from the sociology of knowledge, the very perspective that would normally be expected to raise probing questions about the origin and growth of different bodies of ideas, including those espoused by sociology itself. By such manouvres, sociologists, as one group in society acting as the gatekeepers of knowledge, manage to deflect attention from their own assumptions, and ideological upthrust. In this light, it can be argued that an ideology is a set of beliefs that typically masks or conceals aspects of reality in the interest of dominant social groups. As such, an ideology is one among a series of belief systems in society. Given this understanding, the question can then be raised as to whether the dominant paradigms in sociology are not simply articulated ideologies presenting only partial and highly selective aspects of reality, concealing social contradictions, yet at the same time claiming universality and comprehensiveness.

Paul Baran poses questions of this nature when he argued that bourgeois society appears essentially as a comprehensive world outlook which, while reflecting the class interests of the dominant class, prevents society as a whole, but especially those directly enmeshed in the labor process, from reflecting on the irrationality [of the capitalist system] and from considering historical alternatives to the going concern. Insofar as ideologies typically correspond to the standpoints of class or social group whose vested interest inhibits critical reflection and a total view, they are "false" and "illusory" in the Marxian sense, not taken to mean that the content of idea-systems is a mere reflection of material life, but in the sense that ideas which are thought to be of general or universal validity are, in fact, the expressions of sectional class interests.[5] In this light, ideologies serve to obscure the actuality of the world, thus helping to prevent the possibility of change. By this same token, the beliefs that constitute an ideology have to be sophisticated and

2

relatively consistent, even if their underlying logic
evades us, or they would not be able to withstand, for
any length of time, the constant scrutiny and
assessment to which they are invariably put. This does
not mean that dominant ideologies accurately reflect
reality. Sociologists in the Marxist tradition have
long recognized that the nature, scope and functions of
ideologies change from one historical period to another.
Cultural Marxists, in particular, from Lukacs to
Habermas, have come to argue that the nature and role
of dominant ideologies in "late capitalism" are far
more sinister and far more insidious than in earlier
periods. In the view of the theorists of the
Frankfurt School, ideology in the modern context has
successfully produced, among other things, automatons
charged with the infinite and mindless consumption of
commodities. At the ideational level, what the
<u>knowledge industry</u> produces takes on all the saliency
and features of a "commodity," as well, prized for the
exchange value that is generated rather than for the
intrinsic utility which may be involved. Insofar as
dominant ideologies serve to legitimize and justify the
prevailing distribution of resources, including power,
and to provide the conceptual foundation that upholds a
political system, they cannot be expected to serve the
population at large. Neither can it be assumed that
such ideologies will be shared by the general
population. One suspects, in fact, that one of the
principal aims of dominant ideologies is to encourage
the fragmentation of thought, and thus to cloud the
political and social perception of the going situation,
and indeed to mystify reality. It is thus that John
Rex argues that the layman who seeks to understand and
command the modern world is subject to a double process
of mystification. The first is the mystification of
the world through ideological meanings. The second is
the mystification which arises in sociology itself when,
after arousing a hope of a demystified reality, it then
(a) makes the task seem enormously difficult, if not
logically impossible, (b) uses such language in doing
this that, even if it does claim to point the way to
successful understanding, provides tools of a kind
which only a highly sophisticated craftsman could use.[6]
Far too many sociologists naively believe that
sociology comprises a straightforward dualism: facts
on the one hand, pure untainted and free from values;
and on the other ideology, by which is often meant any
social explanation that unashamedly questions ingrained
assumptions and perceptions. Yet, we know enough in

the sociology of ideas to realize that even in the
secluded world of science competing paradigms win out,
one over the other, not <u>necessarily</u> and always on the
basis of the facts as interpreted by the judges of
paradigms, but often on the basis of ideological
considerations. A consequence of this naive view is
that the ordinary citizens see no need to pose, or are
simply not confident in posing questions about, the
standard definitions of political reality, of concepts
such as "justice," "equality'," or even the ends of
social programs. In essence, the predominant tendency
is to accept all forms of destructive irrationality as
the "natural" order of things.

There is much in the Canadian experience that
illustrates the depth of this type of cultural
resignation and fateful acceptance of social
arrangements. But as Clement[7] has amply shown, neither
is that by accident. Rather the ideology of the
dominant (identifiable) class accounts decisively for
the acceptance of the existing social order. The
mentality of the dominant class has been the dominant
mentality which seeps down to all the other classes -
the former truly dictate what we read as daily news,
what we value in the market place, and how we should
compare our existence with the unfortunates of the
Third World. The discoveries and empirical analysis in
Clement's work are central to the concerns in this book,
for they reveal a number of key points which are highly
problematic in modern social theory. First, the
findings expose the existence of the ideological
citadel that all critical social thought inevitably
confronts. Whether the sociologist retreats from that
reality or seeks to understand and explain that
phenomenon in the socio-historical context of his/her
work is <u>the</u> problem, and no doubt one of the tests of a
critical sociologist. Second, the analysis of interlocking types of domination - economic, political and
ideological, provide clear insight into the reasons for
the intractable nature of resigned consciousness. The
subterranean linkages between knowledge and interests,
as well as between cultural domination and the
production of knowledge, critically influence which
ideas come into communicable prominence in society, and
why. Third, given the sort of structural overview
offered by Clement, it seems inescapable that the
practising sociologist of the modern period could fail
to make a critique of ideology central to his/her work.
If ideology is in fact to be understood in <u>cultural</u>

terms, as we think it should, then it is imperative
that we consider it in terms of the place it occupies
in the broader canvas of socio-political life. We may,
accordingly, come to realize the simple fact that to
the extent that the consciousness of groups and classes
in society (and class societies such as Canada) is
effectively shaped by the ideology of the dominant
groups and their priorities, these same ideologies
foreclose critical reflection and emancipatory thought.
This thesis has been recently documented in the
Canadian context by Marchak. Not only does her analysis helps us understand why populations in advanced
industrial societies happily believe things which are
manifestly contradictory, and things which they are in
a good position to know are false, but _why_ ideologies
live and are thus inevitably embroiled in political and
economic struggles. Thus, she has shown that in Canada
even the dominant ideology of liberalism, for all its
widespread acceptance, simply fails to answer a
number of key "why" questions about society and social
processes. Its "progressional view of history" does
not structurally explain conditions such as poverty in
the midst of affluence, regional disparity despite
equalization payments, the extent of foreign ownership
in Canada, the changes that have taken place in the
social organization of industrial society, and other
paradoxes. Consequently, in spite of vast changes
within capitalism over the past century, it is still
possible, as she puts it, to hear

> speeches to the Chamber of Commerce
> [which] reflect the same _abiding_
> _faith_ in progress, material pros-
> perity and general affluence; the
> same evaluation of private property,
> individualism and achievement; the
> same belief in the existence of
> equality and opportunity.[8]

Liberalism is an ideology which rests on the premise
that the individual is more important than the society,
and does not therefore look beyond private experiences
for explanations of events. Small wonder one never
hears of the _sociology_ of inflation these days, only
the psychology of inflation, and other social processes.
Inflation is supposed to be a national crisis, yet it
is somehow always seen as private trouble, if we are to
believe the pontificating politicians. Liberalism is
also a belief in private enterprise, individual

achievement, and exponential growth, and it assumes classlessness and equal opportunity. Curiously, as the ideology of capitalism, it doesn't even explain (but explains away) economic power, the "Law" of supply and demand, and private ownership. In Marchak's words, there is always a "misfit between theory and fact."

People who perceive the world through the lenses of the eternal verities, of course, never can question the existing social arrangements, which they see as fixed and unchangeable. Neither are they able to imagine any historical alternative to the given situation: alternatives don't occur to them. There is no critical gut to such a world view, which explains why liberalism, while not serving as an adequate explanation of reality, nevertheless persists and thrives. According to Marchak, liberalism's version of the world thrives because in the continuing struggle between competing versions of the real world, liberalism never appears to its adherents as an ideology but as public knowledge; second, the strength of the liberal ideology lies in its apparent accommodation to diversity; third, it explains those realities that people could see, feel, experience even if only partially; and fourth, it establishes goals that seem eminently attainable, even if there are noticeable inconsistencies between the avowed belief and historical fact. As Marchak concludes:

> If capitalism could produce jobs,
> affluence, steady employment, mobility,
> and a sense of optimism and well-being,
> then capitalism could be seen as a
> positive good.

Even with its half-truths, cliches, shibboleths and hidden premises, it manages to "provide positive judgments on the status quo, shows why it is good, makes people feel protective of it." As an ideology which parades as a comprehensive world outlook, but which reflects only the interests of the dominant class, it "legitimates the status quo by selectively informing people what the status quo is."[9] It may very well be, then, as one Marxist thesis has it, that consciousness arises in the process of confronting and solving the problems of existence. But if for most of us there is little opportunity for meaningful input into the definition and articulation of those problems, the development of consciousness must necessarily be fortuitous and still-born. It is in this context that the role and responsibility of the intellectual is revealed. The position being taken here is that intellectuals have a responsibility to develop and espouse <u>critical</u> reason, to undertake ruthless criticism of everything that exists, to carry on rational inquiry to wherever it may lead. In a word,

> The role of the intellectual or the man of reason is to understand the reality beyond the appearances and to uncover the meaning of specific acts within the context of the larger historical project.[10]

For the sociologist who seeks to comprehend contemporary social reality with its diverse and sometimes eventful convulsions, there is the real possibility to make the university something of an ideological battleground in which the problems of society are debated, with passion, but rigorously and with analytical imagination, and outlines of a better society explored. While that in itself is highly desirable and should be part of the definition of the university, in reality the problem of ideology is not negotiated and freely debated, in spite of its multi-faceted relations to science and to a wide body of thought in human society. We often hear that the social sciences don't know enough to foster deep understanding. Yet it does seem that their fatal shortcoming lies in their partial approaches, their pragmatic short-circuiting, their lack of <u>critical</u> insight, and in the fact that they do not <u>incorporate</u> into their corpus of knowledge the understanding of what is historically possible. Any number of disciplines can be ideological or scientific; it depends on whether or not they give an objective account of the socio-economic, political and other structural processes that shape the human condition. If we fail to understand the many complex and powerful aspects of modern capitalist societies, it is not because we are congentially incapable of such under-standing. It is rather because we have consistently pretended that it is not that necessary to foster a critique.

The modern-day discussion of ideology in the social science owes much to Mannheim and Marx, and we shall be discussing their ideas in Chapter 8. Both shared certain fundamental premises relating to the problem of

ideology. Both thinkers argued, for instance, that all
thinking is socially determined, and, too, both concur
that there can be no such entity as disinterested
thought. It is this same point that Habermas makes
when he insists that human knowledge is grounded in
interests. But Marx and Mannheim part company when it
comes to explaining the structural locus of ideas and
ideologies in society. In the context of this exercise,
Mannheim's insights into ideology are, nevertheless,
very important. He distinguished between what he
called "particular" ideologies and "total" ideologies.
The former is a belief which expresses the interests of
a particular social group; as such it provides only a
partial and distorted view of reality. The latter, on
the other hand, is a world view or Weltanschauung. In
reaction to this dichotomy, Plamenatz reasons that
ideologies are nearly always partial, and that stance
clearly takes us to Marx, whose principal concern was
to show that bourgeois ideology, because it was
partial, was also debilitatingly distortive. For him
bourgeois social science was ideological because of its
systematic exclusion of any concept of historical
totality. Where Mannheim divided ideas into
ideological or justifications and defense of the
existing order, and utopian, or designs for a new
social order, Marx insisted that any set of ideas that
lay claim to a comprehensive world outlook, while
systematically occluding the vital historical dimension
is ideological and thereby only partially true.

The Mannheimian distinction is useful in understanding the existence of counter-ideologies or utopian
ideas in complex societies. Counter-ideologies, such
as those found in social movements, pose questions
concerning legitimacy, interest-content and values of
the dominant ideology. As such, utopian ideas in this
strict counter sense hold out the possibility of
changing the status quo. This critique may itself
serve as a harbinger of social change. By the same
token that ideologies (dominant) lay claim to the
legitimacy and veracity of their definition of the
situation, utopias (counter-ideologies) present
alternatives. But in ideological struggles, counter-
ideologies do not always succeed. Not only do they
always have to resist stereotyping, distortion of their
viewpoints and outright malicious devaluation, but they
are often negatively labelled and used as scapegoats.
Hence, they find it difficult to overcome social stigma.

In her study, Marchak points out that the chief reasons for the weakness of socialist counter-ideology in Canada lie outside the socialist movements themselves. They are, particularly, the persistent attacks by established powers against any form of socialist thought and the general prosperity enjoyed by the middle class throughout the postwar period in Canada, so that, as in a zero-sum game, the failure of socialism was a manifestation of the success of the liberal ideology. Furthermore, socialists in Canada have been unwilling to manipulate ideology; the evidence shows that the early histories of the Communist Party in Canada and the CCF were marked not only by organizational difficulties and ambiguity in ideology, but also by aggressive attacks by government-inspired national paranoia concerning "socialism," "communism" or other Left movements. In the liberal version of the world, such organizations posed political and social threats to liberal democracy and to the "free" world, that is, the capitalist world.[11] The history of the Women's Liberation movement and the hippie counterculture of the 1960s and 1970s can also be understood in this ideological frame of reference.

Sociological theory has always suffered from the tendency to accentuate certain partial truths, while at the same time denying the possibility of alternative interpretations. There has always been, for instance, the tendency to systematically exclude Marxian concepts and categories from consideration when constructing theories. This makes it possible for sociologists (e.g., H. Barnes in 1966; Daniel Rossides in 1978) to write the entire history of sociology without indicating that Marx had anything to say about society and social relations. The point is that much of modern sociology is cast in ideological terms, eulogies to the "end of ideology" notwithstanding.

The pronounced inability of so much of sociology to explain the contradictions and crises of industrial society, or to enlighten people about the possible causes and consequences of action, is due in large measure to the assumptions upon which conventional sociology builds. Many of these assumptions are akin to those upheld by the dominant liberal ideology that has come to characterize western democracies. Just as the dominant liberal ideology persists inspite of the myths which it contains, so standard sociological myths persist, inspite of the fact that the theories which

9

they help to shape do not serve as adequate explanations of society and history. A social theory for our times must not only confront the myths of conventional wisdom; it must itself be a theory of ideology and a critique of society.

Theory and the Explanation of Cultural Systems

Giambattista Vico, I believe, pointed out somewhere that humans can understand the historical world (if that world is conceived as humanly created) better than the natural world, which we did not create. Paradoxically, nowadays we can find much claim to understanding the natural world, but not the historical. But why? It is apparent that social theory needs to incorporate, not to exclude philosophical reflections about history, about humanly-instituted relations and the social arrangements that inevitably develop over time. Questions concerning the substantive ends of society cannot be conveniently hidden from ongoing critical evaluation. Removal of these questions from consideration compels the intellectual to become a legitimator of the system, or at best a dissenter from certain policies. Pursuit of this standpoint also negates the critical role which the intellectual may potentially play in the society in which he or she lives.

The student new to sociology, or the student who naively accepts that sociology is value-free, is not likely to be automatically sensitized to the ideological poker game which the vast majority of sociologists play. Behind the facade that is regularly presented, namely, that sociology is only concerned with the facts, is the complex operation of ideological forces. It is one of the principal, if dangerous assumptions of positivistic social science, that the social genesis of scientific knowledge and the use made of it are external to science. From this standpoint, scientists tend to excuse themselves from any untoward social end to which their ideas are put. The problem of knowledge, however, is not that easily dodged, as the sociologists of the Frankfurt School have repeatedly pointed out. Thus Habermas points out that science is ideological, which is to say it puts forth claims which we are encouraged to accept on trust; such trust ensures eventually a greater degree of technical control, or of what we discuss below as instrumental domination. Karl Popper's criticism that

10

the sociology of knowledge overlooks the social and public character of science [12] is not at all valid, in that it has always been one of the key concerns of the sociology of knowledge to question the possibility of cognitive self-interests, values and ideology that might typically interfere with, or color the conclusions of all bodies of knowledge including the conclusions of what he calls the "dry sciences."

It is perhaps not difficult to see the importance of the statement that modern social theory begins with epistemological anxiety. Epistemological problems, notably the problem of truth, is never far from the surface in social theory. The position adopted by the Frankfurt School was that truth was not immutable; nor was it absolute.[13] Each period of time has its own truth, and therefore truth as such was not outside the society but was rather contained in its own claims. Like culture, it was not and could not be epiphenomenal. It was historically bound up with the very process of social living, and this means that at no time could the progress of knowledge, which is advanced by successive approximations, be external to the history of humankind. From these successive attempts at understanding human-in-history a type of truth emerges. This was the basis for Marx's statement that the question whether objective truth can be attributed to human thinking is a _practical_ question. Man must prove the truth, he says. In Marx's philosophy of history, historical truths unfold as an _increasing realization_ of human freedom. This distinctly epistemological provocation means no less than that we must constantly ask to what extent what we say we know exist independently of practical activity. Marcuse's idea is that theory will preserve truth [for] practice follows the truth, not the other way round.[14] Mannheim, on the other hand, uses a pragmatic criterion of truth, and argued that a theory is wrong when it uses concepts and categories which if taken seriously would prevent man from adjusting himself at that historical stage. Specifically Mannheim argues that the truth attainable to man was the truth expressing the essence of historical reality.[15] We will return to these themes in Chapter 8.

Unlike Marx, Mannheim's preoccupation was with the search for pure knowledge, on the assumption that total truth existed in the synthesis of different view-points.[16] Mannheim's claim that all knowledge was rooted in social context, and that truth and knowledge is truth and knowledge from the point of view of a particular social and political situation, might have given the lead for a meta-theory of knowledge. But his idea of free-floating intelligentsia introduced a formalistic illusion which negated the sociology of knowledge's own claims. No social thinker can escape his social origins entirely. Without other criteria for assessing the merits of a viewpoint, and without explicit criteria for situating the theorist (intelligentsia) historically and specifically within a group, class or society, his theory of knowledge remains undialectical, formal and abstract: "Separated from a definite theory of the entire society every epistemology remains formal and abstract."[17] Obviously, this is where the Marxian sketch of a sociology of knowledge has much appeal, for that sketch seeks to situate and ground itself in the center of the concrete process of production and the human involvement in this ineluctable activity. This insight is neatly put in Marx's first thesis on Feuerbach: the chief defect of all materialism up to now, is that the object, reality, what we apprehend through our senses, is understood only in the form of the object or contemplation; but not as sensuous human activity, as practice; not subjectively. This does not mean that what we call the truth is usefully "subjective"; it does mean that the real world from which we distill a version of truth is the very world we historically belong to.

What seems to emerge from the Marxian conception of critical understanding is that truth is but a moment in correct praxis. It is neither fixed for ever nor transhistorical. If that is so, then it follows that every political doctrine, every theory of society, if centered upon the understanding of the historical process, contains its truth in correct praxis as far as this was possible. Or as Jay puts it for the Frankfurt School, what is true is whatever fosters social change. If critical theory can be said to have a theory of truth, it appears in its immanent critique of bourgeois society. If the theory is adequate, its truth can and must be demonstrated by political practice acting upon the raw material of history. And if history does not take shape along the lines intended by political action, the theoretical assumptions must be at fault.[18]

Accepting the truth of critical theory is especially problematic since the general truths that

12

such a theory deals with could not be verified or falsified by reference to the present order, simply because they implied the possibility of a different one. But at least accepting such truths involves coming to define oneself and what it is one thinks one needs and wants in a way quite different from what one had done before.[19] Critical social research seeks to operate in the arena of developing historical possibilities, and such an orientation and commitment is ultimately related to praxis and social change and very receptive to insights generated from people's prescientific experience. Whatever Marx's faults may have been, he certainly indicated that the world we took part in creating was also ours to change. We seem to have forgotten this important lesson. A theory of modern industrial society must take full account of the meaning of these ideas.

The Relevance of the Marxian Perspective on Social Theory

It should not be necessary to justify the utilization of a Marxian viewpoint in the interpretation of any social system seeped in the values of capitalism. Given, however, the distinctly anti-Marxist nature of sociology in Canada where there has been little room for Marxist scholarship and discussion to flourish, it is reasonable to make some preliminary remarks on the relevance of this focus.

Marx had sought social change rather than truth per se, and he had also recognized the validity of utopian thinking, which was philosophical in nature, as the repository of genuine human aspirations.[20] This is the true meaning of his much-quoted statement about "doing as one pleases" in a socialist society, not in the sense that work could be fun, which he also denied, but that humans must seek to transcend given epochs through radical praxis. Essentially, a Marxian social science starts from the premise that the confrontation of reality with reason is the fundamental norm of all thought, whatever the particular historical conception of the nature of reality.[21] Marx's paramount preoccupation was with the critical appraisal of the capitalist order in the light of Reason, that is, in terms of its ability or inability to satisfy human needs as well as provide for the growth and development of human beings. All of his writings were essentially a vast _critical_ effort, an indefatigable onslaught on

13

all ideological activity, and a theoretical synthesis of philosophical and social science knowledge.[22] As Walton puts it in his essay, Marxism is the theoretical and practical force whose major contribution to mankind continues to be the articulation of a radical, dialectical and dereifying theory, striving towards an unalienated culture.[23] Marx's lifelong purpose, clearly, was to concretize the philosophical vision of human possibilities, to search for the human basis of social exploitation and at the same time to stubbornly refuse to accept the authenticity of any solution that was not historically grounded in institutional reality.

The dialectical insights which he inherited from his teachers served as a lever as well as the basis for an immanent critique of bourgeois society and values. As we shall argue below, such a perspective not only offered the type of structural analyses that he was after; it also helped him to put into historical perspective the ontological centrality of labor as the key to understanding institutional and cultural life. The type of dialectical reasoning which he utilized in his vast and intricate study of political economy forced him to constantly question whether science was entitled to proceed in regard to the world of men and women with the indifference practiced in the natural sciences; and to ask whether scientific objectivity, if achievable, is sufficient guarantee of truth.[24] He certainly went far beyond any school or system of thought before or since his time in seeking to grasp all the dialectical connections within a given situation, and especially the social relations that were so integral to human survival and fulfilment. It was only by virtue of his Hegelian insight of contradiction-in-process that Marx was able to empirically demonstrate that contradictions and conflicts were inherent in the capitalist mode of production, since capitalism was not simply a particular stage of economic development but also, fundamentally, a complex structure of social relations.

Marxism was always an intellectual attitude seeped in critical Reason. Indeed, as the theory of the capitalist regime, it can be said that for as long as capitalism exists, Marxism can neither be discarded or ignored, for as Baran puts it, [Marxism] is nothing if it is not a powerful magnifying glass under which the irrationality of the capitalist system protrudes in all its monstrous forms. It clearly possesses the

theoretical tools needed for the analysis of the
economic institutions, scientific possibilities, and
social relations of the capitalist era.[25] To the
extent that the Marxian approach consists of a
systematic analysis of society, it distinguishes itself
from ideology, such as religion, which, because it is
ideological, rests on faith, regardless of the
empirical dead-end that it typically encounters. In
brief,

> the Marxian interpretation of history
> is still, in the 1980s, the most
> comprehensive explanation available
> to us ... By the term "comprehensive"
> one need not mean "true." What is
> true is unknown; comprehensive means
> simply that it appears to provide
> explanations for more features of the
> capitalist society than are otherwise
> provided.[26]

By this criterion, Marxism transcends narrow ideology.
It is a scientific paradigm, that is, a systematic and
comprehensive framework for analysis, and, unlike
ideology which conceals, it reveals.

Having said that, it is important to point out
that this is not a "Marxist book," in any crude sense
of evangelizing a Marxian viewpoint not relevant for
our times. It seeks to stimulate thought and to poke
at questions that are not all collapsable to some
overall Marxian iron stamp, and the reader will
recognize that we have endeavoured here and there to
make Marx's own notion of critique both thematic and
problematic in the evaluation of his own work. It is a
commonplace idea, subscribed to by all but the most
conservative elements, that criticism tends to increase
awareness and that awareness exposes new possibilities
and new visions. We simply want to contribute to that
process, while fully understanding that those
possibilities which we evoke may not necessarily excite
everyone. And then again they might. And they may
very well not be incorporated into social programs.

The age-old Marxian commitment to a critical
position on society as a whole is nonetheless still one
of its most remarkable features, second only to its
"ability to become more relevant each time bourgeois
theorists proclaim its demise..."[27] What fundamentally

distinguishes Marx's views from the other scholars in
the classical tradition, as well as from modern
positivism as Markovic argues, is his always present
radical criticism both of existing theory and of
existing forms of reality. Such a critique begins with
a philosophical vision and a thoroughly critical study
of all prevailing relevant special knowledge,[28] and
conceptualizes science as primarily concerned with the
explanation of totalities. Such explanations are
informed by historical insights which reveal
possibilities, humankind being conceived as the subject
who can change the historical conditions. This is why
the centrality of Marxism remains, in spite of the many
vigorous efforts to disassemble it. Meyer goes as far
as to suggest that it seems impossible not to be a
Marxist, for among all the modern schools of social
science, Marxism is virtually the only one to offer a
systematic explanation of the symptoms of
disintegration and of how they fit together. It seems
to be the only systematic explanation of our troubles
which combines a diagnosis of our sickness with the
prospect of a society in which our ideas can become
reality.[29] For this reason the very attempt to link a
comprehensive critique with the vision of a decent
future remains a great attraction and indeed, for some
intellectuals, an ideal worth striving for. Unlike
Parsons, we cannot claim that as a theorist Marx
belonged to a bygone era. The lasting merit of a
critical theory of society, of which Marxism is a prime
example, is the ability to lay bare the theoretical
reifications of capitalist social relations, to expose
its dramatic contradictions, and to project towards
transcending the immediate. Specifically, we shall
argue that the Marxian theory of dialectics (as opposed
to Engels' version of it) has the conceptual power that
is imperative for the critical understanding of late
capitalism. Critical theory, as Schroyer argued, is a
materialist radicalization of critical philosophy. As
such it proceeds by an analysis of both the blockages
on productive society and the distortions of
communicative praxis.[30] In this light, the generation
of a critical theory of science and society is at the
same time the broadest theoretical framework for
fundamental structural change. However, as will be
discussed later, the really important issue is
precisely how to convince people, intellectuals and
laypersons alike, of the transformative capacity of
certain types of understanding. For, ironically, the
marginality of Marxism to the accepted arena of

knowledge is due in no small part to its ability to unmask and demolish political doctrines and thought-patterns that happen to flourish.

Starting with the empirical generalization that "the economy is the first cause of wretchedness,"[31] critical theory makes the critique of political economy, both theoretical and practical, its central component. It addresses itself primarily to criticism and change, on a further premise that a changed historical situation requires a corresponding development of critical theory. The critical theory of the Frankfurt School sets as one of its prime goals a critique of Marxism, on the contention that Marxism needs to go far beyond the critique of political economy. But yet, this position could encourage a certain amount of intellectual carelessness for, while this is an important criticism, it should also be tempered by the realization that insofar as we have not gone beyond the circumstances that gave rise to Marxism, we can hardly be expected to transcend it without doing exactly what Marx warned against - leaping ahead of history. In the tradition of sociological theory which has been fed to neophyte sociology students for decades, enough attention was never given to the Marxian categories that could lead to a total understanding of advanced capitalism. It seems especially important to return to the Marxian analysis of the commodity form, for example, to grasp how in this period of capitalist development, much of what we mean by "culture" has been appropriated, not to mention debased, in such a way as to reduce society's members to objects - specifically objects of sale or for sale and profit in one way or another. The commodity fetishism of the modern era whereby we cannot, at least in Canada, get public exposure to much of what is regarded as culture unless that exposure is "sponsored," is part and parcel of that commercial gut of capitalism as a structure of social relations which took a different form in the eighteenth and nineteenth centuries. The modern element differs in degree but not in kind from the early operations which ran the forced labor systems in the gold and silver mines of South America, and on the plantations in the Caribbean and the Deep South. The objective was the same: profit.

Those who argue that Marx was an "economic determinist," which is often taken to mean that he somehow saw production determining all of social

17

existence in a one-sided fashion, easily miss the mark of what is central to his thought. And those who are quick to charge "dogmatism" should remember that a theoretical system is dogmatic if it held that any previously reached conclusion is valid independently of the objective conditions existing at a given time, and independently of a concrete analysis of such conditions. Dogmatism, as the belief in things for their own sake, is not part of serious contemporary Marxist scholarship.

NOTES

1. McNall, 1978, p. 4.

2. _Ibid._

3. Althusser, 1969, p. 170.

4. Note, for example, that among "theory" books currently in popular use, those by Ronald Fletcher, Alan Wells, even Jonathan Turner's 1982 edition, to mention only a few, do not discuss the problem area of the sociology of knowledge. It is important to conjecture whether or not these omissions are purely accidental.

5. Giddens, 1971, pp. 41-45, 213.

6. Rex, 1974, p. 10.

7. Clement, 1975.

8. Marchak, 1975, p. 13 (emphasis added). See, further, Gonick, 1975; Clement, 1975; and Allen, 1975.

9. _Ibid._, pp. 13, 35, 137.

10. Baran, 1969, p. 14. Baran further argues that the defetishization of "values," "ethical judgments" and the like, the identification of the social, economic, psychic causes of their emergence, change and disappearance, as well as the uncovering of the specific interests which they serve, represent the greatest single contribution that an intellectual can make to the cause of human advancement (p. 9).

11. Marchak, pp. 147-8, 172, _passim_; cf. Clement, 1975; and Caplan, 1963.

12. Popper, 1961, p. 155.

13. Jay, 1973, p. 63.

14. See Marcuse, 1960, p. 322 and 1968, pp. 147-148.

15. 1936, pp. 36, 84-85.

19

16. Jay, 1973, p. 64.

17. _Ibid_., p. 183, quoting Horkheimer.

18. See Lichtheim, 1974, p. 90 and Jay, 1973, pp. 63, 83.

19. Fay, 1975, p. 107.

20. Jay, 1973, pp. 64, 82.

21. See, especially, Baran, 1969, pp. xviii, 33, 38.

22. O'Neill, n.d., p. 72.

23. Walton, _et al_., 1970, p. 261.

24. See Lichtheim, 1974, p. 174 and cf. Marcuse, 1968, p. 155.

25. _Op.cit_., pp. 41, 89.

26. Marchak, p. xiii.

27. Walton, n.d., p. 35.

28. Markovic, 1974, pp. 1-5.

29. Meyer, 1975, p. 202.

30. Schroyer, 1973, p. 60.

31. Horkheimer, 1972, p. 249.

CHAPTER II

THEORETICAL SYNTHESES IN SOCIOLOGY:
SOME OBSCURE ISSUES

It may never be predicted of sociology, as it was of the "welfare state," that it rides the wave of the future. What can be said of modern sociology is that it still searches for the respectability that has long been accorded the natural sciences. A major part of this search involves several attempts to "synthesize" the conflicting and, in many ways, unreconcilable assumptions on which the different theories of society rest.[1] What is explicit in the many attempts to weave a unified theory is the notion that because the different perspectives in sociology necessarily address the same problem, namely, social behavior and society, they can, with a little fiat, be made to come together into a grand synthesis. Thus, it is suggested in the sociological literature that conflict and coercion theories can be synthesized; or that dialectic and functionalism, or Marxism and Freudianism, can be meaningfully integrated.[2] We are frequently told that the division between competing theoretical schools turns on issues rooted in long-standing differences which cannot be easily resolved, but never explicitly what these differences are,[3] and hence why they persist.

We will argue that the theoretical divide in sociology is much more pervasive than many sociologists believe. Furthermore, the division is likely to persist, given the distinctly different ontologies from which each side begins. The problem is not simply due to the different unit of analysis used, but more fundamentally to the different <u>philosophical</u> and <u>ontological</u> presuppositions on which each builds. Conflict or dialectical sociology, which essentially builds on the ideas of Marx, does not take the nature of humankind for granted, for instance, but rather explicitly inquires and investigates into the ontological structure which constitutes humankind; the search is for qualities which distinguish humans from other animals. The "philosophical anthropology" of the young Marx amply demonstrates this interest;[4] but it is not common to, say, structural functionalism.

Theoretical systems build on assumptions - in this case assumptions about the socio-cultural and hence historical world. And assumptions, unlike definitions,

21

can be true or false. The parallelism in social theory
remains a parallelism because the competing theories
rest on fundamentally different, even opposing sets of
assumptions which simply do not facilitate synthesis,
even if at times there seems to be a grafting, a
symbiosis or a temporary closing of the parallel. The
assumptions of the competing theories are the real
components which preclude true synthesis. Thus the
common point made by structural-functional sociologists,
and others, that sociology does not have and should not
have a political content, is based on the naive (and
patently false) assumption that somehow we can study
human beings, their class relations, their desire for
change, their fears and anxieties, or whatever, without
political input of some sort; yet sociology is
necessarily tied to forms of socio-political structures,
and, as we shall argue below, is a political activity.
In the words of C. Wright Mills, whether he wants it or
not, or whether he is aware of it or not, anyone who
spends his life studying society and publishing the
results is acting morally and usually politically as
well.5 In the majority of cases, people's life-
situations and experiences will be as they are because
of political factors. The "apolitical" positions rest
on the assumption (often unstated) that sociology, like
the natural sciences, utilizes in its practice certain
norms whereby sociologists can study society without
actually living in one and participating in it themselves. The well-known structural-functional analyses
of the 1950s and 1960s in sociology share certain of
these assumptions, together with some assumptions from
Freudian psychology. These assumptions are in many
ways not reconcilable with the philosophical
anthropology of the competing paradigms associated with
Marxian analysis, or phenomenology. It will be
instructive to briefly review these poles.

On The Nature of Humankind: The Freudian View

Explicit conceptions of the nature of humankind do
not abound everywhere. Yet it is quite clear that any
worthwhile theory of society ought to operate on some
assumption about what constitute human beings, as
opposed to animals. Depending on which assumptions we
build, we will come to view humans as being in need of
certain types of control and perhaps requiring
unqualified repression "for their own good" as well as
for the "general good." Our whole system of legal and
juridical restraints in the west (the so-called rule of

law) derive from a set of assumptions, doubtless false, about the inherent aggressiveness and asociality of human beings, if left unrestrained.

It is to Thomas Hobbes more than to anyone else that we owe the inheritance of a rather dismal set of assumptions about the "passions" of the human individual.[6] But, to a large extent, the Hobbesian "problem of order" has given ground to an equally sinister view of humankind in the ideas propounded by Freud. One of the most telling and well-known illustrations from Freud is to be found in his Civilization and Its Discontents where he argues that "men are ... creatures among whose instinctual endowments is to be reckoned a powerful share of aggressiveness." This "view of man" has been taken by many to be "true," that is, based upon observations about human society, and borne out by such experiences as the Nazi excesses, the Vietnam war, among other recent manifestations which presumably demonstrated the law: homo homini lupus [man is a wolf to man]. Yet the key sociological question here is precisely the sort which divides the theories of society: are these excesses explicable as a cumulation of individualistic aggressiveness, or are they to be explained by a theory which considers the social structure including the political values, as the incubator and precipitance of our actions? It is the business of sociological theory to spell out that that which possesses people who perform these aggressive political acts is not a demon or a wolf, but the social system of which they are a part. It is here that the real challenge of social theory lies. The expansive assumption pertaining to the in-born human aggressiveness is a key one on which a good deal of what we call theories of man build. A second Freudian assumption, closely related to the first, is implicit in Lenski's well-known but unsuccessful synthesis. It is that humankind is basically treacherous, and most certainly selfish:

> when men are confronted with important decisions where they are obliged to choose between their own, or the group's interest and the interests of others, they nearly always choose the former - though often seeking to hide this fact from themselves and others.[7]

It is precisely because of this assumption that Freud

directed most of his life's efforts toward a rational understanding of assumed irrational motivations, and to the development of comprehensive theory of irrational drives.[8] The vulgar excesses of this assumption culminate in a reductionist paradigm of human beings, typified in such works as Desmond Morris', Naked Ape, in which one can find the argument that humans constitute a bundle of aggressive instincts and innate brute-like urges. Homo sociologicus is replaced by a veritable selfish animal whose bumptious id threatens the very survival of the (assumed also) social community. The linchpin of Freudian psychology is that basically the human individual is a creature governed by psychic forces which in turn derive their strength from instincts, considered to be deeply rooted in "human nature," that is, in an essentially stable biotically determined structure.[9] A third Freudian assumption may be said to concern the possibility for understanding the world not so much in terms of how it is socially constructed, but rather in terms of how it is unconsciously experienced by the unfree individual. There is some affinity between this idea, and Marx's contention that at bottom man is a suffering being, as we discuss below in chapter four. But the hope which Marx has for humankind is not shared by Freud.

Finally, the Freudian psychoanalytic approach has always rested on the principle that the social process is reducible to the behavior of the individual - the isolated individual so well represented in the utilitarian theories of the nineteenth and early twentieth centuries, to which Durkheim and Marx, in their different ways, were so indignant and fiercely critical. From their quite different positions, both Durkheim and Marx agreed that no theory or analysis which begins from the "individual" in either a conceptual or empirical sense can successfully grasp the specific properties of social phenomena.[10] Let us look briefly at the Marxian view of humankind.

On the Nature of Humankind: The Marxian View

There can be no doubt that Marxian theory operates on an explicit view of humankind, a view which sets his analyses apart from others. This view is clearly expressed by Marx himself and forms the foundation of conflict or dialectical social theory. In summary fashion it can be stated that first, Marx assumed that humankind is an active, purposive being, a subject

24

in the historical process, creating history and himself
by manipulating inorganic nature and "stamping it."
Such a being is further assumed to have the ability to
formulate goals and plan ahead. This voluntaristic
overtone differs from the Freudian in that this view
fully explores the normative criteria regarding the
establishment of those goals. Second, Marx assumed
that in the manipulation of nature the   labor
process is the basic and irreducible requirement of
social existence. Third, Marxian social theory assumes
that humans are purposive beings whose teleological
capacities make them the chief and decisive
manipulators of nature. These ideas are elaborated in
chapter 4 below.

The Modern Arguments for a Convergence of Marx and Freud

Having juxtaposed these two views, let us look
next at the arguments for their synthesis. It is
agreed by those who advocate a synthesis that such a
blend is justifiable on the following grounds. First,
that of all the inquiries into behavior at the
individual level, psychoanalysis reaches the furthest
into the shadowy regions of mass behavior; and of all
the approaches to mass behavior Marxism reaches most
deeply into the mysteries of the behavior of the
individual.[11] This view is sketched in figure 1. This
cross-fertilization of interest is seen as a good
ground for some productive synthesis.

Second, a common ground is said to be the
objective of both views to penetrate facades and outer
forms in order to discover hidden meanings. Further,
the actual discoveries are said to be, for Marx,
society and the warring classes; for Freud personality
and the warring id, ego and super ego.[12] The
implication here is that both sides are essentially
concerned with conflict situations and contradictions.[13]
Third, it is said that both Marx and Freud had
therapeutic aims and that this reveals their common
approach to theory and practice.[14] Fourth, the claim
is made that Marx as well as Freud was keen to advance
a theory of human development and, eventually a theory
of alienation.[15] These reasons for drawing succor from
related theoretical fields are not nearly as articulate
and plausible as those offered by the critical
theorists Jurgen Habermas and Herbert Marcuse; hence a
fifth argument. Habermas and Marcuse do not argue so

	Primary concern	Secondary achievement
Psychoanalysis (Freud)	Behavior of Individual	Greatest insight into behavior of mass
Marxism	Behavior of mass	Greatest insight into behavior of individual

FIGURE 1: The Marxism in psychoanalysis; the psychoanalysis in Marxism

much for a "synthesis" as for a modelling of sociological insight-seeking on the psychoanalytic demystification paradigm. In this connection, John Rex writes that [for Habermas] the psychoanalyst neither seeks merely to discover the laws of the patient's behavior, nor to understand how he sees the world. Rather he offers an explanation of the patient's conduct and, if it is true, it is accepted by the patient himself and liberates him from his fantasies and from the compulsions of his behavior. It is suggested that there might be a social equivalent of this, through which the social scientist, confronted with men whose view of the world is distorted by ideology, is able to offer an explanation which enables them to understand their true conditions and, by understanding, to find their way to freedom.[16]

It is in this vein that Marcuse argues that the achievements of modern technological rationality are based on repression, and that, consequently, we must take seriously the nature of the principal means known to us for the elimination of repression, namely psychoanalysis. Similarly, Habermas takes psycho-analysis as his model in explaining the concept of an emancipatory social science. In psychoanalysis, which can be conceived as a kind of linguistic analysis which deals with systematically distorted communications, the speech and actions of the patient are understood as a system of symbols whose meanings must be revealed and subsequently reconstructed.[17] In his attempt to supplement Marx's theory of value in order to account for the systematically distorted communication within

26

advanced capitalism, Habermas argues that, psycho-analytically, a theory of communicative competence or a theory of ideal communication could conceivably remove repression and unnecessary social control, thus emancipating the depoliticized masses.[18] A communication theory would reveal the systematically distorted modes of communication that permeate all industrial organization. Both Habermas and Marcuse believe that to the extent that science and technology are now the major modes of ideological mystification of power relations, our grasp of society is hamstrung. It is thus that Habermas boldly claims that only critical theory, as derived from the method of transcendental phenomenology, can express the normative character of the cognitive interests that underpin cultural domination. More precisely, only critical theory, (like psychoanalysis) paradigmatically incorporates self-reflection into its method and thus facilitates the "patients" in unblocking and unfreezing reified consciousness. In a word, only critical theory with its well-developed Hegelian concept of <u>reflection</u> can provide the insights into social arrangements to the depth of questioning those arrangements. Such questioning is a precondition for a critique of domination. In Trent Schroyer's important book, <u>The Critique of Domination</u>, Marcuse's works are closely discussed, principally because of the suggestiveness of such works, but also because of the methodological problems posed by Marcuse's "Hegelianized Freud." What the latter point entails is that Marcuse has sought to effect an isomorphism with critical theory and psycho-analysis, notably in <u>Eros and Civilization</u>. As the critical theorists view theory, emancipation from the built-in illusions of late capitalism can be achieved through psychoanalysis by means of a process of <u>self-reflection</u>, a process which presumably, is both therapeutic and liberating.[19]

Habermas, because he takes the goal of critical sociology to be the construction of a general interpretive framework, regards the methodological features of psychoanalysis as a significant clue to the methodology of critical theory in general. In effect, he is reasoning that, with a little ingenuity, psycho-analysis can be <u>reconstructed</u> as a theory of systematically distorted communication. In his view, this paradigm can fruitfully be applied to society as a whole. Its appeal and its relevance are due to the fact that "psychoanalysis ... [is] the only tangible example of a science incorporating methodical self-reflection." In making the transference, the role of the social theorist is to render those to whom he speaks autonomous, by enabling them to understand their own situation in the social world. What in the individual is self-reflection, is, in a society, self-education.[20] The analyst supposedly operates on some sense of commitment, constantly guided by a genuine interest in freeing the patients (or social groups) from the subconscious, dominating illusions that inhibit understanding and freedom, and thereby paving the way for a correct interpretation of an individual, group, or situation. False beliefs, distorted concepts, the meaning of actions and their historical situations, could all then be reappraised, with autonomy, responsibility, and clarity.

Objections to the Proposed Syntheses

Van den Berghe has argued that a synthesis between dialectic and functionalism was a distant possibility given that, in his view, (1) both perspectives are holistic, (2) both "converge" in the role they assign to conflict and consensus, (3) both share an evolutionary notion of change, and (4) both are based on an equilibrium model. But are these necessary and sufficient grounds for a true synthesis, given the traditional limited room for variation on any or all of these conceptions? Besides, as Frank has reasoned, flippant talk of convergence or synthesis on the above claims is illusory and spurious, for functionalism and dialectics do not even ask the same questions about society, so the chances of getting "synthetic" answers are meagre. And on such key questions as the internality of dissensus and contradiction, both perspectives part company in haste. As Frank puts it:

> Of the whole, [functionalists] ask
> no question at all; they do not ask
> why it exists or how, where it came
> from or what is happening to it;
> they do not ask whether they like it
> or not; they simply accept the whole
> system as it is, gladly taking its
> social structure as they find it.

By contrast, it is the sine qua non of the dialectical tradition to precisely first analyze and explain the origin, nature and development of the entire social system and its structure as a whole, and then use the understanding of the whole thus gained as the necessary basis for the understanding of its parts.[21] The difference in <u>historical</u> insight between the two perspectives is severe enough to lead to unbridgable misconstruction of society and social processes.

We would go further than that. In fact the perfectly rational and forceful case must be made on the basis of the understanding that insofar as psychoanalysis and Marxism stand in profound contradiction to each other, they are neither additive or capable of synthesis. Such would do justice neither to Freud nor Marx. Given the differing and clearly contradictory <u>ontological assumptions</u> of Marx and Freud, it is difficult to present the proposal, as some have done recently,[22] that we can "add up" the ideas of these two thinkers to arrive at an overall theory of society. There are several reasons why any adding up must be hazardous, to say the least. First, the Marxian view of humankind is not a psychology, as even one of Marx's most bitter critics admits.[23] If anything, such a view is a critique of psychology and para-psychology, a forceful testament that the seemingly individualistic antics of the actor must be grasped and understood in terms of his structure of social relations, that is, in terms of sociology. Second, the intentionality, purpose and expressivity which are at the very heart of Marx's conception of humankind, is alien to Freud who would rather assume that individuals are governed by psychic forces whose strength emanates from an unalterable "human nature."[24] For Marx, if there is such a thing as unintended behavior at all, that had to be explained, again, by reference to the <u>social system</u> which characteristically possesses the individual. Whether or not he/she is fully aware that his actions are dictated by social forces is itself an important sociological problem. The pessimism which Freud holds about the possibility of a rational society (see his <u>Civilization and its Discontents</u>) is at the opposite pole from Marx's hope for a truly rational society. Third, in Freud, but not in Marx, we operate on a-historical givens,[25] in the form of psyches. Finally, Freud's basic pessimism about the possibilities for social change cannot in any way be squared with the revolutionary hopes of the Marxian perspective.[26] If history, and the human individuals who <u>make</u> it are the result of an unalterable "human nature", then our attempts to achieve a radical transformation of the human condition and the human foundations of the social order are necessarily doomed to failure from the start, and are, in any event, senseless and outside the human ken.[27]

Baran argues that in view of the fact that psycho-analysis today exercises a pervasive influence on social thought, we may do well to take up where Freud left off, in seeking rational understanding of the factors principally determining human behavior.[28] What this seems to mean is that we can emulate the methods of psychoanalysis which would require that we impose rationality and the interpretive scope of critical theory on the understanding of the cultural hegemony of late capitalism. We can perhaps learn from psycho-analysis what it means to use explanation and analysis as liberative or emancipatory forces. But the critical question is precisely how to convince the subject that he/she is under certain illusions, and how then to achieve an acknowledgement of the internalized constraints, conflicts and inhibitions.[29] It is probably very true, as Baran insists,[30] that psychologism points unmistakably to the loneliness, unrelatedness and impotence of men under capitalism, and thus comes nearer the truth than the shallow liberal claptrap which claims that we control and shape our lives as we wish. We are reminded by Marx in the 18th Brumaire that

> men make their own history, but they
> do not make it just as they please;
> they do not make it under circumstances
> directly chosen by themselves, but
> under circumstances directly
> encountered, given and transmitted from
> the past.

Part of what he called "the tradition of all the dead generations" is the ideology of the dominant class.[31]

By far the main objections of the psychoanalytic paradigm tend to be pragmatic ones. For instance, it is suggested that in psychoanalysis the "patient," on the assumption that he or she is genuinely repressed or is under unnecessary illusion, voluntarily allows his symbolic life to be reconstructed by the therapist. Through a process of self-reflection, the patient generally comes to understand his/her situation in the world. This situation is not easily reached in the larger context of societal repression and domination. As Connerton observes, precisely the common purpose of emancipation (normally shared by the patient and the doctor) is absent in societal conflicts.[32] Rather, we typically encounter instead a seeming mutual suspicion. The practical question therefore remains a substantial one: how to have those subject to domination and technical control first of all realize that that situation exists; and second, on the initial knowledge of that reality undertake an emancipatory self-education and critique? These are difficult questions. Furthermore, the theorist may well propose a corrected version of reality or a reinterpretation of a particular situation, but he could never guarantee that it will be accepted by those for whom it was meant. In the final analysis, only the subjects' self-knowledge can eventually ground an analytic understanding of a situation sufficient to effect radical change. Marx, incidentally, was well aware of this possibility (see chapter 9).

Further weaknesses of the psychoanalytic paradigm were recently put forward by McCarthy who pointed out that a precondition of the success of psychoanalytic therapy is the patient's experience of suffering and desperation, and his/her desire to be released from this condition. A second requirement is that the physician not allow the patient's suffering to come to a premature end. Finally, a key to psychoanalytic therapy is the resistance of the patient - a resistance intensified in the course of the treatment. In the context of critical theory, does it mean that the social groups who do not experience profound dissatisfaction with their situation are incapable of political enlightenment? And how can the critical theorist manage the possibility of premature termination of the group's suffering, considering he/she has no institutionally sanctioned control over this situation? Finally, what forms would the intensification of resistance and the exacerbation of conflict take at the social level? For all these problems, and questions, there are no ready answers. This makes for a weakness of the paradigm in the form of what McCarthy calls "disanologies."[33] For some social scientists, the approach taken by psychoanalysis is simply not attractive, since it is seen to have control as one of, if not its chief, concern.[34] Clearly, the relevance of Freud for social theory turns on the fact that he had a theory of culture which (perhaps inadequately) measures cultural institutions, such as the family, by the suffering they inflict on human individuals. And in his own way Freud had a dialectical view of civilization in that, in seeking to understand the unhappiness of involuntarily "socialized" men and women he found their discontent in culture, in institutions, which, even if they fell short, were potentially capable of transforming instinctual impulses into socially acceptable modes of behavior. The idea of dialectics is the subject of another chapter, after we have addressed the issue of theoretical undernourishment in Canadian sociology.

NOTES

1. See, e.g., Sallach, 1973; Cole, 1966; van den Berghe, 1963; and Friedrich, 1972; among others. Cf. Gouldner's obscure argument for synthesis in his The Coming Crisis of Western Sociology, 1971.

2. Adams, 1966; van den Berghe, 1963; Cole, 1966; Kovel, 1976; and Heilbroner, 1975.

3. See Cohen, 1968, pp. 129-73; Horton, 1966, pp. 601-13; van den Berghe, op.cit.; Bruyn, 1966, pp. 23-83; and Dahrendorf, 1958.

4. For an extremely lucid and absorbing exposition of the humanistic and anthropological bias in Marx, see Giddens, 1971, esp. pp. 1-17.

5. Mills, 1959, p. 79.

6. Parsons, 1937, pp. 89-94.

7. Lenski, 1966, chapters 2-4.

8. Baran, 1969, pp. 92-93.

9. Ibid., pp. 92-93.

10. Giddens, 1971, pp. 20-21, 86-88, et passim.

11. Heilbroner, 1975, p. 417.

12. Ibid., p. 420-21.

13. Kovel, 1976, p. 221.

14. Ibid., p. 426.

15. Heilbroner, 1975, pp. 423-24.

16. Rex, 1974, p. 21. It should be recognized, of course, that the psychoanalytic paradigm is not the concern of Habermas and Marcuse alone, but of the entire Frankfurt School, especially in its early days. For important discussion in this regard, see Held, 1980, pp. 111-147.

17. Connerton, 1976, pp. 31-36.

18. Habermas, 1968a, 1968b.

19. The major problems with this assumption are discussed more extensively in chapters 6 and 9 below.

20. Habermas, 1968b, p. 214; and Connerton, 1976, p. 36.

21. See Frank, 1966, for a full discussion of these points.

22. E.g., Heilbroner, 1975, p. 428.

23. Popper, 1945 (II), p. 88.

24. Kovel, 1976, p. 226.

25. Ibid., p. 229.

26. Jay, 1973, p. 86.

27. Cf. Baran, 1969, p. 92ff.

28. Ibid., pp. 92, 97.

29. Connerton, pp. 36, 37.

30. Baran, op.cit., p. 94.

31. See Marx, 1963b, p. 15.

32. Connerton, 1976, p. 37; and Dallmayr, 1972b, p. 223: "While in psychoanalytic therapy both partners are committed to the liberation from psychic constraints, dominant classes view the liberation of the oppressed typically as a threat to their power; under these circumstances, appeals to a therapeutic consensus merely serve to buttress further the prevailing stratification."

33. McCarthy, 1978, pp. 211-212. For more important discussion on the psychoanalytic paradigm, see Held, 1980.

34. For example, Rose and Rose, 1976, p. 107.

THE POVERTY OF SOCIOLOGY IN A
CHANGING CANADIAN SOCIETY*

Introduction

It is customary, and perhaps even fashionable, for Canadian sociologists to blame "Americans" for either "taking over" Canadian sociology or else "undermining" its development (cf. Clark, 1973; Kornberg and Tharp, 1972). The main argument seems to be that an over-abundance of American sociologists are employed in Canadian universities and that they foist upon Canadian students <u>their</u> brand of "professionalism" and <u>their</u> conceptions of sociology.

Yet, it is not always clear how and/or why Americans have tended to dominate, in some departments, not only in terms of their numbers, but also the theoretical orientations of sociology in Canada. Given the fact of a distinctly American flavor in Canadian sociology, and often American interpretation of Canadian issues, we might, in a paradigmatic sense, argue that this situation is an excellent example of the crucial interlacing of economic power and ideational power (cf. Marx and Engels, 1947: 39-63). The paradigm is valid if we recognize the fact of America's global hegemony in contemporary sociology and Canada's historical colonial relationship to the United States. The convergence of theoretical orientations of mainstream Anglophone Canadian sociologists and U.S. sociologists cannot, however, be explained solely in terms of our colonial status vis-a-vis the U.S., for the Quebec nation is as much a part of the "maple leaf colony" (perhaps even more so) as the rest of Canada, yet Quebec sociology (cf. the Laval school of sociologists) is not the replica of U.S. sociology the way Anglophone Canadian sociology is. This reference to Quebecois sociology is not meant to set up Franco-phone Canadian sociology as a model for all sociology to follow. All that we are pointing out is that it is much too simplistic, and altogether unconvincing, to say that the Americanization of our sociology is the reason for many or most of its weaknesses. We must

*Reprinted by permission of <u>The Canadian Journal of Sociology</u>. This chapter originally appeared as an article in the <u>CJS</u> 1(3): 345-362, Fall 1975.

look elsewhere for an explanation of this phenomenon.

In so far as mainstream Anglophone Canadian sociologists have used this situation as a convenient excuse for not developing and sharpening theoretical tools relevant to the critical understanding of their society, they share some of the blame for the Americanization process. In what appears to be over-anxious haste to arrive at the positivistic destination, which, nevertheless, looks suspiciously like a blind alley (Walsh, 1972a: 15), sociology as practised in Canada too often fails to recognize the historical, philosophical, and epistemological underpinnings of the discipline. These concerns are frequently sacrificed on the altar of positivism and for dubious reasons at that. The end result of this orientation is that in Anglophone Canadian sociology we have nurtured a brand of sociology (based on some questionable assumptions) which is obsessed with methodological purism and small-scale quantitative studies.[1] This variety of "academic" sociology is chiefly concerned with men and groups and social institutions as they are influenced by or integrated into the going social order and undermines theoretical development and conceptualization. Indeed, this pedigree of sociology takes us far from the kinds of structural analyses that could deepen our understanding of man and his social arrangements. Like Mannheim (1952: 9), we feel that to look at a thing from a "structural" point of view means to explain it, not as an isolated, self-contained unit, but as part of a wider structure; the explanation itself is based not so much on the properties of the thing itself as on the place it occupies within the structure. (See also Tiryakian, 1970: 13; cf. Watson, 1973.) Structural sociology is fundamentally rooted in the tradition of the sociology of knowledge which concerns itself not merely with the formation of a specific world view, nor with the ideas and modes of thinking that happen to flourish, but with the whole setting in which this occurs. Adopting a structural approach clearly requires the sociological imagination or the ability to see wholes when only pieces appear (Anderson, 1971: 348). A key corollary of the Americanization process is the absence within Anglophone Canadian sociology of a viable intellectual left. Precisely because of this, we feel that although some of the critical remarks in this paper have been articulated before, there is nevertheless some benefit to be reaped from a revival of some of the major criticisms in this book. There

36

can be no last work here. The paper raises many issues and points to problems that are outside the scope of the present work. But it is felt that great benefits can accrue to the Canadian academic community from an airing of these issues, as well as from a vigorous renewal of the critique of Canadian sociology. This renewal can no doubt serve to reshape our own independent intellectual tradition comparable to those which have developed in France, Germany, and Britain since the last war.

The variety of sociology which we have just described has been aptly termed "mindless militant empiricism" (Walsh, 1972b: 43):

> By mindless empiricism, I refer to the kind of sociology in which no explicit theorizing takes place at all. Instead, we are treated to a series of unconnected findings about disparate subjects - I have in mind, here, the immense flow of methodologically "correct" trivia to which most sociological journals bear witness. Militant empiricism could be described as the kind of sociology that specifically eschews theory in favour of what it calls a practical concern with facts.

Such critical remarks accurately describe the current state of Anglophone Canadian sociology, as a review of the literature will quickly reveal. Whilst our review does not pretend to cover every work in Anglophone Canadian sociology, we feel that the ones cited constitute a valid cross-section of those works to which our students are generally exposed. We may next consider, then, some of the criteria we have advanced for the condition that we have termed the "poverty" of such a sociology.

Poverty in Defining the Situation

Historical examination of Canadian sociology reveals that until the end of World War II there was little sociology being done in Canada outside of Montreal and, to a lesser extent, Toronto, and most students were effectively driven to American universities, especially Chicago, or to London for advanced training in the field (Clark, 1973: 205-7). But it is too easy a step to take from that historical acknowledgement to the conclusion that Americans are responsible for undermining the development of the discipline in Canada. Such facile conclusions serve to deaden the movement for a critique of Canadian sociology.

First of all, blame for the impoverished nature of Canadian sociology cannot be laid solely on "the American take-over" of Canadian sociology departments. Canadian sociologists have minds of their own and, by that token, should actively seek to define their situation according to the existential conditions which they confront and experience. Recent trends in Anglophone Canadian sociology do not indicate a move toward a sharper definition of Canadian society. One recent book in Canadian sociology succeeded in discussing "Canadian Social Organization" without so much as mentioning the concept of <u>pluralism</u>; one passing reference was made to this notion and that by way of citing another author. Where is the pluralist model of Canadian society?

Secondly, any sociology may be said to be impoverished if its practitioners do not engage in a systematic <u>critique</u> of the political economy in which they practise and of which sociology forms a part. Thirdly, any sociology which does not try to foster a <u>critical</u> understanding of the "service institutions" (school, church, family, and the whole normative "givens"), which so effectively socialize men into conformity to, and acceptance of, a given political economy, is impoverished. Fourthly, sociologists who avoid serious discussion of the social factors centered on the class-based forces of production and distribution do a disservice to their students and to all who wish to understand the dynamics of social systems. Fifthly, a sociology which does not ground its explanations in structural analyses is clearly much poorer than it need be. On these counts, Anglophone Canadian sociologists score very low; for, with few exceptions, they have not posed a radical analysis of their society, nor have they concerned themselves, for whatever reasons, with exploring alternatives to the going orthodoxy. And Canadian sociologists certainly have not given the subject of <u>class</u> the attention that it demands, in spite of the importance class relations have had in shaping the Canadian past and are having in shaping the present. Class, and "conflict," "racism," and other so-called "sensitive" concepts remain sociological leprae. Or, where mentioned, they seem always to be hedged by apologetics (e.g., Whyte, 1965; Rossides, 1968). In Rossides, for instance, we have the claim that "viable Liberal societies," like Canada, do not suffer from class cleavage and conflicts; they show only considerable incongruity and tension between the major strata (Rossides, 1968: 273). On this critical question of class, we want to make some comments.

Some sociologists naively believe that, because the "progressive loss of power and perceived deprivation" among North American poor has not manifested itself in the emergence of a class consciousness or organized class conflict, this is at once because the poor do not constitute a class, but also that this is a "refutation" of Marxian ideas on class in society (see Whyte, 1965: 183). Such a view is over-simplistic. Indeed, as John Hofley (1971: 104) reminds us: the mythical notion of many Canadians that Canada is a "classless" society has some very profound implications.

> This conception of the reality of our social structure works against our perceiving poverty and the poor, and against seeing the potential intense and violent conflict among various strata in Canadian society.

Hofley rightly warns us not to forget that

> persons in positions of power will stress that society is "classless" and that persons in the lower strata may achieve mobility through personal, rather than collective effort. These are factors that prevent the poor from becoming organized (emphasis added).[2]

Now, while there are some important works on class (e.g., Lipset, 1959; MacPherson, 1953; some of S.D. Clark's pioneering historical if largely uncritical works) and more recently some highly critical analyses (e.g., Teeple, 1972; Ossenberg, 1971) the general Canadian position is one of cautious prowling around the margins of one of sociology's major theoretical concerns. We think, in fact, that it is highly symptomatic of the poverty of Canadian sociology that in the first article of the first volume of Canada's Sociology and Anthropology journal (in 1964) we had the stage set by a Canadian-born sociologist whose clear message was that if we want to do "good" sociology we would be well advised to forget about the concept of social class (Wrong, 1964). Far too many Canadian sociologists have taken this suggestion seriously. If, as Rossides claims (1968: 271), stratification analysis is one of social science's most powerful tools for uncovering the empirical contours of society and for shedding light on a wide range of problems, then it would seem that, in Canadian sociology at any rate, we have nurtured, by default, a conceptually powerless and needlessly diluted sociology.

In the light of the foregoing, it is perhaps instructive to briefly touch on that important aspect of sociology which deals with the sociologists' very grasp of reality. The central problem of sociology, namely that of giving an account of the nature of social phenomena in general, itself belongs to philosophy (Winch, 1958: 43) if we conceive of philosophy as the study of the nature of man's understanding of "reality." If we can agree that philosophy seeks to understand man's construction of world views, man's shaping and sharpening of conceptual schemes, and finally the normative evaluation of these world views and schemes, then these considerations beg a two-fold socio-philosophical question. The first part of the question concerns an inquiry into what the nature of reality is; the second asks how far reality is intelligible. Philosophers and sociologists alike agree that what is termed reality is always problematic (cf. Silverman, 1972: 9; Andreski, 1964: 41-42; Winch, 1958: 7-24, 102) in that, although there cannot be said to be anything "tangible" about reality, we cannot deny, at the same time, that social norms, institutions, and social organizations have effects on social life which it is the business of the sociologist to explain. Applying these ideas to Canadian sociology implies that it is the business of the sociologist to explore and interpret the very human process by which the social world is constructed and by which a reality comes to be defined. The point we want to make then is that if social class, which we take to represent a system of structured social inequality, is to make sense, then the sociologist must at least be prepared to make it a problematic object of his investigation. Instead of trying, therefore, to wish class out of existence, the sociologist should grasp that this type of social arrangement is a "living reality" in the contemporary world. No amount of intellectual shadow-boxing (cf. Porter, 1965: 9-11) can absolve us of the task of coming to grips with it and explaining its impact on human lives in Canadian society. Contrary to what Porter says, social classes represent much more than "artificial statistical groups." As Johnson points out,

> To a Marxist Scholar, class carries
> a precise definition which relates,
> not to the attitudes of individuals,
> but to their external material
> relationships centered on those
> created by the productive process
> (in Teeple, 1972: 143).

It is worth pointing out that the important relationship between Philosophy and Sociology is admirably expounded by several social scientists (e.g., see Emmett and MacIntyre, 1970; Tiryakian, 1962; Rex, 1973; Winch, 1958) and need not be discussed here. Suffice it to say that the relationship is one which, as far as can be ascertained, has been taken very lightly or remains vaguely implicit in Canadian sociology. Yet, any worthwhile philosophy must be concerned with the nature of human society and any worthwhile study of society must be philosophical in character. Thus, it is on the plane of the very understanding of a defined reality that sociology and philosophy are mortised. As Zijderveld (1970: 40) puts it, reality is the socio-philosophical fact that people act meaningfully and that their actions are so defined by others and thus become subjectively understandable.

It is clear that, to some extent, philosophical anthropology has long been aware that social reality consists of subjectively experienced meanings rather than objectively existing systems and structures (see Walton et al., 1970; and Zijderveld, 1970: 36-37). In marked contrast positivistic sociology, which is well represented in Canadian departments, takes for granted the availability of a preconstituted world of phenomena for investigation (Walsh, 1972a: 19) instead of making the process of its constitution the problematic object of investigation.

41

Poverty in "Theory" and Causal Explanations

Stanislav Andreski recently remarked that to deserve his place in society the sociologist must try to enlighten people about the causes and consequences of their collective action (1964: 45). The supreme lessons as to how to foster this enlightenment and how to help men who are not sociologists to understand social structure and the institutions of men as historical creations were given by the founding fathers of social science: Marx, Mannheim, Pareto, Durkheim, and Weber. All of these men, in their different ways, were acutely sensitive to the need for <u>structural</u> analyses that were also <u>causal</u>. All of them, too, were very much aware of the political, moral, philosophical, and historical underpinnings of sociological analysis (cf. Marx,1971c; Marx and Engels, 1947; Mannheim, 1952; Pareto, 1935; Durkheim, 1951, 1960; Weber, 1930). The medium of this enlightenment is theory.

Our argument thus far has maintained that mainstream Anglophone Canadian sociology appears ignorant of or naive towards this sociological tradition. In other words, Canadian sociologists have been unwilling to grapple with structural analyses which seek to explore the "domain assumptions" of social arrangements and which foster understanding of problems of particular milieux as "insets" in a larger structural reality. Nor have they been concerned much with critically evaluating the dominant justificatory ideology of their society. Let us turn to some specifics.

A large portion of what goes under the heading of "Studies on Poverty" in Canada (see Mann, 1970b; Harp and Hofley, 1971) and the studies on "Deviance" (e.g., Mann, 1971b) can be criticized on the grounds that they lack any explicit and thorough conceptual analysis which links these "problems" <u>structurally</u> to the going political economy.[3] In the case of poverty studies, much lip service is paid to the notion that poverty is a structural phenomenon (often recognized as such via the citation of classical theorists such as Simmel and Cooley). Yet, invariably we find the characteristic heavy reliance on "structural functional" explanations (cf. Whyte, 1965) which are notorious for camouflaging in mystifying language (e.g., "structural differentiation," "role obsolescence," etc.) the central sociological fact that we can only understand the phenomenon by a careful and critical analysis of the existing economic institutions of the society and the premises on which they rest. Not surprisingly, structural functional analyses place the blame for poverty on the poor man or woman, which is the only reason why Whyte (1965: 184), who undertakes such an analysis, can speak of the marginal man situation as a consequence of poverty. What is implicit in his discussion is the notion that "it's all his (the poor man's) fault." Otherwise, the sociologist would have spoken of a marginal <u>situation</u>. That situation carries sociological rather than psychological ramifications (cf. Hofley, 1971: 105-6). Conclusions drawn from such theoretical approaches often seem to be somewhat puzzling. For instance, in the study under review, what can we make of the affirmation that the

> conditions of poverty in an affluent
> society are the consequences of the
> extensive social and cultural changes
> which have accompanied technological
> innovations and scientific advance
> (Whyte, 1965: 188)?

It is pointless to make such claims unless we know what kinds of changes are involved, and who institutes them, and whether they are termed "automatic" or are recognized as the activities of men. Obviously, if these problems so-called are seen simply as "accidents," it follows that policies which leave the fundamental structure of the system intact would likely be posed (cf. Howard, 1970: 6).

Obviously, if we conceive of social stratification as <u>structured</u> social inequality, then it will not be difficult to understand that stratification and poverty are interlaced in Canadian society. Hence, it certainly is of more than mere academic interest that in Canada there has been relatively little change in the distribution of family income over the last fifteen years. In particular, the share of total income received by the bottom one-fifth of families has altered only fractionally, even in the period 1951-1959, which was a period of unprecedented prosperity in Canadian history. This observation refers to family income before tax. And when it is further realised that the overall tax system in Canada is regressive at lower income levels - i.e., the poor are relatively "overtaxed" (Harp and Hofley, p. 36), then it seems that the conclusions that one can logically draw are pretty obvious.[4]

Another convenient point of departure for revealing the poverty of Anglophone Canadian sociology in addition to the failure to appreciate the need for structural analyses, which are per force historical,[5] is the denial that sociologists should be concerned with causal explanations. One of the best examples of this stance is to be found in S.D. Clark (1962: 281-282) who argues that

> It is not the task of the social theorist to seek to discover whether social change is caused by the thoughts men hold, the tools they employ, or the way they order their economic lives ... it is not what causes what but what is related to what that is the concern of the social scientist.

Clearly, if that is the case, then we may as well abandon the works of the truly great sociologists mentioned earlier and totally discourage our students from ever reading them. For at the very core of the works of these social scientists was the idea that causal rather than merely functional analysis should be the concern of the genuine social scientist. The whole purpose of any science is to discover the causes of the phenomena it investigates, and genuine science is causal explanation. But Clark seems to be proposing a totally new brand of social science in which we are to avoid asking for the causes of social action. To avoid asking for the causes of social action is to avoid the need for theory or for theoretical understanding of man and society. And to avoid theoretical questions is to end up counting heads, or finding out "what is connected to what," which any level-headed citizen can do. If, then, this is the sort of sociology we practise and teach, we may succeed in training students as good technicians but hardly as sociologists; we may also conclude that the raison d'être of our sociology is badly in need of reformulation.

To a large extent, this is the kind of sociology that is in vogue in Anglophone Canada, as an examination of the standard literature will expose. The theoretical dearth of Canadian sociology seems to be hinged on a form of positivism aptly described by Walsh (1972a: 26n) as a "belief in the transcendental objectivity of formally rational procedures." In their anxious pursuit of scientific respectability based on certain dubious premises (a concern shared by other sociologists elsewhere, notably in the United States), Canadian sociologists have restricted themselves, unnecessarily and inflexibly it would seem, to what, in comparison with the range of methods available to them in principle, is a meagre and stereotyped set of techniques and theoretical frameworks. From these, they can glean only the shallowest message at the most superficial levels of meaning (e.g., see Whyte, 1965; cf. Seeley at al., 1956). Even the more intrepid works in Canadian sociology, such as Porter's (1965), suffer from what Wolf (1970: xix) aptly calls "theoretical innocence," or as Heap (1974) says, "Porter's documentation becomes a substitute for theory." The theoretical innocence of mainstream Canadian sociology has strong connections with the "fetish of concepts" (Szymanski, 1971: 101; Mills, 1959: 28) and with the "enumeration of categories" (Colfax, 1971: 89) as well as with the belief in positivism as noted above (cf. Hyman, 1971: 21). This orientation also means that, as far as understanding Canadian society is concerned, there is much theoretical irrelevance in Canadian sociology. This point we shall elaborate on later when we discuss social change. Much of this irrelevance comes via structural functionalism,[6] because, in the words of Rex, we seem to be "seeking an American future in purely empiricist, positivistic or functional studies" (1973: 191). That we are seeking this future is clear from reading Porter, 1965; Clark, 1962: 279-97; and Rossides, 1968, among others.

It is evident that positivism has been pursued partly at the expense of any kind of thorough theoretical or epistemological understanding of why social arrangements in Canada are as they are. There does not appear to be much concern for insights which could be expected to unite "data" with the phenomenal world of acting and innovating human beings caught in historical nets of social arrangements.

This point is very much overlooked in contemporary sociology, but especially in orthodox criminological studies whose aim is usually the practical one of prediction, an aim best explained in terms of the social problem orientation as opposed to the sociological problem orientation. We must make some critical remarks on this. In effect this approach means that the practical concerns of the agencies of law and order in society, which revolve around problems of the detection and prevention of crime and delinquency, are treated by criminologists as the central problematics of their investigation.[7] The criminologist's position is summed up by Vallee and Whyte (1971: 570-571) thus:

> As society moves through the phase of advanced industrialization the idea gets more firmly implanted that human behavior and human nature can be mastered ... through the application of scientific methods and techniques" (emphasis added).

This is a point of first importance, for it exposes the fact that if sociologists accept this somewhat deterministic idea without question, they will as a consequence take social control as one of their major concerns. But, above all, we should firmly ask: whose idea it is that "gets more firmly implanted?" Such a question begs for answers that must be plucked from a structural understanding of society, which understanding is itself rooted in the sociology of knowledge (see Marx and Engels, 1947: 38-43).

Another failing is clearly illustrated in Canadian studies on "minority relations" (e.g., see Elliott, 1971; Henry, 1973) where there is little systematic attempt to utilize a theoretical perspective such as that offered by the sociology of knowledge to "flush out" or probe under the cloak of notions men and women have about themselves and society (see Marx and Engels, 1947; Mannheim, 1952; Berger and Luckmann, 1966). Such a perspective could prove useful in helping us to grasp the Canadian Weltanschauung on ethnic and other minorities in a stereoscopic way, thus enabling us to recognize how cultural socialization shapes and supports the all-important attitude structures and belief systems that are so crucial in "minority theory."

It is the business of the sociology of knowledge to call for and undertake analyses of the structural forces, that in any epoch bring about and consolidate a world view, and the whole thought-pattern that happens to be dominant. Neither Elliott nor Henry go far enough, we feel, in grounding their data with a view to discovering the styles and methods of thought that undergird ethnic relations. What is needed in these analyses of "minorities" and "immigrants" is a radical conceptualization that would systematically relate the marginality of the immigrants and other minorities in Canadian society to their position in the system of capitalist social relations of production. This means that, however political it might become, the sociologists specializing in the study of minority and ethnic studies will have to relate the intergroup process which fall within this orbit (e.g., assimilation, integration and so on) to the historical, political and economic structural contexts. Prejudice and discrimination may seem like psychological aberrations; they are explicable only social-structurally.

Micro-Sociology, Structural Understanding and the Question of Values

In mainstream Canadian sociology, there is a noticeable neglect for the understanding of structures of social relations and of cultural definitions of the situation. It is this neglect which has spawned so many micro-quantitative studies, the cumulative results of which, by and large, do not (perhaps cannot) open our eyes to the problems of social structure and culture or tell us anything sociological about social systems as ongoing dynamic realities. A review of the recent literature reveals that the concern with small-scale empirical studies is a persistent one. Many of these studies are guilty of perpetuating what Tiryakian (1970: 119-120) refers to, after Whitehead, as "the fallacy of misplaced concreteness" in that they mistake the analytical part for the concrete whole (see also Walsh, 1972c: 67). Clearly, if these studies were put into the more general context of structural studies and history or were situated in power contexts, then we would have no quarrel with them. But invariably they remain dismembered, isolated "studies," often a-theoretical, and they seemingly bear no connection with the human issues in society and history. Alas for the positivistic notion that somehow these studies will "add up." This curious but firmly rooted notion of "Abstracted Empiricism" (Mills, 1959: 67) comes home to rest in Canadian sociology. For these studies do not add up when they are bound together as "Readers" or as "Collected Essays" or as "Anthologies" (e.g., see

47

Blishen et.al., 1971; Mann, 1970a; Mann, 1971a; et passim). This is our central point. These micro-studies do not "add up" to a full-fledged organized science of man and society, and they often are, for lack of a theoretical focus, conceptually irrelevant because the variables selected are not placed within the meaning of a larger social structure.[8]

All this, of course, is not to deny the significance of statistical manipulation in social sciences or the importance of micro-studies. But there is the danger, as Rex (1973: 35) warns, that, as we develop more sophisticated ways of counting and calculating with the aid of the computer, we shall lose the capacity to think. This danger is all too real in Canadian sociology, with its dominant focus on survey methods and "quantification" and the limited concern with seeking out the process of the social construction of reality and the "whys" of social action. If sociologists spent more time looking behind the facade of social roles and paid more attention to men and women as acting thinking beings rather than small pieces of statistic, they would no doubt enlighten people about the causes and consequences of their action.[9] Sociologists would then have earned their place in society, not as mystics, or as sorcerers (Andreski), but as social scientists.

The preoccupation of mainstream Anglophone Canadian sociology with empiricism carries many significant implications for the development of sociology in Canada. We have already remarked that inasmuch as this orientation is developed at the expense of theoretical development and conceptuali-zation, we have inhibited our understanding of man and his arrangements in Canadian society. But the strong concern with empiricism also serves to focus attention away from social structures and onto the narrow historicity and metaphysical aspects of social life. The combination of these two points make for a third, perhaps more serious, result, which is that the search for methodological rigor serves to keep most sociologists from having to examine the values implicit in and underlying their work (Colfax, 1971: 35; cf. Silverman, 1972; Taylor et.al., 1973: 33-36, 273).

By avoiding issues of values, many sociologists feel that they can remain "objective," "scientific," and uncontaminated by the political implications of their enterprise. This position is linked to the mistaken notion that sociology can be value-free (see Mills, 1959; Gouldner, 1968; Horowitz, 1968; Rose, 1956; Gray, 1968; Furfey, 1959; and Lynd, 1939). Being a notion which seems to be implicit in much of Canadian sociology, if forms a further target of the criticisms in this essay. On this important problem we wish to make a number of comments.

First of all, it can be strongly questioned whether the purposes of scholarship are necessarily served by lack of involvement or through "neutrality." In sociology, at any rate, under some circumstances scholarship purposes may be properly attended to only if the sociologist becomes involved in his subject of inquiry rather than remaining aloof and becomes committed and empathic to those he studies rather than pretending to be neutral (Howard, 1970: 8).

Secondly, it is never to be forgotten that scientific inquiry is a series of confrontations and refutations. This point is not inconsistent with Thomas Kuhn's idea of paradigm-shifts. In essence this means that science, properly understood, is not an inhuman enterprise that requires us to dismiss the human task of selecting things to see and seeing them with a bias. In the world of social phenomena, then, we only become sociologists, rather than mere grubbers of miscellaneous information about man and society, when we investigate the confrontations of social life from the point of view of meaning and purpose (see Weber, 1947). The very touchstone of science is to articulate the bias and clarify explicitly why we choose to see what we are looking at and defining, whilst refuting other alternatives (cf. Chambliss, 1973: 463; Myrdal, 1969; Lynd, 1939; and Gouldner, 1962, 1968). But, if it is argued that the standpoint is "subjective," then it would be a recognition that understanding is subjective, and, perhaps by this criterion, "Unscientific." If this argument is pursued and upheld, the whole of science (which ostensibly seeks "understanding") becomes subjective. The concept of understanding as a goal in science and all of systematic inquiry do themselves nest in some kind of "subjectivism." When all is said and done, of course, it must be conceded that we do agree, firmly and often dogmatically, on things subjective. This being so, the major task of the sociologist is precisely to determine how, in cultural and historical

49

terms, we come to agree on the subjective elements in life.

Thirdly, as Bredemeier (1973: 127) reminds us,

> among all other things it may be said to be, science is also a morality, in the sense that it includes values, and scientists have a stake in the morality that pervades society.

Social sciences have, by their very nature, a special connection with morality, because as normative sciences they cannot avoid propositions about what "ought to be the case."

Fourthly, and finally, critical sociological analysis contains a substantive political content. In this sense, the sociology which is worth its salt cannot avoid discovering and debunking cherished values and illusions (cf. Colfax and Roach, 1971: 14); nor can it avoid bringing to light what many would like to conceal. As Andreski puts it, no important understanding of social phenomena can be made without offending adherents of various dogmas, loyalties, and material interests (1964: 45). In short, we know enough about the sociology of knowledge to recognize that the practice of sociology is in part a political process.

It is highly doubtful whether mainstream Canadian sociology has ever fully confronted these problems. The fact that Anglophone Canadian sociology has traditionally remained in the safe and shallow waters of academic empiricism, has displayed an unwillingness to develop structural analyses, and has never posed a radical critique of Canadian society, means that this sociology has failed to embody an explicit political position which is critical of our social arrangements.[10] By default or by intent the makers of Canadian sociology (and anthropology, for the reasons expressed by Goddard, 1972) opt for the status quo. To single out and to attend to what are considered important issues, of course, is not, per se, radical. To be radical about something is partly to grasp that something "by its roots" and partly a question of how one asks one's questions (see Howard, 1970: 5; Mills, 1943).[11] The vital question about what is radical and

50

what is not in the above terms may be best answered by the specification and utilization of a theoretical viewpoint which is critical of political economy.

In summary, Canadian sociologists must be prepared to ask questions about the reified social arrangements that somehow face men as gods on the Durkheimian principles of externality and constraint. These man-made arrangements are never immutable, in spite of the process of "externalization" (Berger and Luckmann, 1966: 58-60) which does tend to weaken our understanding of persistence and change in society.

Poverty in the Understanding of Change

If we are to follow S.D. Clark as an exemplary path-breaker in Canadian sociology, we may hardly be able to understand the process of social change. On the one hand, we have in Canadian sociology a sparsity of structural analyses, and, on the other, an umbilical reliance on "structural functionalism" as a theoretical perspective.[12] The latter condition has led some sociologists on to what seems to be a confusing trail about what social theory can and cannot do (e.g., Clark, 1962: 279-80; cf. Wheatcroft, 1971: 545-58). Clark makes the point that "only in a very limited way has sociology succeeded in fitting social change into its general framework of theory" (1962: 295).[13]

But this statement is as much an indictment of contemporary social theory as it is a revelation of the ignorance of Marxian social theory which made the concept of change its very leitmotif. If the sort of theory Clark has in mind is structural functionalism, then his statement is hardly surprising. Parsons himself confessed that change internal to any system was difficult for his theory (1951: 483, 486; cf. Parsons, 1961); and, furthermore, even change within a system could only be partially dealt with.

Now, a theory of society which cannot handle change is no theory at all, and a theory incapable of explaining conflicts such as struggles between classes or industrial conflicts, both of which are characteristic of modern industrial societies, cannot hope to explain a changing Canadian society. It is distressing then, that in spite of Parson's own confessions, Professor Clark holds such unjustified expectations of Parsons's "theory" which Parsons himself does not hold. As Clark puts it:

> certainly if there is to come an
> advance in the theory of change,
> a heavy reliance upon the
> theoretical work of such sociologists
> as Talcott Parsons can be expected
> (1962: 297).

This attitude toward American sociology is uncalled for.
To take issue with Clark, of course, is not to deny his
very significant contribution to Canadian sociology or
to belittle his stature as a sociologist; we would not
wish to be misunderstood on this. Nor, indeed, are we
suggesting that Clark alone is responsible for shaping
the Canadian apotheosis of a static model of society
and change. Others are easily recognized (e.g., see
Porter, 1965; Seeley et al., 1956; Whyte, 1965). But
it must be remembered that Clark's work in question has
been for some time a standard text in sociology courses
on "Canadian Society." Most sociologists know (even
though they perhaps do not admit) that structural
functionalism cannot handle change. At best this model
can recategorize a society after the changes have
occurred, and this task does not seem to us to be
particularly creative or even useful. Rather than
accepting the Marxian theory of change, a theory which
very explicitly speaks of change as, more often than
not, rooted in structured internal conflicts (i.e.,
between the forces of production and the relations of
production), Canadian sociology seems prepared to do
without any theory at all, unless, of course, we can
squeeze something of the sort from say, Mann's
"Collected" volumes on "Social and Cultural Change in
Canada." This is very doubtful.

Few would question the validity of Marxian theory
in providing powerful tools for the analysis of
change.[14] Indeed, as Mack (1965: 397) reminds us:

> We have seriously underutilized a
> promising theoretical focus in our
> relative neglect of social conflict.
> Surely, it is not because conflict
> theory has been tried and found
> wanting. It has been little tried
> and, when tried, remarkably
> successful ... Continuing and more
> intensive attention to power,

52

stratification, and conflict will
surely advance the science and our
ability to make use of it.

One of the great contributions that social theory can
make to our understanding of society is to foster
causal explanations of the relations between parts of
the social system. All worthwhile theories do this,
and critical social theory with its emphasis on the
structural and ideational elements of social systems is
very capable of accomplishing this (cf. Chapters 8 and
9 below). In this context, the implications of
Francophone Canadian sociology for contributing to a
conceptual understanding of Quebec and Canadian society
should be grasped. Insofar as Quebec sociology is
<u>critical</u> and insofar as the critique is <u>structurally
informed</u>, it carries vast implications for change. For
what we think about society will change society, and
the more critical that thinking the greater the
possibilities for change. What we seem to need, then,
is a fresh exploitation of energy and thought toward a
<u>structural critique</u> and a structural vision of the way
Canadian society might be changed in other than the
agreed liberal terms. Critical sociology assumes that
radical change is at least possible. To the extent
that such a sociology provides the knowledge of how
society works, it makes a distinctive contribution to
the struggle for socio-political change. For the
critical sociologist, knowledge of society is a means
to transform society. This posture, needless to say,
creates its own set of problems, for there never is an
automatic connection or isomorphism between knowledge
and social action.

Conclusion

As far as we can state a conclusion to this
chapter, it has two facets: one theoretical, the
other methodological.

Theoretically, we would argue that, if we are to
give constructive direction to Canadian sociology, then,
at the very least, we would do well to shape a
reflexive sociology which is also a "sociology of
engagement" (Howard, 1970: 7-8) which explicitly
questions the background assumptions that shape the
orthodoxy of Canadian sociology. The crucial task of
demystifying the reified products of human activity,
such as class, exploitation, racism, and coercive

social control, is yet to be undertaken. If such a task were tackled, it would be inevitable that the sociologists engaged in such an activity take note of a sociology of conflict and of power relations, not only in the formal sense, but in a way which accounts for human beings not as passive objects but as active subjects engaged in creating themselves and hence history.

Such a theoretical position could bring into the arsenal of sociological analysis a structural critique of the Canadian political economy. But it seems, at this point, that nothing short of a radical rethinking of Canadian sociology and of sociological theory along the critical plane will assist us in becoming social scientists with accumulated knowledge about social systems.[15] Any sociological theory worthy of the name ought to take full account, therefore, of the complex problems of reification and alienation whereby men and women hypostatize the outcome of their social relations and feel estranged from, perhaps even in a sense resolutely driven and crippled by them. Only a critical sociology promises to deepen our understanding of these important theoretical issues. Only a critical perspective promises to incorporate methodical self-reflection into its method. This is precisely the dimension that positivism closes off. In proposing that a critical sociology can counteract the reifying tendencies of the "techno-structure" by revealing them, we should not be led to believe the future of sociology lies with "criticism" alone. Criticism is one of the many challenging tasks a sociologist has to face. Nevertheless, the task of forceful critique is particularly urgent in our period of the twentieth century, for, as we have argued elsewhere, the new technological work-world of advanced industrial society is quite capable of amputating and absorbing the critical function of the imagination. Theoretically and methodologically we need to re-examine both our practical procedures and our conceptions of the utility of knowledge.

Methodologically, we would agree with Rex (1973: 6-7) and with Tiryakian (1970: 129) that the best hope for the future of sociology lies in a careful and considered application of the anthropologists' technique to the analysis of the problems of large-scale societies, i.e., the adoption of participant observation, coupled with the interpretation of what is observed in terms of the purposes, and always of the culture observed. Since, as we have already argued, the anthropologists have been, by and large, more problem oriented and have been more sensitive to the philosophical and epistemological issues involved in studying people, it seems reasonable to state with Tiryakian (1970) that, for an adequate sociological approach and particularly for a mode of explaining social change, we must embark upon the closest collaboration with history and anthropology.

But in concluding thus, we should not be so naive as to think that switching techniques alone will do. Only by deliberately rejuvenating our theoretical perspective on Canadian society will we be able to move away from the current orientation to the nit-picking, narrowly empirical shallow waters of sociology, to the deep substratum of social reality in all its inter-subjective and spontaneous diversity. As conclusions these are modest suggestions, but we feel that they point in the direction that promises to alleviate some of the poverty of sociology, of the type we have discussed, in a changing Canadian society.

NOTES

1. We do not happen to agree with the claim made by Curtis and Scott (1973: viii) that "thus far, research in this country shows greater emphasis on ... analyses at the macro level" and that "attention has only begun to turn to micro-level studies." This claim is altogether incorrect, because apart from the pioneering and truly macroscopic work of Porter (1965) and a few others which address problems at a macro level (e.g., Westhues, 1972 and S.D. Clark's mainly historical works) most of Canadian sociology is of the micro-quantitative sort which lends itself to "objective" quantitative rather than to macroscopic understanding.

2. For more important inroads into an understanding of this problem in modern industrial society see the works of Herbert Marcuse, especially his One Dimensional Man (Boston) 1964; and his Counter Revolution and Revolt (Boston) 1972, cf. also Engels's insight into this problem of "working class apathy" in his Condition of the Working Class in England in 1844 (Preface to the 1972 edition), and cf. the useful essay by Norbet Wiley. "The Ethnic Mobility Trap," Social Problems, 15 (Fall) 1967: 147-159.

3. It must be remarked that Hofley's own contribution to this volume is a refreshing exploration into conceptual thinking and marks a clear departure from the common crop of barren approaches associated with structural functional analyses.

4. See Harp and Hofley, 1971: 16-17; Rossides, 1968: 250-252; Porter, 1965: 112-125.

5. It is much too easy to overlook the historical relevance of many of the everyday concepts we use in sociology. Andreski (1964: 65) gives a timely reminder that "a term such as 'structure' can only be meaningful when used as an historical expression to denote a set of relations known to have endured over a considerable period of time." In this sense, a historical explanation is a sociological explanation in so far as it is an explanation as distinct from a narrative, i.e., descriptive non-continuous account.

6. One should not overlook that, for all its pretentiousness, Porter's work is a functionalist analysis of Canadian society, with all the dubious functionalist premises. Thus, his focus on class composition and ruling elite of Canada, on functionalist premises, forces him to believe, like all good functionalists, that the need for order in society requires institutions (perhaps coercive?) and elites which coordinate and regulate these "functions." Elites, in Porter's terms, are functional for Canada. But how do we penetrate them? And for whom are they functional? This is a gigantic question when asked in the multi-cultural context of Canadian society. The political implications of this theoretical position are many, and they clearly reflect what Mills (1958) suggested, namely, that the possible "causes" of World War Three depend in the final analysis on the political decision of a handful of men (Porter's elite?) over whom we have no control (cf. the December 1973 "incident" involving Canada's implication in the Colorado-based North American Air Defence Command, NORAD). Every Canadian knows what happened!

7. See Hackler, 1968 for such a focus; and cf. Walsh, 1972b: 47; and Taylor et al., 1973: 268-282 et passim, for some critical notes.

8. Only a very small proportion of these studies is explicitly concerned with theoretical questions of any significance. Often we find it difficult to cross that bridge from "private troubles" to "public issues." This is the case with Jackson (1966) where it is difficult to grasp the theoretical bridge between "community conflict" in "Normanville" and the wider societal context. To some extent, this holds true for Scott and Curtis (1973) where the truly Canadian data are less illuminating than the rest of the non-Canadian content of the book. Here, we still do not know whether, say, the fact of mobility carries political implications, and, if so, what they are. Or even whether the fact of mobility upsets, or in any way threatens, the elite model of Porter's Canada.

9. Clearly, as Hofley (1971: 114) points out, one of the grave short-comings found in much of the

literature on poverty (cf. Mann, 1970b; Harp and Hofley, 1971) is the over-reliance on survey data such as the Census. No one is disputing the usefulness of these types of data in sociological work, but, as we have already intimated, over-reliance on them characteristically tends to divert attention from the larger structure of social arrangements of which they are mere reflections. To overlook this fact is to severely underplay the fundamentals of the construction and definition of reality as the existential-phenomenological task of human actors.

10. An independent Canadian sociology capable of effecting a break with the colonial past and of establishing a critical structural understanding of social arrangements, will come only from those sociologists willing to question the basis assumptions on which our economic and political system rest.

11. Howard, in Deutsch and Howard (1970: 5), puts the point well: "Radical sociology asks whether the problems generated by social structure are inherent within it (a consequence of 'internal contradictions,' if one will) or simply 'mistakes or unintended consequences'?"

12. It is obvious that the lack of structural analyses in Canadian sociology has been recognized by some sociologists (see e.g., Wheatcroft, 1971: 556; Vallee and Whyte, 1971: 566). But whether the desire to face the inadequacy has been taken seriously is another matter. For attempts to at least address problems in structural/historical terms see Clairmont and Magill, 1970, and for works that have departed from narrowly-conceived consensus models see Ossenberg, 1971; Westhues, 1972.

13. It is instructive, of course, to note that Wheatcroft (1971: 545-558), in analyzing social systems over time, does not explicitly speak of social change, or contradictions, or dialectic, but "trends" and "counter-trends." Nor does he speak of conflict. Now, all this seems a curious hedging, for it can be argued that the term "trend" is one that is shorn of any dynamism; indeed, it smacks of the notion of equilibrated consistency,

which is altogether an unrealistic depiction of a culturally plural social system. The point here is that the choice of concepts _is_ very important in constructing a realistic and dynamic theory of man and society (cf. Card, 1968).

14. In this connection, see Worsley, 1968; Saran, 1963; and Hobsbawm, 1959. Cf. also, some of the illuminating essays in Ossenberg, 1971.

15. With much concern nowadays about the Canadianization of sociology (which is taught in Canada), perhaps our students may indeed become hopelessly confused and intellectually under-nourished if they attempt to understand sociology, in all its rich philosophical, historical, and epistemological tradition, by keeping to the books and journal articles ostensibly Canadian. In the CRSA, except for rarities like Jackson (1966) and the enthographic studies, most are of the positivist types which we have criticized in this paper.

A Postscript to Chapter III

As we noted in the Introduction, the preceding chapter appeared here in the form in which it was published in 1975, when it <u>was</u> true to say that Anglophone Canadian sociology was needlessly obsessed with micro-explanations, concomitant with the promotion of methodologically impeccable, if theoretically naïve, accounts of Canadian society. Then, it was justifiable to say of the vast majority of Canadian sociologists that they kept well away from critical structural interpretations of their society (as the review of the literature cited above reveals).

It is now evident that since 1975 much work has been done, in mainstream sociology alone, to flesh out our understanding along the lines suggested in the article. Many issues have been sharpened in the intervening period, as attested to by the crop of important publications since the original article appeared.[1] Yet, many of the criticisms aired in 1975 are still applicable today; besides, the essay represents the original programmatic beckoning (and hope) of the author, a realistic hope for a theoretical synthesis which would follow the lead of a critical theory relevant to the explanation of the contradictions and crises within western industrial societies and liberal democracies such as Canada. Nothing here is suggesting, of course, that the developments which occured since the publication of "the poverty of sociology" are causally related to the thrust of that critique. Many of the works to which we now draw attention were obviously formulated <u>before</u> the critique was ever conceived. We can only say that it is gratifying both for students and teachers to be able, now, to draw upon a wide (and growing) range of macro, and in many ways critical material, in systematizing a structural analysis of modern Canada.

There are, to be sure, some badly neglected points of interest yet to be teased, and we have sought, in this small book, to point to some of them with appropriate commentary. For example, the question of pluralism in the socio-cultural sense is still a vexed one in Canadian sociology, as is the relevance of the sociology of knowledge to the interpretation of world views and idea-systems. And, finally, the long-standing problem in sociology - the question of class and <u>class conflict</u> - is yet to be given the formulation that befits it as a structural characteristic of capitalist society. Here, the works of Forcese, Hunter, Osberg, Marchak and Brym and Sacouman are in the forefront. We must fiercely resist any attempt by social scientists to present a theory of Canadian society which does not take fully into account the ideological salience of what we as Canadians daily imbibe, often without reflection or critical analysis. What Alvin Gouldner (1976) terms "epistemological anxiety" is still a major characteristic of sociology, as a discipline. To some extent this is unavoidable, for as we have already said sociologists do not have a monopoly on truth - no one has. Yet the explanations which we give of the cultural world - the humanly created world - have a special validity or status, not because of any unspecified claim to superior insight, but on the important basis of their search for structures of social relations which are rooted in a philosophical conception of humankind. What this conception implies is an untramelled effort to delineate and establish the humanness in constructed reality. The dialectical questioning which underpins a sociology of knowledge as a hermeneutic method, helps to assuage the anxiety which so many social critics experience at one time or another. But it does not eliminate the anxiety. Also, the willingness to engage in critiques of society does not carry an inevitable implication that those who pursue independent criticism and judgment necessarily subscribe to a dogma of certainty. Rather, it is that right to investigate into and conjecture about accepted doctrines and conceptions of reality which motivates the critical theorist toward the formulation of alternative perspectives.

Up to the middle of the 1970s, it did seem as if Canadian sociologists feared retribution of some sort, to judge from the tip-toe posture which characterized the mainstream of the discipline. The kind of synthesis that was groped for in the foregoing article, and which is still now evident in the rest of this book, has a direct bearing on the author's belief that the only sociology which will stand the test of time is the one which explicitly fosters a non-atomized understanding cognizant of a concept of historical totality. Such an understanding would serve, undoubtedly, to counteract the popular tendency of assuming the existence of historical patterns as timeless "laws" of nature. Typically, explanations of the latter type ignore the contextual location of thought patterns in general and what Habermas calls the "knowledge - constitutive interests" in particular.

A good portion of the intellectual anxiety experienced by academics stems from, or is in a significant way related to, the unnecessary fragmentation of thought, which often aids in creating an abyss between, say, theory and practice; economic life and political struggles; self-knowledge and societal context; the object of history and the subject of history; fact and value, and so forth. At bottom, then, part of the epistemological uneasiness in so much of social science thought derives from the apotheosis of these false dichotomizations. Therefore, the concept of dialectical totality which was only implicit in "the poverty of sociology" and which will be spelled out in more detail in the next chapter, was designed to show that a critical theory must be concerned with a double dialectic: the interaction of nature and humankind; and the interaction among humans.

It is this thrust, according to Hamilton, which is brought out in Lukács's conception of dialectical social science: the value of the dialectical method consists in its reliance on holism and in the fact that it does not take the structure of existing reality as "given," and that this "given" reality is shown to be a mere appearance obscuring an underlying reality. This tendency to look at the totality of the social world in the explanation of "facts," rather than facts isolated from it, constitutes what distinguishes dialectics from accepted social science. This type of social science merely takes the laws of capitalist society as given, as the unquestioned basis of its scientific method. Marxism - in its properly dialectical form - shows the necessity of dialectical and historical analysis of the facts, and thus can penetrate to the historically specific core of the laws of capitalist society: it can make distinctions between the "real existence and inner core" of phenomena, and understand the relation between the two in terms of their historical context. True knowledge, freed from the ideological obscuration of ahistorical "bourgeois" conceptual systems, is thus made possible when the "isolated facts" of social life are integrated into a totality, a knowledge based on a "conceptual reproduction of social reality."[2]

The quest for a critical, structural formulation of theory, the centrality of the sociology of knowledge to sociological theory, the necessity for a plural model of Canadian society and the search for a philosophically informed social theory were all prefigured in this programmatic essay. The search continues. What we present here in the rest of the book are the first approximations of some of the ideas we feel are worth careful examination from the vantage point of the 1980s.

Notes to the Postscript

1. Among the notable works filling this bill, the
    following deserve special mention: Wallace
    Clement, The Canadian Corporate Elite, 1975; idem.,
    Continental Corporate Elite, 1977; Alfred A.
    Hunter, Class Tells: On Social Inequality in
    Canada, 1981; Lars Osberg, Economic Inequality in
    Canada, 1981; Dennis Forcese, The Canadian Class
    Structure, (two editions: 1975, 1980); Richard
    Ossenberg (ed.), Power and Change in Canada, 1980;
    John Allan Fry (ed.), Economy, Class and Social
    Reality, 1979; Robert J. Brym and R. James
    Sacouman (eds.), Underdevelopment and Social
    Movements in Atlantic Canada, 1979; Norman Penner,
    The Canadian Left: A Critical Analysis, 1977;
    John Richards and Larry Pratt, Prairie Capitalism:
    Power and Influence in the New West, 1979; J. Paul
    Grayson (ed.), Class, State, Ideology and Change,
    1980; M. Patricia Marchak, Ideological
    Perspectives on Canada, (two editions: 1975, 1981);
    Cy Gonick, Inflation or Depression: The
    Continuing Crisis in the Canadian Economy, 1975;
    Allan B. Anderson and James S. Frideres,
    Ethnicity in Canada: Theoretical Perspectives,
    1981; Wsevolod Isajiw (ed.), The Impact of
    Ethnicity in Canadian Society, 1977; Leo Driedger
    (ed.), The Canadian Ethnic Mosaic, 1978; Jeffrey
    G. Reitz, The Survival of Ethnic Groups, 1980.

    At the Introductory level several important
monographs have been added to the growing
literature on Canadian sociology. Here the
McGraw-Hill Ryerson series in Canadian society has
gone a long way towards buttressing the ongoing
task of building Canadian sociology. And one must
also mention that G.N. Ramu and Stuart Johnson's
Introduction to Canadian Society, 1976, as well as
Dennis Forcese and Stephen Richer's Issues in
Canadian Society, 1975, contains substantive
discussions concerning the current direction of
Canadian sociology. This is not by any means a
"comprehensive" updating, and those whose works
are not included here may well feel that we are
not aware of their publications and ongoing
research. Such a reaction would be understandable,
but it would not necessarily reflect the true
state of awareness which now exists in Canadian
sociology departments about the "coming of age" of

sociology. This is simply to record the exciting
current developments which, in time, will
probably render the critique in the foregoing
chapter somewhat obsolete.

2. Hamilton, 1974, p. 41.

CHAPTER IV

THE CONTEMPORARY RELEVANCE OF
DIALECTICAL THINKING IN SOCIOLOGY

The Meaning of Dialectics for Social Theory

What is perhaps one of the most important observations concerning social science theory and the problem of reflexivity was made by Anthony Giddens in two of his books dealing with social theory in its philosophical union. He remarked that the conceptual schemes of the social sciences express what he calls a double hermeneutic that has no parallel elsewhere, relating both to entering and grasping the frames of meanings involved in the production of social life by lay actors and reconstituting these within the new frames of meaning involved in technical conceptual schemes.[1] Sociology necessarily shares this double hermeneutic because sociology stands in a subject-subject relation to its field of study, and in common with other social sciences cannot separate itself from its heteronomy, since there is no morally separate or transcendentally "neutral" meta-language in which to couch the vocabulary of the social sciences.

All social theory must deal with the reflexivity of human society in one fashion or another, and it is of the essence of Marxian social theory to constantly focus on the transformative capacity of human action. This is the key element in the notion of praxis,[2] that Hegelian notion of universal self-creative activity as that through which human beings create their world, themselves, and initiate practical change, thereby exercising a direct influence on all of social life. Praxis and dialectic are two fundamental concepts in Marxian social theory, and both concepts embody the idea of reflexivity.

It is generally recognized that the idea of dialectics can be traced to Plato and ancient Greece, or that, at any rate, it is as old as the practice of philosophy. Notwithstanding, some modern philosophers argue that this particular idea has only a very tenuous association with the Greeks. For the purpose of our discussion, we are primarily concerned with the post-Enlightenment bouyancy of dialectics, and most specifically as it has reached us through Hegel, Marx, Feuerbach, and Engels, but especially Hegel and Marx

whose ideas were greatly influenced by "the greatest of
the modern philosophers,"[3] Immanuel Kant. But here
again scholars tend to disagree on whether Hegel or
Marx had very much to do with a systematic formulation
of the idea of dialectics. Thus, for instance,
according to Lichtheim,[4] the dialectic is not essential
to Hegel's system, and the terms "thesis - antithesis -
and synthesis" occur nowhere in Hegel's writings.
Similarly, Cornforth[5] suggests that Marx and Engels
never and nowhere worked out a fully systematic
statement of dialectical materialism or the "laws of
dialectic." What they did, so Cornforth avers, was to
cite examples of phenomena corresponding to these laws.
Finally, Bottomore and Rubel,[6] argue that "Marx himself
never used the terms "historical materialism" and
"dialectical materialism."

Without getting into the centre of these claims,
we would like to draw substantially on the work of Marx
(and comment on the exegitical labors of Engels) to
illustrate how these men were responsible for investing
the idea of dialectics with historical specificity and
scope. Their keenness to apply this critical method to
the understanding of society contributed to a high
degree of systematization, and clearly facilitated the
relevancy of this idea to modern social science.

What, then, is dialectics? Dialectical analysis,
or reasoning, employs a method which necessarily begins
with a particular existing condition or society, and
goes on to theoretically analyze that condition and its
transformation in its entirety, with a view to understanding what may be called macro-relations. In
Kantian terms, however, there could be no analysis
without synthesis, and no synthesis without analysis.
Thus, basically, dialectics is the mutual inter-
relation of analysis and synthesis. But as a
processual approach to phenomena, it is further joined
to the conception that all social and historical
conditions are permeated by a negativity or immanent
contradition which to a large extent "determines their
content and movement."[7]

The key to dialectics turns on an understanding of
interconnections or structural relationships, as well
as on an understanding of totality and the immanent
negativity of historical phenomena. In the Marxian
paradigm, a major empirical assumption informing the
dialectical approach is that capitalist society has,

built into its very structure, a series of contradictory and conflict-ridden social relations which generate its "laws of motion." Specifically, the idea is that historical events (and, Engels thought, Nature as well) operate on some knowable dynamic. It is the aim of Marxian oriented research to discover the human causes and structural tendencies of social change, to chase after these apparent "laws" and make them socially comprehensible. This approach will not ascribe behavior to "human nature." The relevance of thinking in this way quickly registers in the mind when one realizes that in everyday speech and conception of reality, the dialectical fact confronts us. It is revealed, for instance, in the use of terms such as: "paradoxical," "ironic," "feedback," "two-edged sword," "mixed-blessing," "ambivalent" and so on.

Some common examples of what can be understood as dialectical processes will help to concretize the idea. By the dialectical token, man's mastery over nature and himself is almost without exception the destruction of the individual as subject, thus negating the very purpose of that mastery. Or again, democracy, by serving as the basis for bureaucracy, calls forth its own destruction - to succeed, it requires the one thing which will destroy it. And, the process of life gives rise to death; death only happens as the negation of life, unfortunately a terminal negation. Finally, to use a more elaborate example, Kuhn has shown in his influential little book The Structure of Scientific Revolutions, that the revolution in science is dialectical, not cumulative. For while normal science is a phase of cumulative understanding, the process of expansion in normal science calls forth anomalies, that is, events or phenomena not explicable within a dominant paradigm. When these anomalies increase (as they are bound to, if scientific work is continued), then they produce a crisis. It is this crisis stage which necessitates the fall of one paradigm and the rise of another. This stage, termed by Kuhn revolution, is the one where major advances in science are made, and is the period during which great changes in scientific status take place. Each time a new paradigm is enthroned, the stage is set for a new dialectic in science to revitalize itself. It is contradiction within the given explanatory science which, ideally, become stressful and initiate new developments and change. But, as Hegel argued, contradiction was never eliminated, once and for all.

Everything was inherently contradictory, and thus the new paradigm would, in time, encounter its own special anomalies.

The above illustrations are perhaps sufficient to indicate the pervasive quality of this idea. This pervasiveness explains, partly, why Engels was not content to simply state that dialectics is "the science of interconnections, in contrast to metaphysics,"[8] but anxiously wanted to amplify dialectics to cover all of Nature, not just part of it. But it must be grasped that Engels' enthusiasm which came after Marx's death, cannot be squared with Marx's views of the dialectics, if it can be called dialectical at all.[9] For, in seeking to transcend Marx, and by applying dialectics to Nature, Engels divorced it from the mediation of consciousness.[10] By arguing that there is in all of Nature a dialectical evolution at work of which the dialectics of concepts were mere reflections, Engels brutalized the dialectics.

Marx had kept clear of extending the dialectic into a universal science of the laws of nature, and had instead confined his dialectic to cover the human and only the human side of history. The problem which Engels carelessly stumbled into, and which Marx studiously avoided was, therefore, that of deducing the necessity of a future society from some general "law of nature." For Marx, any deduction had to be rooted in a critical analysis of a going thesis; to do otherwise, is tantamount to leaping ahead of history. It is only in this light that one can grasp that Soviet society, as shaped by Stalin, was never an application of Marxian ideas, but an application of Engels' version of the dialectic. This version amounted to a cannonical expression of certainty, an objectivistic and scientistic natural law and ideology, a blueprint which provided Soviet theoreticians with a program for tyranny. Avineri articulates this point extremely lucidly:

> Marx ultimately maintains that only
> a socialism that knows of a fully
> differentiated system of private
> property can abolish it and replace
> it by a new, non-possessive
> relationship between man and man
> and between man and his artifacts
> ... According to Marx, any break-

> through to the final end not
> mediated through [this] dialectical
> ambivalence is doomed to end either
> in Cloud Cuckoo Land or in a new
> authoritarianism that will not
> begin to grasp what freedom really
> is.[11]

Avineri is not the only one to have drawn attention to the fact that with his excursions into natural science, for the purpose of amplifying the dialectic to cover all of the universe, Engels discarded dialectics. His editorial exercises, after Marx's death, conferred a privileged status upon his own writings, culminating in a monistic materialism and mechanistic Marxism directly opposed to Marx's own dialectical understanding of social life and organization.[12] What Engels succeeded in accomplishing in the end was the abandonment of dialectics in favor of positivism, as is clearly expressed in his bold statement about ultimate causes: the ultimate causes of all social changes and political revolutions are to be sought not in the minds of men, in their increasing insight into eternal truth and justice, but in changes in the mode of production and exchange; they are to be sought not in the philosophy but in the economics of the epoch concerned.[13]

Clearly then, Engels' flirtation with natural science problems is not to be mistaken for Marxian dialectics. As Lichtheim remarked, Engels' extension of the dialectics to nature and science drastically oversimplified the infinitely complex historical processes and in effect invented a peculiar ontological system of metaphysical materialism (called "dialectical materialism") which has only the remotest connection with Marx's own viewpoint.

The Marxian Heritage of Dialectical Philosophy

It is an oft-repeated, if dimly understood point in sociological theory, that at some stage during Marx's life he stood Hegel "right side up." Accompanying this is also the observation that to try to understand the philosophy of Marx as a self-contained body of thought is like trying to understand the fourth chapter of a book of which one has not read the first three. For Chapter One we have to go back at least to Immanuel Kant in the eighteenth century. After Kant had written the first chapter, Hegel came

71

along and wrote an additional chapter of such intrinsic power that he thereby gave his name to the whole tradition of German philosophy from that point on. Those who came after him were ostensibly commentators on the chapter he had written, calling themselves Hegelians or neo-Hegelians or post-Hegelians, Old Hegelians or Young-Hegelians. Ludwig Feuerbach, the best known of these Hegelians, transformed Hegelianism, and then Marx transformed Feuerbach's transformation.[14]

We are here interested in a display (albeit a tiny one) of the harvest of ideas in social theory and social philosophy which dates back to Kant, in order to understand why it was absolutely necessary for Marx to turn Hegel on his feet or right side up.

At the expense of some oversimplification, the philosophy of Kant may be summarized as a gigantic synthesis of Cartesian rationalism with its emphasis on so-called universals, and Lockean skeptical empiricism. Descarte's idealism (or mathematical determinism) amounted to the conviction that the senses were untrustworthy. He therefore sought, instead, something more "self-evident," and chose propositions in mathematical laws. Cartesian rationalism is built on the notion that pure mathematical laws govern the universe. Kant's task was to find a middle ground between these two apparent theories of knowledge. In his grand synthesis, mind was given primacy over matter. But perhaps the most distinguishable aspect of Kant's philosophy is his duality between two worlds: the phenomenal, which is the world known to our faculties of perception, and the noumenal world, the world of things in themselves.[15] According to Kant, reason through mathematics could discover scientific truths concerning phenomena, but reason was incapable of attaining similar truths about the realm of human belief and values - the noumenal realm. Thus, in Kant, reason confronts a barrier and confesses a certain impotence for dealing with certain otherwise important cultural creations. This duality, according to Halle, is "not unlike that found in the Judaeo-Christian tradition: between the perfect and the imperfect, God and the devil." It is the kernel of the "fact" and "value" dichotomy of contemporary social science.

Hegel inherited much of this philosophical system. For Hegel, too, matter is organized by mind, and our historical concepts possess true generality because

they relate to mind as a universal agent that unfolds
through the histories of particular peoples and
civilizations. For Hegel, particular knowledges were
always partial. Beyond that, however, he objected to
the Kantian duality and sought, instead, to achieve
wholeness. For him, human actions are the objectifications of their beliefs and as such both action and
beliefs fall into the realm of Kant's phenomenal: all
being is basically one and indivisible - the "Absolute
Idea."

But Hegel's epochal discovery could be said to be
that contradiction or negativity is built into the very
structure of reality. In other words, that
contradiction is not external to reality but is part
and parcel of it.[16] There was always a tension between
any present state of affairs, and what it was becoming.
Second, Hegel may also be said to have discovered that
world history is the process of man's self-creation or
labor. Marx, in fact, showed much honesty by arguing
that the outstanding thing in Hegel's Phenomenology was
that Hegel conceived of the self-creation of man as a
process in which man's own labor is germane. However,
while Hegel grasped labor as the essence of man, his
comprehension was limited by a one-sidedness which
recognized only abstractly mental labor. In other
words, Hegel conceived of labor not in its real,
existential, humanly-grounded form, but in abstract,
spiritual form - in an alienated form.[17] Third, (and
this compensates somewhat for the acute criticisms from
Marx) Hegel achieved the great intellectual breakthrough by showing the relationship between actual work
and consciousness, and how philosophy impinged upon the
central concerns of political and social thought. As
brought out in the same Phenomenology of Mind, there
was always a continuous and intricate interaction
between social realms, notably consciousness (mind) and
reality. His error, as Marx was to point out, was in
insisting that all the different levels of action could
in fact be comprehended in a single dialectic of Geist
or Spirit.

Whatever Hegel's faults, (and Marx chalked up
several) he never made the mistake of supposing that
the human element could be removed from the equation of
theory and praxis. Nor did his philosophy lend support
to the notion that history was subject to inexorable
causal laws, set aside from the unique dialectical
logic of human historical action. It is in this German

dialectical tradition that Marxism, in its original, philosophical form, is rooted. More specifically, it derives its life from the potentially stimulating content of German idealism; - not in the trivial biographical sense, but in the sense that Marx's "materialist" inversion of Hegel conserved the problematic enshrined in Hegel's earlier critique of Kant.[18]

Ludwig Feuerbach, generally regarded as the principal link between Hegel and Marx, succeeded, even in Marx's terms, in mounting a successful transformation of Hegelian philosophy.[19] Apparently, his Essence of Christianity effected a transformational interpretation of Hegelianism which completely seduced Marx. The key to this interpretation was the distinction Feuerbach made between the manifest content of Hegel's philosophy, which anyone could glean for himself by reading Hegel's words, and the latent content, which could be brought out by interpretation.

According to the manifest content of Hegel's philosophy, God is the ultimate reality of which existential men and things are incomplete aspects. This manifest content, however, contains a hidden, esoteric, and recondite revelation. The revelation is that, while existential man and God (qua idea) stand in an alienated relation to each other, the reality is not God (as in manifest Hegelianism) but man, God being merely a projected figment of man's imagination. One might say that the latent truth in the statement that God created man in his own image is that man has created God in his own image. This is the positivistic mirror-image of the idealist conception.

By inventing religion, Feuerbach said, and by projecting an image of an external God, man alienates himself; he externalizes his noumenal self. "The relation of thought to being," Feuerbach wrote, is as follows: "Being is subject, thought is predicate. Thought proceeds from being, not being from thought." Man is being; God is thought. Whereas Hegel sees the "real" as emanating from the "divine," Feuerbach argues that the divine is an illusory product of the real. This revolution in Hegelianism is one of the foundations of Marxism. It also has implications for the meaning of alienation: by attributing all his best and most essential qualities to an external God, man denatures himself, converting himself into an impoverished and essentially alien being. According to Feuerbach, man's alienation was rooted in his religious alienation; it follows that emancipation from religion is one escape from alienation. For Marx, this was a fantastic insight, but the alienation which Feuerbach had seen in religion was even more explicit in political economy. Thus, in both realms, the problem was that human beings had somehow come to attribute to a system of human values a degree of independence and autonomy which was misleading. Not only did this invert the true relationship of men and ideas; but it misled men and women into the rather senseless thinking that they are somehow independent of their social contexts. Marx went beyond Feuerbach then and suggested that man's alienation was a function of his existential situation, of which the illusions are merely a symptom. This hypothesis directed him into a full-scale study of economics where Marx hoped to discover the material basis for human self-alienation, and indeed the hidden meaning of Hegelianism.

Enter Marx. Marx liked, and accepted, Feuerbach's insights, but over time came to realize that while Feuerbach made something of a breakthrough, he missed some key connections, and did not go nearly far enough. Eventually, he tangled with Feuerbach.

There is little doubt that Marx clearly approved of Feuerbach's dialectical thinking. In fact, at one point he remarked that Feuerbach was the only one who had a "serious, critical attitude to the Hegelian dialectic and who had made genuine discoveries in this field."[20] The Left Hegelians, headed by Feuerbach, had unmasked the truly human roots of religion; and Marx in turn unmasked the historical roots of the Left Hegelians, calling this his "settling of accounts with his erstwhile philosophical conscience." The effect of the many profound insights which he derived from these Hegelians, but especially from Feuerbach, was to apply a transformative and radical criticism to the under-standing of the material world. Especially crucial was the prospect of shaping a philosophy that combined analysis and criticism, and applying the result to the sphere of political economy. His confrontation with Feuerbach became even more pronounced, as he continued to search for "the unholy forms" of alienation.

Feuerbach failed to properly "connect" the elements of his anthropology. For instance, Feuerbach treated material reality as the determinant of human activity; but he failed completely to analyze the modification of the objective world by the subject, that is, by the activity of men. Yet, just as society itself produces men so is society produced by him.[21] Feuerbach therefore, like Hegel, committed a "double error." They both misunderstood the dialectic and ignored the historical process, to the degree that they soft-pedalled the fact that ideas are the product of (social persons, and experientially derive from human transaction with) a knowable material world; ideas are not founded independently of existence. On this Marx rebuked them both:

> The production of ideas, of conceptions, of consciousness is at first directly interwoven with the material activity and the material intercourse of men, the language of real life. Men are the producers of their own conceptions, ideas, etc., real, active men, as they are conditioned by definite development of their productive forces and of the inter-course corresponding to these ... Consciousness can never be anything else but conscious existence, and the existence of men in their actual life process.[22]

In other words, as Giddens writes, human consciousness is conditioned in dialectical interplay between subject and object, in which man as subject actively and consciously shapes the world he lives in, which in turn resolutely shapes him. And it is, paradigmatically, the dialectic of labor which reveals this nexus between man as conscious subject and society as a product of human subjectivity. Unfortunately, as expressed in the Third Thesis on Feuerbach, it is precisely this major point that Feuerbach had failed to grasp - the fact that "circumstances are changed by men and the educator must himself be educated."

But yet, Feuerbach, more than others, was close to something, as Marx and Engels attest. We quote at length to illustrate Marx's concern with this problem:

> Certainly Feuerbach has a great

advantage over the "pure" materialists in that he realizes how man too is an "object of the senses." But apart from the fact that he only conceives him as a "sensuous object," not as "sensuous activity," because he still remains in the realm of theory and conceives of men not in their given social connection, not under their existing conditions of life which have made them what they are, he never arrives at the really existing active men, but stops at the abstraction "man," and gets no further than recognizing "the true, individual, corporeal man" emotionally, i.e., he knows no other "human relationships" "of man to man" than love and friendship, and even then idealized. He gives no criticism of the present conditions of life. Thus he never manages to conceive the sensuous world as the total living sensuous activity of the individuals composing it ... As far as Feuerbach is a materialist he does not deal with history, and as far as he considers history he is not a materialist.[23]

To Marx, this was part fact, part romantic fiction. Feuerbach accomplished this much: He did at least have human beings in his anthropological model, and he had an anthropological (as opposed to a theological or metaphysical) frame through which to view human beings. But the "materialism" which he invoked to explain them was mechanistic, hence reified and, ultimately, reactionary. By assuming what had to be explained, he not only shrouded the ontological significance of human-in-society, but presented a materialism which squeezed every bit of sensuous activity from the humans in his model, making them, essentially, "judgmental dopes."[24] In addition to his one-sided, static ontology, Feuerbach also omitted the labor process from his anthropology, the very process that defines the "human essence,"[25] and his de-emphasis on the socialization of humans was a serious error.

Against Hegel, Marx reasoned that if there is such a thing as a universal agent that unfolds in history, it is not mind, but human activity or praxis; that is, the practice of humankind struggling to subdue Nature and to develop their own latent powers. Not only does Marx object to Hegel's conception of history which tends to become detached from the people who make it, and is seen as superior to them,[26] but he is also dissatisfied with the way Hegel conceptualizes human beings. In Hegel, the real, living human being is obscured - he is not visualized as the true architect of history, nor is his existential situation as a suffering being fully grasped: "Man, as an objective, sensuous being is... a suffering being - and because he feels what he suffers, a passionate being."[27] Marx contended, therefore, that the defect in Hegel was very serious. Hegel realized that there was a self-formative process, but he failed to see that in the historical ways in which human beings form themselves, reside contradictions, such as systematically distorted communication. So while human beings create their own history, they do so under conditions only partly disclosed to them in terms of their own, limited grasp of appearances. To this Marx reacted that the purpose of social analysis is precisely to transcend the apparent consciousness of human actors and uncover the real foundations of their activity. That done, it would soon be realized that what often passes as human history is written upside down, that is, from the standpoint or within the orbit of, the dominant classes and their interest-laden ideas. What is in Hegel is good; only, it seems to be upside down.

In search of a conceptual victory, Marx hoists as his epochal discovery the ontological centrality of labor as that which not only maintains life, whether civilized or savage, but that which also truly dramatizes the human "essence." This idea was also at the heart of Hegel's philosophy, but it was latent; it had to be activated. As conceived by Marx, the dialectic of labor is the very substratum of human history, a process through which humankind fulfills himself and creates society as social relations. The labor process is that purposive activity which, step by step, tries to achieve the changes desired. Labor, Marx says, is in the first place a process in which both man and nature participate and in which man of his own accord starts, regulates and controls the material relations between himself and nature.[28] It is the expression of the productive capacity which defines the "essence of man," and his ontological status, as we shall see later. As Schroyer recently argued: Just as work is the "outwardizing" of human potential, ... so too is the rational insight and reflex understanding that accompanies the reciprocity of work the "inwardizing" side.[29] As man produces, he comes to know his powers and limitations. Labor makes possible "material production," i.e., production by social individual.[30]

But, within the workings of the capitalist structure, Marx detected some serious structural problems, based, essentially on two of capitalism's intrinsic qualities: private ownership, and the greed for profits. One of these problems is alienation, another key idea which Marx inherited from Hegel. There can be many different origins of alienation, but Marx insisted that the root of all alienation is economic alienation, which in turn shapes and conditions other types such as political alienation or ideological alienation.

It was in order to grasp the inner processes of labor that Marx constructed his well-known analysis of alienation, that complex process whereby under the aegis of private property and profit, men and women are forced to sell their labor-power as a commodity. There are several aspects to this structural condition. First, under capitalism, with its intricate division of labor and private ownership, the worker is related to the product of his/her labor as to an alien object. The object he produces does not belong to him, dominates him and tends in the long run to stabilize if not increase his poverty. The product of human labor is transformed into a commodity, that is, an abstract value that can be exchanged in the marketplace. Under these conditions, production is not so much in order to satisfy human needs, but for exchange; whatever object is produced by labor is objectified and eventually lost by the worker. This is because the worker lacks control over the disposal of his products, since what he produces is appropriated by others, primarily for exchange and invariably in such a manner as to promote the interests which are not the worker's. This is alienation from the product of human labor.

Second, there is alienation of the worker in the work task itself. Here, what is being probed is the

79

fact that under capitalist production labor does not offer intrinsic satisfaction which would make it possible for the worker to develop his/her many potentials, including his mental and physical energies. It is not work which is entered into freely, and on the worker's terms; rather, it is labor which is imposed by force of external circumstances alone, a means to an end, rather than an end in itself, a factor which explains why, as Marx puts it, "as soon as there is no physical or other compulsion, men flee from labor like the plague!"

Third, there is alienation from nature and from the species. For while human beings always live in an active interplay with nature, alienated labor reduces human productive activity to the animal level of mere adaptation to the environment, rather than forging a mastery of it. This cannot help but to detach or further estrange the human individual from his own species.[31]

The importance of this analysis of alienation cannot be overemphasized. For Marx, labor itself does not inevitably entail alienation. As a historically determinate condition of capitalist society, alienation is historically abolishable, but obviously only if there is a critical understanding of its causes and consequences. What he discovered was that in so far as a given social arrangement obliges people to sell their labor power as a commodity, they not only mortify themselves, but also lose the real connection with nature: Their own deed becomes an alien power opposed to them, which enslaves them instead of being controlled by them.[32] Labor becomes alienated to the extent that it becomes an object which was "not the satisfaction of a need," but a "means to satisfy needs external to it" - particularized needs. It thus ceases to be voluntary; it is forced labor.[33] Alienated labor is a negation of man's generic nature and potential. The internal dynamics of this mortifying process, classical political economy never clarifies, but covers up:

> Political economy conceals the estrangement inherent in the nature of labor by not considering the direct relationship between the worker (labor) and production. It is true that labor produces for the

rich wonderful things - but for the
worker it produces privation. It
produces palaces - but for the
worker hovels. It produces beauty
- but for the worker deformity...
It produces intelligence - but for
the worker stupidity, cretinism.[34]

To fail then, to fully clarify the complexity of
the dialectic of labor, and in particular the process
of alienation, is to fail to understand the totality of
our involvement with society, as well as to fail to
connect the seemingly disparate elements of human
society. Labor, and its dialectics, stand our for Marx
not only as the life-blood and the pre-condition of
human existence, an existential irreducibleness, but
the praxis whereby men and women transform themselves
and nature. Where history records this process of
transformation and its objectification, it is human
history. Where it does not, it is, as he puts it, "not
history but old Hegelian junk, it is not profane
history - a history of man - but sacred history, a
history of ideas."[35]   Marx therefore understood, as
Schroyer points out, that the moving dialectic of work
is the means by which man satisfies the needs which
confront him as an active natural force. And this
"critical materialism" of Marx is also his
phenomenology of work. The understanding of the
phenomenology of work under capitalism exposes that man
does not fulfill himself through work or in work, for
work in capitalist social structures, as forced work
for particularized interests, breeds alienation, and
deforms man by making the product contradict the
intention of purposive activity, or by negating the
dialectic of work, thereby denying the reflexivity of
work. Thus "Marx concludes that work under capitalism
is its own negation; it is the exhaustion and
debasement of man, not his self-realization."

The central importance of the Marxian critique of
alienation is to dramatize the need for material
emancipation from the exchange rationality and the
attendant fetishism of commodities. Marx, clearly,
does not intend to take lightly the work activity.
Rather, he seeks to abolish alienated labor and class,
not labor and property which are for him the praxis of
free humankind. The discussion of Marx's phenomenology
of work highlights two crucial sociological problems.
First the problem of reification, and second, the need

within the human consciousness to overcome domination
either symbolically or actually.[36] It is one of the
characteristics of reification to artificially isolate
man as subject from the social arrangements he makes.
Hence Marx was highly critical of political economists
who analytically separated the production processes
from the totality of social institutions, and of those
who treated these as if they were natural processes
that could not be mediated by the consciousness of man.
This is, indeed, a fundamental problem in sociological
analysis. Not only is the essential, human topic of
the tyranny of work under capitalism typically down-
played in sociology, but the whole business of
dehumanized and meaningless work is overlaid by the
rubbish of liberal ideology, making it virtually
impossible for the workers to understand why their
lives are as they are. All they can see is a "natural"
order of things. A second point then is that
conventional sociology has not explained, through
structural analysis, why workers in the industrialized
west have not deployed the kind of revolt predicted by
Marx, and this is because we have tended to view the
labor process (in Feuerbachian style) as unrelated to
anything else that we think or do in the modern world.
What has not been done in liberal social science is the
situating of the work process squarely in the broader
perspective of the social and political organization of
capitalist society, including the prevailing set of
beliefs and ideology in the society.

Against this backdrop, and against this understanding of contemporary society, an ideology-critique
cannot be viewed simply as a past stage of social
thought. Indeed, the totality of the liberal world-
view, with its half thought-out notions, cliches,
dubious value assumptions, and no small number of
cloudy ideas, is fundamentally that which is to be
explained by social science. But it is important to
note, too, that in North America, those academics who
have taken up the challenge to spell out how and why
work under the auspices of capitalism alienates workers
from their species being and acutely devalues social
activity, have been publicly reprimanded and maligned
by the "liberal"-dominated establishment. Thus such
academics have been denied jobs, or tenure, or entry to
visit the country. This is not apocryphal; the names
of Bertell Ollman, Richard Pfeffer and Istvan Meszaros
come readily to mind in sociology, and Paul Sweezy and
Samuel Bowles in economics.

For Marx, it is man above all that is alienated. It is not, as Hegel thought, "spirit" or anything manifest in man. Simply man in his dialectical journey toward self-knowledge, working to satisfy his natural appetite, and constructing social life in the form of institutionalization in the process. Unlike Hegel, Marx does not treat history as the unfolding of a meta-physical substance. In Hegel, history took place only in the past; in Marx history is the incessant production of both human surroundings and of man himself: our conception of history, he writes, depends on our ability to expound the real processes of production, and to comprehend the form of intercourse connected with this and created by this as the basis of all history.[37]

In wrestling with nature, under all and varying modes of production, human beings come to realize their essence. Human labor was man's nature; it was an ontological category, and this both Hegel and Marx had understood. But here Marx was adamant, and perhaps more perceptive than Hegel, in wanting to extend it beyond mental labor. Even Habermas, who is otherwise quite critical of many aspects of Marx's thought, has shown in his many works the imbeddedness in Marx of the distinctly Hegelian ideas of the dialectic as self-reflection of the _subject_ of history, and of the material transformation of nature through human labor.[38]

What distinguishes one stage in history from another then, and one economic system from another, are the instruments employed in production, the form of cooperation required, and the relations (especially property relations) between the worker and the means and products of production. Any analysis of the ways in which various forms of class rule come into being and are maintained is really an analysis of different forms of alienation which prevail within each society. Thus understood, whatever the increase in the _consumption_ pattern and style of the modern working-class may have been, neo-capitalism has not modified the basic nature of work under capitalism, as alienated labor,[39] forced labor under the tutelage of a hierarchy which dictates to the worker what he has to produce and how he has to produce it. It is under such tutelage that the modern consumer (contrary to classical economic theory) is literally told what to consume and when to consume it, what to think, and when to think it.

Now, the importance given to the labor process
does not belie the fact that in time labor produces its
own negation.   Like alienation, this negation is rooted
in the labor process itself, which, Nicolaus has
remarked, presents itself in western society as "the
surplus class."[40]   As labor becomes more and more
productive, it produces its own opposite, that is, as
less and less people are forced to produce more and
more, more and more people are forced to produce less
and less.   It matters little whether one calls this
slack labor "surplus class," "industrial reserve army,"
"structural unemployment" or "persistent unemployment."
What does matter is whether we locate the root (that is,
human) causes of it within the internal workings of the
established labor processes.   Needless to say, these
unfolding possibilities of capitalist production were
clearly envisaged by Marx.[41]   This is the whole point
in dialectics.   In the words of Habermas, the
dialectical concept of society as totality demands that
analytical tools and social structures act upon one
another like cogwheels.

In order to fully understand the Marxian
dialectics, it is important to move towards his
informed ontology - towards his thoroughly
philosophical view of humankind.   Only then can we see
in broader outlines what surely is the lasting and
indispensable feature of dialectical thinking in
sociology.

In his letter to Kugelmann, about Capital,[42] Marx
went as far as to equate reality with the "inter-
connection of things."   But we get the clearest
manifestations of a distinctly Marxian dialectics, when
Marx himself demonstrates that he is, as Martin
Nicolaus wittily puts it, "under the spell of Hegelian
choreography."[43]   Nowhere is the idea of dialectics
brought out more clearly than in the Grundrisse,
especially in the discussion undertaken there on the
double nature of commodities.

From Feuerbach, and from Hegel, Marx inherited an
obviously revelatory conception of dialectics, but not,
however, without questioning the epistemology of his
inheritance.   We have already indicated his agreement
with Feuerbach on certain matters.   He also spoke,
however, of the "outstanding achievement" of Hegel's

phenomenology.[44] He explained his commitment to the
dialectic quite vividly in the Afterword to the second
German edition of Capital. To the reviewer of his "Das
Kapital" who remarked that Marx's method of inquiry
into political economy was "severely realistic" but
unfortunately "German-dialectic," Marx replied that he
was not using the decandent interpretation of the
dialectic. In his well-known words:

> My dialectic method is not only
> different from the Hegelian, but
> is its direct opposite... I...
> openly avowed myself the pupil of
> that mighty thinker [Hegel], and
> even here and there, on the chapter
> on the theory of value, coquetted
> with the modes of expression
> peculiar to him. The mystification
> which dialectic suffers in Hegel's
> hands, by no means prevents him
> from being the first to present its
> general form of working in a
> comprehensive and conscious manner.
> With him it is standing on its head.
> It must be turned right side up
> again, if you would discover the
> rational kernel within the mystical
> shell.[45]

What immediately concerns us here is the pronounced
difference between his application of the dialectic and
his chosen unit of analysis, and Hegel's. As Nicolaus
observed, the context changed, the content changed, but
Marx remained captivated by the spell of the Hegelian
dance - the dialectical movement of human history.

In turning Hegel on his feet Marx is arguing that
there is no need whatsoever to mystify the dialectic by
applying it to the explanation of some far-fetched
(idealistic) notion of Absolute Idea, or Spirit, with
the real world being external and epiphenomenal. For
if in fact, one applied it to an understanding of
political economy, to the analysis of real humans
caught up in their own social arrangements, then one
could lay bare the "law of motion" of bourgeois
society.[46] One could then easily recognize the
"anarchy of production," the connections between the
misery prevailing in different aspects of human
existence under capitalism, and the irrationality of

the total, and, crucially, the social foundations on which the whole process rests. One could, as a result, discern an essential negativity of capitalist accumulation, a negativity reflected in the estrangement of labor, and the thingification of labor power, and hence of human creative powers, into "commodities" which essentially conceal the exploitative quality of the entire social structure of production. Praxis in Hegel was "spiritual" self-creation. Marx, for his part, wanted to invert this image, or at any rate reinterpret an otherwise useful idea by applying it to the realm of material production, whereby labor was to be conceptualized as the source of all wealth and as that activity through which human beings prove themselves as a species being.

To turn to Hegel on his feet is to switch the subject and predicate in the key propositions of Hegelian theory. Unlike the Hegelian position, Marx insisted that one should realistically set out from the premise of real, active men, and on the basis of their life processes demonstrate the development of their ideology, and the "echoes of this life process."[47] Only this approach, carefully and systematically grasped, would help to make the connections between being and thought. By ascending "from earth to heaven, and not from heaven to earth" one could come to grasp that "life is not determined by consciousness but consciousness by life."[48] In taking issue with the abstract nature of Hegelian dialectic, Marx succeeded in grounding it in human existence. He explained:

> We proceed from an economic fact of the present... Do not let us go back to a fictitious primordial condition... such a primordial condition explains nothing; it merely pushes the question away into a gray nebulous distance... The object before us, to begin with, material production. What is meant is always production by social individuals... [Dialectics must] grasp the essential connection between private property, greed, and the separation of labor, capital and landed property, between exchange and competition, value and the devaluation of men,

monopoly and competition, etc.[49]

In switching the content and context of dialectic, Marx triumphed in demystifying Hegel, and substituted a materialist (humanistic) dialectic for idealist dialectics. As Halle remarked, the duality of noumena and phenomena was kept, but the relationship between them, as primary and secondary, was reversed. The material world was given primacy over the world of ideas.[50] Marx's dissatisfaction with German philosophy must be understood against the background of his grasp of how one might use the dialectic to interpret history. Feuerbach, and those who thought like him, missed some key connections, which is the same as saying that they actually distorted reality. In arguing against the Hegelian interpretation of history, and in putting philosophy and history in dialectical perspective, Marx forcefully argued that reality can be depicted, philosophical speculations and empty talk about consciousness can cease and real understanding begin, if the premises on which one starts an analysis of society rest on "real active men, and their real life process." Marx & Engels argue:

> The first premise of all human history is the existence of living individuals. Thus the first fact to be established is the physical organization of these individuals and their consequent relations to the rest of nature.[51]

The critique in Marx moves resolutely from theory to practice: from a critique of Hegel's (and German) philosophical conceptions to a critique of capitalist society.

Marx's materialism is dialectical in the sense that it seeks to portray the interaction between theory and practice or between conscious activity and the material preconditions of existence, themselves the product of past history.[52] Such a dialectic does not imply logical necessity or some "law" of inevitable historical development. Such a notion belongs to Engels, not Marx. For the latter, the future is not determined. It may, however, witness the expression of human social possibilities as these derive from a critical insight into the nature of society.

87

Dialectics and Its Relation to
Critical Sociology

In Marx's own analysis, the emergence of
European feudalism from the wreck of ancient society
was never regarded as a matter of logical necessity.
What his historical materialism does claim to have
discovered was an indispensable approach to the understanding of historical constellations and to have
focused attention on the nature of the principal
energies responsible for their emergence, transformation and possible disappearance. The latent
structuralism in Marx's work revealed that no partial
aspect of social life and no isolated phenomenon could
be fully comprehended unless it is structurally related
to the historical whole, that is, to the social
structure conceived as a macro entity. Thus, it is
only as men come to understand their environment
(natural & social) as the product of human activities,
and learn to adapt it to their purposes, that they
cease to look upon it as alien, hostile and mystifying.
Then, and only then, can men and women come gradually
to see their social and cultural world as the medium in
which they develop their specifically human capacities.
And the material conditions of human existence which
formed the primary datum for Marx could be altered if
human beings were to reach their full stature.

The dialectical approach in Hegel and Marx is
preeminently a critical method for analyzing the interconnections of phenomena by grasping facts not as
isolated, rigid and external data, but as part of an
all-embracing process.[53] It was materialist insofar as
it sought to shed light on what Marx called the "real
life process" in which humans are engaged in production
and reproduction of material existence. This vantage
point ruptured any "idealist" procedure wherein
ordinary material history was treated as the unfolding
of principles laid up in the speculative heavens.[54]
The materialism, moreover, may be said to be
revolutionary, because when applied to society it
discloses what the idealist hypostatization of "spirit"
obscures: namely, that human history is a constant
struggle in which human "nature is formed and
reformed."[55]

The dialectical approach is an open-ended critique,
not a body of eternal truths. It is not dogmatic so
much as it is emergent and this-worldly speculative,

and Marx was always careful to specify the unique historical preconditions which make possible the unfolding of a new mode of production. For Marx, one could not leap ahead of history. The historical process may indeed have an internal logic, but investigation into the actual sequence of socio-economic formations is a matter for empirical research. Marx, in his own time, used the dialectic essentially as a tool, a critical method for the analysis of political economy, and specifically in the interpretation of concrete historical situations, as in the Class Struggles in France, and in The 18th Brumaire. Now, whatever may be said in criticism of this approach, it is quite independent of any metaphysical assumption about the ontological priority of an absolute substance called "matter."

Dialectical analysis fuses a philosophical view of the human condition with empirical analysis and thereby incorporates philosophical anthropology with empirical analysis. But the grounding of historical into philosophical does not necessarily entail the further step of suggesting that human history is set in motion and kept going by a dialectical process of contradiction within the "material basis."[56] What it does is to confront the question of the meaning of history directly, and to expose a cluster of philosophical assumptions that are central to the sociological understanding. These assumptions are first that the world is an historical being, that is, it is a product of humans acting on antecedent natural surroundings; second, that humans have certain specifically knowable potential capacities and dispositions for action; third, that there is no necessary limit to the process of history-making; and finally, that given freedom from animal needs, human's consciousness can grasp reality and indeed change it.

It has often been remarked that dialectical thinking seeks to forge theory with history or theory with practice. What this seems to imply first and foremost is that the middle way between empiricism and ontology is a dialectic of theory and practice which measures social actuality against historical possibility.[57] So said, the essence of dialectical analysis is the constant shuttling between theory and empirical observation in order to penetrate beneath the surface of particular phenomena and to disclose the contradictory movement or structure.

Marx's special version of dialectics derives from an immanent critique of the Hegelian theoretical apotheosis and reification of civil society. The optimum aim of his rebuttal was to empty philosophy of its other-worldly speculative content. Thus he was led to charge, too, that classical German philosophers such as Hegel and Feuerbach failed to grasp that the dialectic of human sensuous activity is explicable in the process of production in which man makes himself, and hence history. They also fell into another trap then. They failed to see the dialectical tragedy whereby in mastering nature man succeeds in creating society, society which turns on him like a Frankensteinian monster. One of the reasons why Feuerbach's transformation was not as radical as it could have been was that he somehow dabbled in the myth of "human nature." For Marx, there could be no nature apart from man, and there is no such entity as "human nature," only man in nature.[58] What man makes of himself depends on the interaction with his environment, including crucially, as part of that environment, his own man-made institutions. One cannot postulate a human nature as passively dependent on the environment, since there is always a dialectical <u>active</u> interplay between both entities. Against this background, it is not possible to understand Marx's account of, and hope for humans, unless one grasps that he operated on a distinctively philosophical view of humankind. This view forces him to conceptualize human purposive activity and its outcome as the key to understanding history. "Society," for Marx, thus becomes the unity of social man and nature, a unity forged through <u>praxis</u>.[59]

What amounts to an informed ontology, a socio-philosophical view of society and humankind, emerges from Marx's debacle with his teachers. It will be necessary to sketch the outlines of this ontology which Marx sees as a corrective to the "human nature" fallacy. Giddens has pointed out that because of concentration upon the critique of the political economy of capitalism, Marx never managed to return to the more general problems of ontology that preoccupied him in the early part of his intellectual career.[60] Nevertheless, we do have the broad outlines of such concerns which we shall briefly comment upon.

It is fundamental to the Marxian approach to the study of human society that there is no such entity as an external, timeless, and fixed (invariant) "human nature" which inhabits man, such as the egoism of "economic man." Over and above what may be considered biotic constants, the character of man, for Marx, is the product of the social order in which he is born, in which he is culturally socialized. Man's nature is something created through relatedness and purposive interaction between the world and human, between human and human. As such, "human nature" cannot be a fixed entity, for humans are assumed to be active, creative agents who not only possess the unique capacity to form symbols, but also a sense of identity. This latter was always the product of human beings' conceptual powers and teleological capacity, as opposed to the non-dialectical immediacy of animals.

Especially important here is the stinging criticism Marx and Engels made of Feuerbach for falsely supposing that there is such a thing as "man" in the abstract. Rather, they insisted, there are different sorts of men and women who exist at different times and places. And these men and women are social beings whose nature changes quite decisively with the sort of life they lead; and that, in turn, is liable to change according to the ways in which they make a living. For this reason, one has to be suspicious if the ruling class claims to speak for the working class. The classes have different interests, different existences, different ideas about what is "fair," what is "just," about religion, about truth.

The philosophical position that "human nature" is not, and can never be, fixed once and for all, but rather is a constantly unfolding idea, establishes Marx's unmistakable philosophical anthropology. It is a critical standpoint in that Marx conceived of man as "generic being," as a potentially free, creative, rational social being, whose potentiality becomes limited and crippled in a system (industrial capitalism) in which he is effectively reduced to animalistic pursuits. Simultaneously, his labor power, as a potentially creative force, becomes simply a quantity of energy which can be efficiently objectified and exchanged in the market.

In this anthropology, the uniqueness of the human being is his/her sociality, plus his ability to think conceptually. The historicity of human nature is a necessary consequence of his anthropological

naturalism.[61] But it is only in and through society
that men and women become conscious of themselves, and
they only truly produce in freedom from physical needs.
This is the meaning of his statement in The Holy Family,
that if man is shaped by his environment, his
environment must be made human. If man is social by
nature, he will develop his true nature only in society
and the power of his nature must be measured not by the
power of the separate individual, but by the power of
society. Specifically, human activity is not
deterministic but involves self-determination;
similarly, human nature, unlike animal nature is not
fixed, but evolves in response to the changing social
context, to the changing human history.

One of the most persistent problems posed by
Marx's predecessors, notably Kant and Fichte, and by
Hegel and Feuerbach, is the view given by them that the
essence of man lies in his generalized individuality.
As Marx polemicizes, it is the matrix of social
relations, the dialectical interplay between
individual thinking and the shaping of that thinking by
the socio-historical context.[62] There are some
particularly illuminating sections in Marx's writings
where he forcefully attempted to dispel these illusions.
In the Manuscripts, he says:

> "The human essence" is no
> abstraction inherent in each
> single individual. In its reality
> it is the ensemble of the social
> relations. Conscious life actively
> distinguishes man immediately from
> animal life activity. In creating
> a world of objects, by his
> practical activity in his work
> upon inorganic nature, man proves
> himself a conscious species being,
> i.e., as a being that treats the
> species as its own essential being
> ... Admittedly animals also
> produce. They build themselves
> nests, dwellings, like the bees,
> beavers, ants, etc. But an
> animal only produces what it
> immediately needs for itself or
> its young. It produces one-
> sidedly whilst man produces
> universally... Certainly eating,

drinking, procreation, etc., are
also genuinely human functions.
But abstractly taken, separated
from the sphere of all other human
activity and turned into sole and
ultimate ends, they are animal
functions.[63]

Later, in the German Ideology, he again returns to
the key point that human beings are special and it
makes a vast difference whether we assume them to be
mere brutes, or creatures with empirically demonstrable
qualities that set them apart from animals. [Thus, he
continues]

Men can be distinguished from
animals by consciousness, by
religion, or anything else you
like. They themselves begin to
distinguish themselves from
animals as soon as they begin to
produce their means of substance
... The nature of individuals
thus depends on the material
condition determining their
production.

Marx's contention that the only world we know is the
one we have constructed, the experiential world in all
its intersubjectivity, might seem to present important
ramifications for epistemology. For since society is
made and not given, the knowledge of it cannot be
regarded simply as a reflection or mirror of objective
realities. But the subjective nature of this
experience is checked by its social character, which in
turn is rooted in the permanent constituents of man as
"species being" who comes to himself in society. There
is, in the strict sense, no epistemological problem for
Marx.[64]

From the very early phases in his analysis, Marx
warned against the short-hand tactic of postulating
"society" as an abstraction vis-a-vis the individual.
"The individual is the social being," in that his life
is an expression and confirmation of social life;
individual life and the life of the species are not
different things.[65] Thus, it is never enough to say,
glibly, that man is a zoon politikon, a social animal.
One must add the important criterion that man can

develop into a <u>social</u> animal <u>only in society</u>.[66] That
point, essentially, demands that "society," the product
of human living and the genesis of the social, must at
all times be the subject of thorough and critical
evaluation. Society is only as abstract as the
individuals who compose it, no more, no less.
Interestingly, although there seems to be some general
agreement that Marx's ontological assumptions form the
kernel of his sociology, Bottomore and Rubel argue that
he was not concerned either with the ontological
problem of the relation of thought and being, or with
the problems of the theory of knowledge.

In opposition to this view, we will quote at
length from Marx to illustrate that the Marxian
philosophical view is an explicit ontology comprising
at least three major analytical elements: one, that
man is tool-maker <u>par excellence</u>; two, because of that,
man is the primary manipulator of nature; and three,
man possesses special reflective features, or what one
author calls "teleological capacity." What sets man
apart from animals then is his capacity to use his
"conscious life activity" to practically work upon
inorganic nature, thereby transforming it, and
"stamping" it. As he poetically puts it:

> We presuppose labor in a form that
> stamps it as exclusively human. A
> spider conducts operations that
> resemble those of a weaver, and a
> bee puts to shame many an architect
> in the construction of her cells.
> But what distinguishes the worse
> architect from the best bees is
> this, that the architect raises his
> structure in imagination before he
> erects it in reality. At the end
> of every labor-process, we get a
> result that already existed in the
> imagination of the laborer at its
> commencement.[67]

It is only by establishing this epistemological premise
in Marx that we are able to move from crude
psychologism to conscious man, from particular animal
to universal man. The important point is that Marx was
never a Feuerbachian, for reasons that should now be
clear. He was deeply influenced by the insights of
Feuerbach, but was keen to plot and pursue his own

94

independent social theory. The consumation of the Marxian ontology (of which we have barely give a sketch), sees man's species life as distinctly characterized by purposive praxis and reflective consciousness.

In summary, not in fixed man, but in human beings in their actual historical activity lies the Marxian view of human nature. Such a view seeks to understand not only the dialectics of on-going liaison with inorganic nature, but also the historical possibility of human existence as that is conceived by human philosophical insight. The double dialectics of Marx in this context concerns human-to-human dialectic; and human-to-nature dialectic. The external world, as it exists in and for itself, is irrelevant to a materialism which approached history with a view to establishing what men have made for themselves.

The Consequences of Non-Dialectical Sociology

It is our contention that the absence of dialectical thinking and reasoning in modern social science is largely responsible for the atomized, ahistorical and reified accounts of modern society. The well known end-of-ideology thesis of the 1960s can perhaps be used to illustrate the point. Having completely lost (if ever they had) any sense of "connection" in modern society, a number of social scientists proclaimed and celebrated, in the early 1960s, what they called the "end of ideology." According to this doctrine, in the modern west, but especially in North America, there was an "exhaustion" of political ideas. Humanity had reached the end of a search for the good life and the good society, quite simply because, as everyone could see, "success" was everywhere. Conveniently mortised with the dogma of "value-free" social science, that thesis naively held that not only was ideology spent, but that it had been replaced by something deemed superior: a strictly factual science. There was no need to question the social ends sought - those were solved once and for all by the techno-structure which could be left to go on its own steam, perpetually. In the tradition of structural-functional approach to social life, this perspective sought to remove the question of the social ends of society from critical consideration and evaluation. Another meaning of that thesis, as

Clement points out, was "an end to a prevalent ideology in opposition to the dominant ideology."[68] The point is that liberal industrial societies are class societies, and cannot be understood as uni-ideological, for the different class circumstances necessitate the formation of different kinds of ideology. Class societies are always multi-ideological.

Ironically (dialectically?), the end of ideology claims were made on the eve of what turned out to be one of the most ideologically-charged decades in recent North American history.[69] It cannot be that these social scientists had a grasp of the relations within the social structure they were trying to explain. Daniel Bell, Seymour Lipset, and others were able to eulogize the passing of ideology, precisely because the atomization of understanding and their own philosophical naivete, as well as their uncontested ideological hegemony over social science served to vitiate a "dialectical grasp" of reality. More recently, an allied thesis continues to impress on us that we have reached the post-industrial phase in the modern west, and that such a phase is to be characterized above all in terms of knowledge explosion, freedom from conflict and the finesse to manage crises of any proportion. We will assert, polemically, that the first case was more than simply another instance of wrong prediction; it was a case of total misunderstanding of some built-in negativity of modern industrial society. The second thesis also dramatizes the intransigence of the standard world view. The ideological scars of the 1960-1970 decade will not heal for a long time; and despite the treacle of the post-industrial prophets, we are not at all convinced that modern social science has tried to foster that understanding of existing society which would reveal society's own contradictions. In other words, we cannot see the knowledge explosion.

Against the claims that the dialectic consists of a set of "metaphysical assumptions that are not nullifiable empirically,"[70] we would contend that what Marx propounded as dialectics is a transformative method of inquiry in social science. For social science to incorporate dialectic into its method, it must attempt to foster an understanding of existing society which would reveal society's own contradictions. To the sociologists who complain that they cannot be content with asserting the essential negativity of all

96

existing phenomena, we would reply that if sociologists understand the dialectic as a critical method for grasping the totality of immanent contradictions in social reality, they would by that token understand that the dialectical approach is not all negativity. It also focuses on the unfolding of inherent possibilities of a structure. The alternative to a dialectical view is to reify, or as Marx would put it, to "take every epoch at its own word and believe that everything it says and imagines about itself is true."[71] Obviously, if one has no dialectical understanding of that which is, or a misunderstanding, one cannot be expected to have notions about the future, since how one shapes things to come depends on having an adequate understanding of existing situations.[72] Critics who charge dialectical social science with "utopianism" forget this, at the same time as they reveal a certain ignorance of the role of theory in social science, and indeed of the sociological significance of utopia. Whatever misgivings we might have about the turbulent events attendant upon the anti-bureaucratic and countercultural critique of the 1960s, they had the effect of shaking many academics out of the smug complacency of Cold War politics, halted the premature benediction on the end of ideological and other struggles, and assailed the comfortable certainty that we were, in the West, inaugurating the decline of politics. It was, we now know, the dawning of a new zeal in questioning. We probably now know, also, that for as long as there are class societies, there are bound to be bitter contests of legitimation and ideological cleavage.

There remains a great challenge in modern social science to transform utopian fears into philosophical visions and political programs. But if the social world is not seen or understood as being of our own making, there is no way we can change it. And if we have no chance of changing it, it is quite conceivable that we are all wasting our time in social science. Not only should social science theory generate new knowledge, but such knowledge should be a means of transforming society. The dialectical approach dramatizes this fact. But beyond that it also sensitizes us to another fact, namely, that men and women are more than mere objects existing in the natural world. They are the creators of the liveable world - the cultural world. It is a tragedy if they cannot change what they have created. Here, then, is

97

the crux of Marx's Theses on Feuerbach, and the background against which to assess the eleventh thesis: "The philosophers have only interpreted the world differently, the point is, to change it."[73]

In conclusion, we would argue that to understand the dialectic between human beings and society is one of the great challenges in social sciences. To miss this key connection is to be left with an ultimately reactionary and reified account of "sacred history" instead of human history, as Marx polemicizes against Proudhon, Feuerbach and Hegel:[74] the social history of men is never anything but the history of their individual development, their material relations being the basis of all their relations. Insofar as Proudhon did not regard social institutions as historical products, he could hardly be expected to understand that men who produce their social relations in accordance with their material productivity, also produce ideas, categories, that is to say the abstract ideal expression of these same, social relations.[75]

In response to Proudhon's claim, then, to have explained poverty, not through an historical analysis of social arrangements, but by taking refuge in a fiction, Marx retorted that one can give credit to Proudhon for having grasped the fact

> that men produce cloth, linen, silks... What he has not grasped is that these men, according to their abilities, also produce the social relations amid which they prepare cloth and linen.

Furthermore, because Proudhon lacked the historical knowledge,

> he has not perceived that as men develop their productive forces, that is, as they live, they develop certain relations with one another and that the nature of these relations must necessarily change with the change and growth of the productive forces.[76]

Of course for Proudhon and others who sought to explain the historico-philosophical sources of economic relations, but who were either lazy, or ignorant of historical origins, it was convenient to invent myths, such as that "Adam or Prometheus stumbled on the idea ready-made and then it was adopted."[77] One method of counteracting myth-making and of providing an antidote to the fallacy of misplaced concreteness, is the method of the dialectic which we have sketched in this chapter. The lasting merit of dialectics to social science is its critical acumen. And the critical theory of society must be grounded in a critical philosophical understanding of humankind. When Marx "threatened" to "leave philosophy aside, to leap out of it and to devote oneself like an ordinary man to the study of actuality," he was grasping for such a critical philosophy which was to be, like the social science of which it is a part, the display of an intellectual, and eventually practical effort which was not to be satisfied with accepting the prevailing ideas, actions and social conditions unthinkingly and from mere habit. The social function of philosophy is in the development of critical and dialectical thought, and action.[78] Human self-understanding and therefore human development is inescapably dialectical.

From the phenomenology of labor, as analyzed by Marx, we can derive a key element which sets Marxian social theory apart from all others. That is the dialectical relationship between society-as-social arrangements, and nature. It is the on-going and continuously developing interchange between human beings and nature which establishes the main problems of a truly social science, for instance, the fact that such interchanges create social relationships among humans, while at the same time progressively transforms those relationships.

The exhortation of Marx in his Eighth Theses on Feuerbach is the fitting conclusion to the chapter:

> All social life is essentially
> practical. All the mysteries
> which urge theory into mysticism
> find their rational solution in
> human practice and in the
> comprehension of this practice.

This is the thesis that separates Marx's prime unit of analysis (human society as social relations) from Feuerbach's vague "genus," that quasi-biological unit in which the socialization process is apparently unimportant. After this exposition of Marx's humanism and philosophical anthropology, it will be instructive to bring under discussion the well-known and controversial thesis of Max Weber that the fact of our time is characterized by rationalization and intellectualization, which, in effect, guarantees that there are no mysterious incalculable forces controlling humanity. Rather, Weber avers, we have the reverse: the world is like a gigantic artifact governed by formal rationality and bureaucratic coordination. More precisely, the "formal rationality of economic action" is intended to maximize the quantitative calculation which is technically possible in the Western World. Such a rationality was to be guided by a "given set of ultimate values no matter what they may be."[79]

What seems to have happened in modern times is that formal rationality has been pursued with pronounced indifference to substantive rationality, that is, to the question of whose set of values, and what social ends, are embodied in given courses of action. The next two chapters will offer some preliminary and basic ideas on these issues.

NOTES

1. Giddens, 1976a, pp. 79, 146; 1977, pp. 12, 28. McCarthy made a similar observation when he says: "if the social scientist is not to proceed with his head in the sand, he must reflectively take into account the dependence of his conceptual apparatus on a priori understanding that is rooted in his own sociocultural situation. He must become hermeneutically and historically self-conscious." McCarthy, 1978, p. 179.

2. Giddens, 1976a, p. 110.

3. This statement derives from no less a figure than Bertrand Russell himself, one of the great philosophical figures of the twentieth century.

4. Lichtheim, 1964, p. 7.

5. Cornforth, 1968, pp. 36, 99.

6. Bottomore and Rubel, 1961, p. 36.

7. See Marcuse, 1960, Preface and p. 27.

8. See, e.g., Engels, 1972; 1940; 1968, p. 84.

9. Avineri, 1968, p. 65.

10. Ibid.

11. Ibid. For further, interesting discussion on dialectics and totality, see Swingewood, 1975, esp. Chapters 1 and 2.

12. Lichtheim, 1974, pp. 66-67; Lukacs, 1971; Wellmer, in O'Neill, 1976; and Rose and Rose, 1976.

13. Engels, 1972, p. 292.

14. This interpretation belongs to Halle, 1965, p. 29.

15. Ibid., p. 30; and Lichtheim, 1974.

16. See Lichtheim, 1974, p. 126; and Markovic, 1974, p. 22.

17. For more on this, see Marx, 1964, p. 177.

18. Lichtheim, 1974, pp. 74, 161.

19. The following two paragraphs draw substantially on Louis Halle's little known but very insightful article in which he successfully situates Marx's philosophical vision within the broader span of the German idealist tradition (Halle, 1965).

20. Marx, 1964, p. 172.

21. Ibid., pp. 137, 175.

22. Marx and Engels, 1947, pp. 13-14; 1963b, p. 47.

23. Ibid., pp. 37-38.

24. This term is borrowed from Harold Garfinkel's Studies in Ethnomethodology, Prentice-Hall, 1967. It is Garfinkel's thesis that man in society can be conceptualized as a "cultural dope" insofar as he is socialized to accept, and sees no reason to question, the various officialized definitions of reality by which his life is governed (pp. 67-69).

25. In the Sixth Thesis on Feuerbach, Marx wrote: "the essence of man is no abstraction inherent in each separate individual. In its reality it is the ensemble of social relations," Marx and Engels, 1947, p. 198.

26. Marx, 1964, pp. 175-93; Marx & Engels, 1956, p.100.

27. Marx, 1964, p. 182.

28. Marx, n.d., p. 173.

29. Schroyer, 1973, pp. 77-79.

30. Marx, 1973, pp. 83-85.

31. Marx, 1964, pp. 106-109. It is not to be overlooked that alienation is one of a number of contradictions emanating from the labor process. Under capitalist production one must recognize at least two other critical processes that are a function of the existential situation in capitalism. These are: the extraction of surplus value; and the conception of labor power as a commodity. For more, see Marx, 1971b.

32. Marx, 1964, p. 108; Marx & Engels, 1947, p. 22.

33. Marx, 1964, pp. 110-111.

34. *Ibid*., pp. 109-ff.

35. Marx, 1963a, p. 182.

36. Schroyer, 1973, p. 97.

37. Marx and Engels, 1947, p. 28.

38. See Habermas, 1968a; 1968b; and 1974.

39. Ernest Mandel, "Workers and Permanent Revolution," in Fischer, 1971, p. 173.

40. Nicolaus, 1967, pp. 38ff.

41. Marx, 1973, pp. 450-51, 700-706.

42. See Marx & Engels, 1965, pp. 209-210.

43. Nicolaus, 1967, p. 23.

44. Marx, 1964, p. 177.

45. Marx, n.d., p. 29.

46. In the Contribution to a Critique of Political Economy, Marx puts the matter this way: My inquiry led me to the conclusion that neither legal relations nor political forms could be comprehended whether by themselves or on the basis of a so-called general development of the human mind... the totality of which Hegel embraces with the term "civil society"; ... the anatomy of this civil society, however, has to be sought in political economy (p. 20).

47. Marx and Engels, 1947, p. 14.

48. *Ibid*.

49. Marx, 1964, p. 107; 1973, pp. 83-85. The juxtaposition of the ideas in this quotation is deliberate and significant: ideas from one of Marx's earliest works to one of his latest. This exercise might not be enough to dispell the modern

day thesis that Marx experienced on "epistemological break" somewhere between his early life and the writing of the <u>Grundrisse</u>. But as Walton has argued, if there is a break in Marx, it is an empirical or conceptual break, <u>not</u> an epistemological, philosophical or ontological break. Briefly, the break is Marx's shift from merely viewing capitalism as extracting surplus from labor to his demonstration of how this is based on the extraction of surplus-value, and in demonstrating that this distinguishes it from feudalism. See Paul Walton, n.d.

50. Halle, 1965, p. 31.

51. Marx and Engels, 1947, pp. 7, 15.

52. Lichtheim, 1974, p. 25.

53. Swingewood, 1975, p. 33; and see Marx, 1963b, p. 110.

54. Lichtheim, 1974, p. 72.

55. <u>Ibid.</u>, p. 69.

56. Farganis, 1975, p. 490.

57. Lichtheim, 1974, p. 174.

58. "But nature, too, taken abstractly, for itself - nature fixed in isolation from man - is <u>nothing</u> for man," Marx, 1964, pp. 191, 112, 43.

59. The Marxian position is penetrating: "man is not an abstract being, squatting outside the world. Man is the human world, the state, society," cited in Avineri, 1968, pp. 148-149.

60. Giddens, 1976a, p. 126.

61. Lichtheim, 1974, p. 69.

62. Marx, 1964, 1963a; Marx and Engels, 1947.

63. Marx, 1964, pp. 111, 113.

64. Lichtheim, 1974, p. 70.

65. Marx, 1964, pp. 137-138.

66. Marx, 1973, p. 84.

67. Marx, n.d., p. 175.

68. Clement, 1975, p. 274 (emphasis in original).

69. Colfax and Roach, 1971.

70. See, e.g., Rytina and Loomis, 1970, p. 312.

71. Marx and Engels, 1947, p. 43.

72. Marx, 1963a, p. 192.

73. Marx and Engels, 1947, p. 199.

74. Marx, 1963a, p. 181.

75. Ibid., pp. 186-89.

76. Ibid., pp. 186, 189.

77. Marx, 1973, p. 84; cf. Marx, 1963a, p. 186.

78. See, especially, Horkheimer, 1972, p. 270.

79. See Weber, 1947, pp. 184-218, but especially pp. 184-5.

CHAPTER V

INSTRUMENTAL RATIONALITY:
ITS RELATION TO REIFICATION

The Legacy of Weber's Sociology:
A Comment

In this chapter an argument is presented that one of the most influential and respected models of capitalism - Weber's theory of rationality - is not immune from theoretical fog if not outright mystification, and that the model we have inherited serves to conceal the image of the whole.

Most students in the social sciences are familiar with Max Weber's thesis on the rationality of bureaucratic structures. What is perhaps not so well known are the reifications and the determinism implicit in Weber's "domain assumptions." In essence, Weber argued that the cumulative "spirit" of bourgeois capitalism encysted in bureaucracy is the most rational form of industrial organization because such spirit makes possible a high degree of calculability of results at the same time as it guarantees "imperative control over human beings." Besides, the bureaucratic rationality is presented as being an indispensable, "practically indestructible" and immutable form of domination.[1] In Weber's words, if bureaucratic administration is, other things being equal, always the most rational type [of organization] from a technical point of view, the needs of mass administration make it today completely indispensable.[2]

This chapter is a critical set of comments on Weber's general thesis on bureaucratic rationality. The problematic distinction between formal rationality and substantive rationality is not often made in discussions of Weber. By all accounts, the formal rationality of action refers to the degree to which conduct is organized according to rationally calculable principles.[3] Thus understood, modern science and technology are premised on formal rationality, for the whole purpose of relegating so much of social life to the scientific mill is in order to stamp such actions or conduct with a high degree of calculability and hence controllability. Substantive rationality, on the other hand, refers to the application of this idea of calculability to the furtherance of definite goals or values, or _ends_.

According to Giddens, modern rational capitalism, measured in terms of substantive values such as efficiency or productivity, is no doubt an advanced type of economic system. But this very quality of rationalization which envelops such a system has consequences which cut across some of our most cherished values such as that of individual creativity and autonomy of action:

> The rationalization of modern life, especially as manifest in organizational form in bureaucracy, brings into being the "cage" within which men are increasingly confined.

It is this seeming contradiction which we seek to fully understand, to review, and to put forward for open discussion and thought. It is true to say that what currently concerns critical sociologists most is the fact that the domination and the highly questionable logic of capitalist social relations are not taken as _problematic_. The apparent success of formal rationality occludes consideration of futures that are alternatives to what the present priorities plot; furthermore, the necessary critique of, and resistance to, this rationality is defused or arrested. All of this is not to deny that Weber has been criticized before; but, as we all know, the somewhat feeble and deferential criticisms have tended to congeal around the structural-functionalist position that whilst Weber pointed unmistakably to the functions of bureaucratic rationality he neglected the "dysfunctions." At no time did mainstream criticisms establish ideological and cultural domination as problematics. Instead, the claim is often made that Weber's thesis provides the site of human freedom.[4]

It can straight away be said that, as a general rule, sociologists always approach the Weberian altar on ritualistic bended knees, dwarfed by the apparent far-reaching and deep understanding of human society and history he provided. Here, Weber's very signifi-cant contribution to the formalization of sociology is not minimized; no one who has been exposed to sociology can doubt that the importance of his wide-ranging studies. But in the context of twentieth century history we are forced to question any epistemology which suggests that there are inevitable, even less eternal "laws" independent of human action which dictate social processes. In other words, we agree, with Weber, that under certain historical conditions human behavior actually obtains thing-like properties; but at the same time we are very wary of reification, of forgetting that the world we live in has been produced by human praxis, purposively, on the basis of human beings' own philosophical visions and materialist imperatives. In this short book, we can only sketch the outline of some of what seems to us to be significant themes demanding closer attention. We do not expect to get away "scot-free" with this exercise in iconoclasm; we do not even believe that the exercise will be successful in the sense of dethroning Weber. But that is not the intention. If this discussion can serve to focus critical attention on the well-established ideas of sociological theory, and if as a result of reading this book students and teachers feel obliged to reconsider the value cornerstones of modern society, then the intent of this book would have been served. Being polemical is in no way inconsistent with being serious, logical and analytic. It is one thing to study things as they are; it is quite another to formulate ideas regarding things as they might historically be. Part of this exercise then is to suggest that perhaps our theory of modern industrial society is badly in need of overhauling, beginning at the very roots of the edifice on which we build.

Weber's Position in Brief

By rationalization Weber means the principle of subjecting all areas of social life to the criteria of calculation and rational decision, that is to say to the type of decision which would guarantee a high degree of productive output, and which would optimize both means and ends. He envisioned rationalization as a developmental trend of contemporary society, as a "fate" which, once in motion would effectively obliterate magic, guesswork and other mysterious forces and impose mastery of all things.[5] This veritable law of rationalization was proposed by Weber as part of a larger explanation of the emergence and vitality of bourgeois capitalism in the Western world. It was, in fact, nothing less than the logical and indispensable counterpart of capitalism's built-in pursuit of profit as an end in itself by means of continuous enterprize.

An important corollary of this principle is that optimization of means and ends cannot be achieved except through mechanisms of formal control and domination; these are the elements which make bureaucracy as rational-legal authority, far superior to charisma or traditionalism as systems of administration. In sum, the process of rationalization, as a necessary prerequisite and concomitant of bourgeois capitalism seeks both the fragmentation and the fine-tuned calculability of human labor (conceived as a commodity) and its many products, to the extent where they became amenable to the "formal" economic logic of capitalism.[6] This process of rationalization becomes an imperative to the Calvinist believer who finds the signs of grace in the prosperity of his enterprize when this enterprize is seriously organized as if it were a calling.[7]

Weber concluded that in so far as the process of rationalization represented a liberation from magic and traditionalism it was an inevitable density of any Western society which adhered to the Judaeo-Christian ethic. This is the meaning of his widely misunderstood phrase "disenchantment of the world." The important concept of calling provided the psychological sanction of systematic conduct and literally compelled strict and methodical calculation and control; in short, the rationalization of life.[8] This instrumental rationalization of life is assumed to make possible the development of the socio-cultural institutional preconditions for modern capitalism and, indeed, the entire rationalized western social structure. It is a corollary of this position that modern capitalism has need not only of the technical means of production, but of a calculable legal system and administration in terms of formal rules and eventual imperative control over human beings. The rationalization of the modern world, seen in these terms, is firmly rooted in the Calvinist rationalization of religious life. Indeed, this spirit or attitude which seeks profit rationally and systematically and forever renewed profit by means of continuous rational capitalistic enterprize[9] succeeded on two counts. First because it was sanctioned by the theology of Calvinism which assigned authority and status on the basis of material signs of grace; and second because it was intrinsically a form of domination based on material self-interest.[10] It was instrumental rationalization, to be achieved through organizational means without regard to person.[11]

Weber argues that the decisive reason for the success of bureaucratic organization has always been its purely technical superiority over every other form,[12] and that in the final analysis capitalism, which provides the necessary resources for bureaucratic proliferation is the most rational economic basis for bureaucratic administration.[13] The two are mortised, as illustrated in figure 2. Profit for its own sake eventually becomes domination for its own sake.

In terms of Weber's epistemological position, it is important to note that what Weber called the rationalizing process was originally a product of the economically ruling classes and the intelligentsia that served them,[14] and that as such we ought to be somewhat suspicious of any claim to universality of thought. Besides, it is quite legitimate to radically interpret the many qualities which Weber assigned to bureaucracy, or formal rationality, as leading, decisively, to all kinds of human deprivations, if not a totally schizoid existence for the bureaucrat and his/her many spheres of social relations. But if we are to accept Weber's position, all of this is unimportant alongside the overall goals of the organization - corporate self-interest and the maximization of profits. There is, whether we are willing to admit it or not, a built-in irresponsibility and moral indifference in capitalism.

We fully recognize the sorts of confusion and uncertainties surrounding the use of the concept of rationality. By the criteria which Weber utilized in his analysis for _formal_ rationality viz. the extent of quantitative calculation, to be directed toward _Erwerhen_ or profit effectiveness, we can still say that within capitalistic systems social forms are not as formally rational as the state of our knowledge could facilitate. The recurring phenomena of crises within twentieth century capitalism, of poverty and squalor amidst affluence, the under-utilization of production capacity (for a variety of reasons), the persistent unemployment among people who want to work, not to mention the physical destruction of the environment, are all outstanding examples of _irrational_ "formal rationality." This means, as well, that the goals of this interpretation of rationality fall, by Weber's own set of criteria, far below their maximal coordination and hence throw into deep doubt the avowed aims of that which exists as "rational bourgeois capitalism."[15]

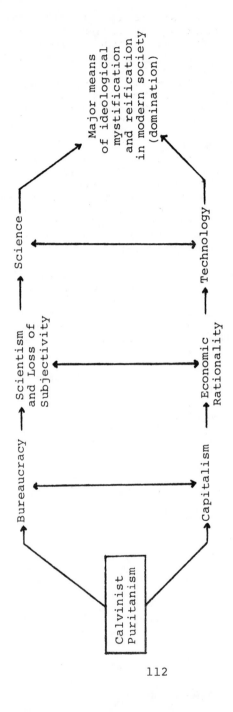

FIGURE 2: The relation between bureaucracy, capitalism, and domination

Among the students of capitalism, it was Marx who pointed to the need for a radical critique of cognition and for a sociology of knowledge which would expose the categorical framework of a critical materialism - that the ruling ideas at any given time are the ideas of the ruling class. Given the class nature of modern industrial societies in the west, some sort of reflection upon the formation of consciousness is imperative, in order to discover that management ideology and worker ideology, for instance, are often fundamentally at odds, and that the worker who toils under modern capitalism is integrated into its culture, not necessarily because of commitment to the ideals of production and overproduction, but by a special type of domination which amounts to an overdose of management ideology. Such a "diffused" domination produces a form of consciousness which is neither profound nor coherent, and which cannot therefore, intelligently assess, criticize or deny, the spurious claims of the technological era. Such a type of consciousness approximates what we mean by reified consciousness. It is, by virtue of being emasculated by bourgeois cultural apparatus, quite harmless, or at any rate incapable of speculating or conjecturing about post-capitalism alternatives, or of harboring the possibility of transforming social arrangements through human praxis and intentionality.

It is unfortunate that although "functionalism" has had as part of its theoretical scheme the notion of social action or "voluntarism" there is, notwithstanding, a lack of any concept similar to or carrying the same theoretical aim as that of transformative praxis in Marxist theory. The latter clearly assumes the human potentiality for transformation of society through purposive activity; the former does not carry any such positive assumption. We simply have not given sufficient thought, analysis and general encouragement toward the understanding of the market mentality: the reified (mis)understanding of the production-exchange-consumption matrix as they obtain in the contemporary world. The schizoid route by which the modern consumer arrives at his/her supposed "needs" gives us an unmistakable set of clues regarding the cultivated reification that is nowadays inseparable from commercialism and euphoric consumption. Are these in any way related to the value structure of capitalism? To answer this we will make a few comments in the form of an objection to some of Weber's claims for bourgeois capitalism.

The Main Objections to Weber

In this section, the main objections to Weber are raised. It is not our intention here to become entwined in the problems of Weber's methodology; this aspect of his work has been addressed over and over again.[16] Rather, our focus turns on a theoretical critique of three central assumptions dealing with (a) the rationality of bourgeois capitalism, (b) the inevitability of the rationalization of all institutional life, and (c) the presumed immutability of rationalized structures of domination. We will discuss each in turn, before returning to the idea of reification.

(a) In his famous essay on "Science and Technology as Ideology," Jurgen Habermas argues that what Weber called rationalization realizes not rationality as such but rather in the name of rationality a specific form of unacknowledged political domination; that in fact science and technology as we know them help to legitimate domination.[17] And Marcuse echoes this thesis in his equally famous essay "Industrialization and Capitalism in the Work of Max Weber."[18] Small disagreements aside, both theorists fear that the growth of industrial society has facilitated the extension of instrumental rationality into every sphere of society, at great social cost. Habermas goes as far as to suggest that the interest of instrumental rationality, like that of natural science, is that of technical control, and that where social science conceives of itself as a strict science (as opposed to a hermeneutic or critical science) it implicitly shares the theoretical concern (interest) of the strict sciences, namely maintaining technical control.

There is ample evidence to illustrate the fact that sociology has a technical character, and that it insists on the positivistic premise of producing knowledge which is purely instrumental in form, and which therefore, is claimed to be "neutral" with respect to values. There is another side to this professed neutrality however. Social sciences have come increasingly to adopt the methodology of the established natural sciences on the premise that thereby they can guarantee scientific accuracy and respectability. In actuality, such techniques also

114

serve effectively to manipulate and dominate human beings, given that the knowledge-constitutive interest of positivistic social science, is, as Habermas says, that of domination. Marcuse points to the idea that the very fact of being socialized into the principles of technological society - into its pattern of work, consumption and leisure, serve to deaden the critical faculties of modern populations. One should of course add to this the further point that requirements of the production system are only part of the problem. The rest has to do with the whole system of exchange that underpins bourgeois society - the competition, supply and demand, hoarding - in short, the market, with its own built-in irrationality and hedonism.[19]

Predicated upon this instrumental conception, science, as we know it, typically serves ideological ends and represents above all a form of activity not uniquely dominative, but which, given certain cultural imperatives, is more dominative than less. Besides, however, instrumentally interpreted, science tends to effect a double concealment of the actualities of life: first, it hides exploitation in dubious logistics; second, it hides its dominative side with a camouflage of cultural myths,[20] most notably by presenting the notion that the actual is rational and that given its very calculating potential, it can be relied upon to rescue us from all and any evil which may befall us. At the level of practice, instrumental science goes hand in hand with capitalist values. And no one with so much as a hunch about the modus operandi of modern capitalism will deny that there is much in this system that is basically irrational and hedonistic in the less-than-efficient sense, from the wanton and monumental waste of non-renewable resources, to the care-free modification of behavior through psychosurgery and neuro-biology.

It is one of the great merits of the sociologists of the Frankfurt School that they have chosen to grapple with the rather uncomfortable realization that "technology" and "instrumental rationality" of the modern era have been turned into an awesome means of ideological domination, a domination which threatens the human race's emancipatory interest.[21] The popular fad of the industrialized world of legislating all and any group of disgruntled striking workers back to work is but one of the more common manifestations of domination in "liberal" democracies. It is one way in which state-manipulated "truth" is stapled on to the consciousness of the population. Insofar as this domination transpires under the auspices of capitalist social relations, where the spell of the commodity form is well choreographed, it is not easily recognized as such. It would not be far-fetched or sensational to suggest that such developments could be taken as dress-rehearsals of 1984 in the Orwellian sense. Second, however, such ideological domination smothers creative consciousness, thereby reducing, if not eliminating, the possibility of constructing alternative conceptions of reality. Third, this ideological crisis serves to prolong the life of capitalist exploitation for selfish, private ends, whilst a reified consciousness is carefully juggled with, as just another commodity, and a highly unimportant one at that. Processed information assumes all the characteristics of a fetishized commodity, and typically occludes the central structural issues that generate strikes, protests and discontent. In short, then, domination, predicated upon instrumental rationality, distorted communication, and the full-scale appropriation, even debasement of all culture in the service of commodity production and exchange, are all distinguishing characteristics of late capitalist societies.

A related concern has to do with the very physical status of the worker in modern industrial society. In one of his many indictments of political economy, Marx pointed out that "political economy knows the worker only as a working animal, as a beast reduced to the strictest bodily needs." Essentially, he remarked, "it does not consider him when he is not working, as a human being; but leaves such considerations to criminal law, to doctors, to religion, to the statistical tables ... and to the poorhouse overseer." There is, alas, a startling resemblance between the situation depicted by Marx, and the industrial carnage which modern-day anthropologist Elliott Leyton has discovered in his examination of one group of workers under modern capitalism.[22]

The Frankfurt sociologists have argued that the one-sided instrumental concept of reason, as it has developed under the tutelage of bourgeois ideology, blocks our capacity to recognize the socio-cultural significance of our acts and thereby vitiates any emancipatory idealism among the mass population. Not surprisingly, this realization disturbs them, even

116

moreso when it appears to them that in the midst of these realities (surely unrecognized) the working classes have willingly collaborated in their own subordination and reification, to judge from the relative passivity of urban proletariat in developed capitalist societies. France may be the exception here, as the events of May 1968 suggest; but one can hardly envision a similar revolt in Canada. Canadian workers are so accustomed to being "forced" back to work that they have lost sight of their relative strength as a political force themselves.

Obviously, it is quite wrong to assume that capitalist society <u>necessarily</u> produced a class whose essential interest is emancipation. Indeed, the history of socio-political events in developed capitalist societies such as Canada tend to deny the presumed catalytic role of the proletariat, or the labor movement for that matter. Amongst the congregation of critical theorists, generally regarded as pessimistic, Marcuse seems to be more utopian than others, for he at least hopes to find a medium, preferably a material medium such as a social class within instrumental rationality, and optimally a "new science," where the humanness of nature can be actualized,[23] where, through reason, men and women can learn to throw off the shackles of repression; and then through reason use science and art to create a society in which to nurture new freedoms. The idea of a new science has earned Marcuse the title of "romantic utopian." As a new conception of reality, the new science would require a totally new <u>leitmotif</u> and a totally new climate and set of goals other than those currently guiding instrumental science. Thus, in <u>Eros and Civilization</u> he argues that human beings are not totally dominated or contorted by bourgeois instrumental rationality - that in fact human subjectivity cannot be totally reified. It is nevertheless terribly <u>repressed</u> and smothered by an overlay of ideological pleasantries and bureaucratic ethic. This means that there is still <u>some hope</u> for emancipation and still scope for the awakening of erotic political freedoms, and expressions of new sensibilities. More than that, <u>if</u> science and technology were utilized differently, these same forces could bring the dawn of human liberation and freedom, freeing men and women from scarcity and stuporous work. Because Marcuse's ideas underwent drastic change from one period to the next, it is not surprising that some have claimed that Marcuse holds a defeatist position. If anything, Marcuse's Marxism is _ambivalent_, for he does say in _One Dimensional Man_ that advanced industrial society generates new and all-pervasive forms of social control. In this popular work, he abjures today's technological states, fearing that the all-pervasive sense of affluence dulls the sensibilities of people. But yet his _hope_ for men and women forces him to make the perfectly reasonable assumption that human beings have an inexhaustible reservoir of creative (libidinal) force which will eventually deliver emancipation. This element of hope is clearly rooted in his ontological assumptions about humankind's ability to purposively change their situations.

There is very little within conventional sociological theory which explicitly questions the apparent fixity and permanence of social arrangements. Typically, the arrangements are defined as fulfilling an indispensable integrative function for society. The conception of the struggle for change is one of the salient characteristics that distinguishes a radical sociology from conservative or traditional one. A radical sociology looks for explanations of social life and theories of society which assume that radical change is at least possible, and resists those theories which root inequality, domination, or other arrangements in "inescapable facts" of biology or social structure. Furthermore, a critical social science either knows or seeks to know that the laws of society are not given in the same sense as laws of nature. Therefore there is no "dynamic" of society which could not be changed. The society is created by men and women and can and ought to be changed by them. Otherwise, men and women become slaves to the pseudo-naturalistic forces of history and society.[24]

Given this level of conceptual understanding, we could claim that the arts and sciences (to take common examples) _do_ achieve _economic rationality_, which does not however mean isomorphism between economic rationality and fulfillment of human beings. It will be instructive to reflect on some recent illustrations. Important parts of physics and chemistry have been pressed into the service of war and destruction; whilst much mathematical and statistical ingenuity has been turned into an auxiliary of monopolistic market control and profit maximization.[25] The computational concept

of rationality, nurtured, as Hans Dreitzel puts it, by
the prevailing positivistic fashion in social science
research,[26] is a system of rules, procedures and habits
of thought which seek not the satisfaction of human
needs, but the technical control of human beings. The
ideological ends which psychologists (and other human
scientists) unconsciously accept typically lead them to
present a model of man which dehumanizes him, and
obscures rather than clarifies the way in which
society's goals are mediated by the individual, and
attempts to reify its values under the disguise of a
spurious objectivity.[27] Thus psychology has become a
prostitute of "motivational research" and personnel
management,[28] psychiatry a peddler of anti-depressant
drugs and tranquilizers, whilst biology is made into
the handmaiden of pharmaceutical rackets, or else
serves, through its techniques of manipulating and
controlling of people, as an ideological justification
of the status quo. The debate concerning this
development has gone on for years amongst radical and
conservative chemists, biologists and doctors. The key
point, of course, is that

> according to the parameters of
> neuro-biology and psycho-
> pharmocology these drugs "work" in
> the sense that they "pacify"
> individuals even if they do so by
> reducing them to cabbage.

The outcome is regarded, on the whole, as less
important than admitting criticism of social
structure.[29]

Similarly, art, language, color and sound are
often not developed in the interest of human
satisfaction so much as to maintain a steady and firm
consumer demand for commodities that may serve a
"psychological utility" rather than a pragmatic
utility.[30] What comes in daily through every pore of
modern mass media represents a degradation of resources
and talent into instrumentalities of advertising, and
one can easily recognize, if one is critical, the
pervasiveness of the consumption mentality associated
with the commercialism in which we are enmeshed. Now,
this is not to say that science has not provided
positive ends or that it lacks the potential to be
humanizing. This is not thoughtless anti-scientific
pessimism; it is not even to summarily reject the

119

accoutrements of scientific advance. Because science has produced the birth-control pill, helped men to conquer space, modified the weather, and so on, it is not fashionable to criticize instrumental science and instrumental rationality generally. Yet, as humanists, or as social analysts, we fear that as technological rationality becomes political rationality we abdicate the emancipatory role of science at the same time as we deny the role of reason in human affairs, that is, the critical capacity of thought to understand the going reality, to criticize it and to project alternatives. The longer we leave partial reason unchallenged, the greater will be the hegemony of instrumental domination and the productive principles which go hand in hand with it.

Perhaps, then, what we want to say is that we do not so much question the rationalized _effort_ as the patently irrational ends of science, if we can make that distinction meaningful at all. More to the point, "computational rationality" has done nothing to prevent the present disastrous state of world affairs. University social scientists and administrative technocrats have been proved wrong in their predictions that what is called "post-industrial" society would produce a greater degree of political rationality or reason - a failure in judgment that is in sharp contrast to their self-advertised strategical cleverness.[31] According to John Rex, twentieth-century barbarism involving the destruction of human life on an unprecedented scale in world wars and colonial wars, the practice of genocide and torture, the crude recurrence of financial and political corruption in public life, and the irresponsible destruction and consumption of natural resources to a point at which the survival of mankind for more that a few more generations cannot be guaranteed, has clearly demonstrated that the promise of a scientifically managed social order was not to be fulfilled.[32] There clearly is no basis for the powerful belief, inherited from the optimism of the Enlightenment, that science will save us, or that by all the objective criteria available we are moving toward the universal satisfaction and _unquestionable_ betterment and fulfillment of human life. The facts of _social structure_ have thrown such free-flowing ideas into disrepute and, for some, contempt.

Not unreasonably, therefore, critical theory

charges science with deifying domination, and with being unwilling to judge given situations in terms of their historical possibility. In Horkheimer's view, the goals and interests of instrumental reason have, over time, eclipsed practical reason,[33] and, ironically, the "success" of the technical control of nature achieved by instrumental reason has effectively blocked the realization of practical reason. The moral is that we need, as part of our program, a critique of instrumental reason. The critical theorists all place some urgency on the need for a critique of instrumental reason, and of "mass culture." This concern is illustrated, for instance, in Adorno's work on music, and Benjamin's on literature. At bottom, they recognize that the intellectual tools for criticizing human culture and activity are severely blunted by/in traditional theory which clearly has failed to provide the basis for criticizing the status quo. Instead of being liberating, reason, instrumentally deployed, turns out to be an effective means for domination, repression, and the circumvention of basic freedoms. Thus, Marcuse, Benjamin, Horkheimer and Adorno, among others, do not for a moment equate instrumental reason with Enlightenment or progress. Economic rationality may be rational economically; this does not say it is thereby rational socio-politically and morally. Like C. Wright Mills, they view rationality without Reason as a rationality which is not commensurate with freedom but the destroyer of it. Enlightenment is as totalitarian as any system, for the Enlightenment's attitude to things is the same as the dictators of men: they know them insofar as they can manipulate them.[34]

Clearly, the naive optimism and the falsehood of the Enlightenment harbors then a pernicious idea, namely the mindless domination of humanity via the domination of nature. As Giddens puts it in his own inimitable style, the progenitors of the Enlightenment set out to effect the disenchantment of the world, to replace myth by solidly founded knowledge, and by the application of that knowledge in technology. In so doing, they prepared the way for the domination of modern culture by technical rationality: the under-mining of Reason against which Hegel struggled and which, with the disintegration of the Hegelian system, became largely lost to philosophy. In the name of freedom from the domination of myth, the Enlightenment created a new form of domination, hidden from view by its own philosophy: domination by instrumental rationality.[35] It must be strongly accentuated then, that the "dialectic of enlightenment" means that the Enlightenment spun its own internal contradiction and negativity, best exemplified in the tyranny of modern science and the loss of subjectivity in social life. It is this realization which has turned into a permanent nightmare of all critical intellectuals, in the natural as well as in the social sciences. However difficult it may seem,

> until we can bring the social
> relations of men under control,
> we remain victims of a dilemma
> whereby every outstanding victory
> in the scientific and techno-
> logical mastery of nature entails
> the real possibility of an
> equally great catastrophe.[36]

We will return later to some more ideas of critical theory.

(b) But now we must introduce a _second_ point: the assumed inevitability of rationalization. In arguing that those subject to bureaucratic control cannot escape from it,[37] Weber in effect introduces into his historical analysis an element of determinism which betrays the human hope in praxis and emancipation. Unlike Marx who conceived of history as the purposive creation and actualization of human beings, Weber foresaw a mechanically predetermined history shaped at every stage by the purely technical superiority of bureaucratic organization. Quite in contrast to Marx who places his utopia in the future, where it rightly belongs, Weber leaves his in the present, in the sense that he reasoned that history mechanically progresses until a certain point when the totally bureaucratic state is reached.[38] Such a philosophy of history, of course, is premised on an "ideal-type" social organization or the "spirit of capitalism" which "seeks profit rationally and systematically" and forever renewed profit.[39] The trend is irreversible and unstoppable.

(c) The third point then deals with the contention that once bureaucracy becomes routinized, it will not change, and presumably is not changeable. Implicit in this claim is a version of historical determinism which does not belong to a philosophy of history, but to

ideology.[40] Kolko has aptly remarked that Weber's
bureaucratic determinism not only predicts 1984 but
helps create the conditions for its establishment; his
determinism is essentially a-historical, for one can
see the future in the present.[41] Given Weber's
historical grasp and sophistication, it can only be
with great trepidation that anyone accuses Weber of
being a-historical. But it is nevertheless the case
that Weber found himself in this trap in which he was
forced to argue that if humans succeed in refining a
process of domination, then they would have to live
with it since there would be no possible way to
eliminate it. We do not take Weber's position to mean,
as so many of his followers have suggested, that
because he foresaw an irresistible advance of bureaucratic forms of life, in which men and women would be
robotized, he thereby had a _universal_ historical
perspective. There is a distinct point of view in
Weber's analysis which regards "dehumanization" as a
preferred state of human existence if that state
discouraged personal, emotional and other "irrational"
elements in social affairs. It is a legacy of the
Enlightenment world-view of which we spoke earlier.

If Weber can be said to have even hinted that
bureaucratic structures tend to develop absolute
permanence over time, he must be held responsible for
introducing reification into his analysis. This seems
to have been the case where Weber says that once the
bureaucratic apparatus of authority exists, the ruled,
for their part, cannot dispense with or replace it, and
that the achievements of big industrialists cannot be
dispensed with - not by trade union, not by state
socialist official.[42] This position must be understood
as a cue for the introduction of the reductionist
methods of natural science into social relations, a
beck and call to the "behaviorism" of psychology which
seeks to reduce human subjects into objects, the
potentially active into passive salivating creatures,
whose every response is couched by the "laws" of reward
and punishment.[43] Thus, since World War I, and
increasingly since the Hawthorne experiment at Western
Electric in the 1930s, up to the present day, theses on
"scientific management," industrial sociology and
psychology have turned to studies of small groups and
the subjective condition of the workers. And the
"music while you work" pacifier which characterized
British factories up to the 1960s, was also geared more
to the subjective attitude of the workers and not the

conditions of the worker; the intent was to increase production,[44] and to numb the reflective or enquiring potential of the dominated class.

It is not difficult to ground these ideas in the concreteness of Canadian society. In fact, it was recently pointed out by a political economist how the thesis of "scientific management" is aimed primarily at removing all brainwork from the shop floor and into the planning and laying-out department of businesses. It is considered bad policy for workers to have a real understanding of the work they do. The secret of this "science" is to keep the true nature of the labor process and its socio-cultural ramifications hidden from conscious reflection. As Gonick has written, "clever university professors" daily instruct countless thousands of students in the economics of the Canadian economy according to the tenet of a text on economics "that excludes all but economic variables from its purview."[45] Cultural Marxists have long recognized that capitalism's resiliance in the face of severe structural crises has been possible only because of an integrated administrative structure of domination.[46] However, that the so-called "spirit of capitalism" inveigles men and women to relent to political and cultural domination is not some sort of a law of nature but a fetishtic reification of human relations.

Now it is true, and it has been frequently remarked, that Weber was not completely sanguine about the existential consequences of a full-blown technological rationalization, and he in fact spoke in rather chilling terms, of the "polar night of icy darkness and hardness" which lay at the end of the bureaucratization process. He remarked:

> No one knows who will live in this cage in the future, or whether at the end of this tremendous development entirely new prophets will arise, or there will be a great rebirth of old ideas and ideals... Of the last stage of this cultural development it might well be truly said: "Specialist without spirit, sensualists without heart; this nullity imagines that it has attained a level of civilization never before

achieved."[47]

Indeed, from these remarks, one might conclude that Weber might very well have viewed the direction of the social change initiated by instrumental rationality with distaste and deep cynicism, or stoical resignation. And many defenders of Weber have pointed to his melancholia as an indication that Weber did not like the trend and would have liked to reverse it. What we are concerned with here is the theoretical blueprint. The problem of rationality cannot but disclose that instrumental rationality is a form of domination which, in Weber, is claimed to transcend its specific historical forms. Such a portrayal, needless to say, closes off any dialectical understanding and immanent critique of rationality as a distinctive type of . consensual validation. The view is one-sided and fatalistic and in a sense violates Weber's own imperatives, especially his thesis that the ideas and values men and women have in social life are necessary for influencing the course of social change.

Quite simply, we object to any philosophy of history which fatalistically assigns men and women to live (presumably forever) in the "iron cage" of bourgeois capitalism and political domination. Weber, in fact, encouraged the social science to assist in building a world he could not stand.[48] His "law" of rationalization does not contain sufficient ingredients that could coagulate around the possibility for changing the situation which was, after all, a human social arrangement.

Beyond the Objections: Weber and the
Problem of Reification

There seems to be no way in which we could over-state the importance of a theoretical criticism of Weber's position and claims. We have already argued that to the extent that Weber's thesis reifies social relations, it makes it difficult for us to recognize our own deeds and our own arrangements. Brian Fay, in his excellent little book, offers some pertinent comments on the reification of economic history:

> The so-called "laws of economic
> system" (in Keynesian economics)
> are taken to be natural necessities
> like gravity, with the effect that

the relationships which these
laws describe are taken as given
parameters within which the
specific problem...must be solved.

Similarly, on the same issue, Allen has observed how
economic theory has been elevated as a science with
laws, beyond the comprehension of ordinary people, to
be believed because it embodies the "truth" about the
economic order, to be accepted because of its
irrefutable logic and scientific rigour.[49] What the
dominant liberal paradigm of society has accomplished
then, above all else, is the portrayal of a reality
which is reified - presented as a matrix of laws and
eternal verities, beyond criticism, beyond reproach.
But there is another point which should be articulated,
and that is that the metaphysical concern for
continuity, inherent in the theory, obscures the
problem of domination. Indeed, there could be no
greater justification of an existing type of political
structure, economic organization or any type of
domination, for that matter, than to claim for it not
only that it is the most technically efficient, but
that it was so efficient that it was permanent and
inevitable, and unassailable.

There is absolutely no doubt that Weber grasped
the dominative nature of bureaucratic administration,
which he said was "formally the most rational known
means of carrying out imperative control over human
beings." While we are not suggesting that Weber
provided this image as a blueprint for the Prussian
State, we nevertheless find its presentation
insufficiently critical and reflective, considering
that the rationalization of the world through bureaucratic effectiveness is the antithesis of the
humanization of the world through creative praxis. Not
all sociologists share the interpretation of the modern
world as being sewn together by domination and the
denial of creative praxis. But then this is precisely
the germane point. The very nature of the material
reality in present industrial societies tend to foreclose the historical understanding of structures of
social relations. Instead of structural understanding,
we typically find a posture which is the nursery of
reification, archetypally falsely conscious; certain
social relationships are taken as "natural necessities"
given by nature. The intransigence of this type of
thinking is clearly illustrated in George Homans,

Austin Turk, and John Porter, among others, all of whom can be said to encourage a permanent illusion in that they subscribe to the idea that we can simply, and always, take historical creations and institutional structures as "given," and work uncritically with them, as Homans says, "for the time being."[50] A related point here concerns the danger of uncritically accepting either a so-called value-neutral definition of social problems provided by bureaucrats or governmental idealism, and presumed good intentions, as the basis for policy-research. These problems take us into the realm of reification.

The concept of reification is germane to the aims and posture of critical theory, for it is a concept which refers to the problem of ideological masking and mystification in society.[51] In its most concentrated form, reification refers to the human tendency and ability to conceptualize a socio-historical experience or situation as though it were "natural," that is, given by nature, fixed and unchangeable. Marx, and Lukacs after him, used the term specifically to describe the nature-like, mechanical quality of certain social relations that transpire under capitalism. It is not surprising then, that the theme of reification is a permanent one in most of Marx's works. In fact, it could be said that Marx's unmistakable and distinct thrust was one of anti-reification. For instance, in The Holy Family, and in The Poverty of Philosophy, he reasoned against reifying history; in Capital he discussed the fetishism of commodities and the secret thereof as the manifestation of reification, while in the 1844 Manuscripts and in the German Ideology he strongly warned against reifying society thereby missing the key to social relationships, and so on. His overriding concern was to disclose how classical economics, and aspects of philosophy, typically left the impression that human beings could be easily under-stood in total isolation from, and unrelatedness to, the matrix of the commodity form. Marx pointed out how in the exchange process, we typically lose the linkage between the commodities and their human origins and the circumstances of their realization. This forgetting gives rise to the ideological litany that commodities have living human powers. In what Marx refers to as the "mystery of commodities" the human agency was systematically detached from the dynamics of the labor process. This involved, crucially, "commodification" of all inputs into this process, including the human

127

beings, who become an exchangeable commodity along with
all the others deployed in the making of the
exchangeable commodity. The final reification takes
place when money is hoisted (as a fully developed
commodity form) as the power which will command goods
over human desires. The formal relationship which
money creates masks the qualitatively different
contents of the objects exchanged. There is,
ostensibly, an exchange of equivalents, a quid pro quo,
but in the process, something is lost, or "forgotten,"
or extinguished, namely, use-value. Here, the mystery
of the commodity form, and the phantasy of the market,
can be detected. But not by everyone. In this context,
the general perception of social reality amounts to a
mystification which not only hides the source of
profit and surplus value, but establishes an abstract
"fairness" as an appearance which hides real relations.
Clearly, the notion of a fair day's work as equivalent
to a wage makes no sense at all unless understood in
ideological terms, that is, in terms of the distortion
of living labor into an arbitrary, quantifiable
exchange value.

The complexity of this process carries some
important implications for a critical theory of society.
For, to the extent that human beings comprehend the
products of their labor (typically encrusted in social
institutions) as autonomous, objective forces, totally
unconnected with human praxis, we can expect an
attitude and a consciousness that manifests resignation,
adaptation, and an uncritical acceptance of "destiny."
We can expect, in short, a frame of mind which will not
entertain the idea of the changefulness of social
arrangements.

In the context of our overall discussion, the
latent reification in Weber's thesis encourages a
tendency to view social roles and activities
independent of their humanness, or "detached from their
intentionality and expressivity, to the extent that
they are transformed into a seemingly inevitable
destiny for their bearers."[52] This interpretation of
reification helps to explain why it is often suggested
that "all reification is a forgetting," a sort of
social and cultural "amnesia"[53] whereby in the course
of our daily lives, at least under capitalist
structures of social relations, through a relentless
commodification we "forget" that it is human activity
which brings commodities into existence. The

forgetting makes us victims of our own human powers and subjectivity. The metamorphosis of a social into a natural condition, obviously bestows ontological status on social roles, commodities, ideas, and institutions, thereby masking relationships, and distorting the historical totality of human relations. But it is equally clear that the reification process is not simply that of amnesia, but also that of eternalizing partial explanations. In other words, some aspects of social life are conveniently forgotten, at the same time as others are given constant reinforcement and elevation to the level of "laws." There are many such "laws in economic theory, and sociology is not far behind in suggesting that there may be "natural laws" governing a good deal of the behavior in modern society. To the extent that these so-called laws ignore the historical totality of human existence they invariably reify and hence distort social understanding.

Our next concern then is to discuss briefly, some of the implications of this forgetting. First, by reifying and thereby fetishizing, we lose sight of the historical fulcrum, and foolishly harbor an existentially-induced false consciousness in the sense that human relations are conceptualized as things-in-themselves. Second, to invest social roles and institutions with their own ontological status is to ascribe to them an almost boundless mandate and a capacity to conceal their true social and historical character as human objectifications. The form reacts upon its own content and takes possession of it; the thing turns man into its thing,[54] disguising its own origins and the secret of its birth, namely, that it is the product of specific human interrelations. Third, to the extent that institutions are reified, they are mystified, and this mystification effectively dispossesses human actors of reflective self-understanding and philosophical visions. Reification amputates or occludes utopianizing, and utopia, in the Mannheimian sense, as opposed to ideology, should stand ready to disturb the existing body of ideas, even outlining a new horizon. Fourth, reifying social relations and institutions postpones, unnecessarily, social change. To reify existing ideas about what things should be done and how they should be done is to inhibit change by putting these ways and ideas beyond question.[55] To the extent that humans cannot conceive of the social and cultural world as being of their making, they can hardly be expected to change it.

Understood in these terms, reification cannot be divorced from the larger problem of alienation in human society. For this reason we think that Berger and Pullberg are quite mistaken in their belief that one can make a letitimate division between alienation and reification.[56] If they insist on this divide, then they themselves reify, that is, present a form of analysis which claims that reification is a condition having a life of its own. Reification and scientism, in this sense, go hand in hand, scientism being understood as science's belief in itself and the fallacy that the scope of knowledge-production is restricted to the production of strict data and timeless information.[57]

We might, accordingly, invoke some ideas from critical theory to bring to bear upon the topic. Critical theory conceives of itself as having emancipatory potential by virtue of its ability to reveal relationships and to dispell illusions and distortions. This phenomenological-reconstructionist task is facilitated by critical theory's anchorage in epistemological self-reflection and practical Reason. Critical theorists argue that instrumental science operates on the norms of instrumental reason, which, by dint of its logic and structure, participates directly in the process of domination;[58] in practice, political domination is underwritten by the norms of technological/instrumental rationality.

We will return, in Chapter 9, to a more extensive discussion of critical theory. For now it should be remarked that the generalized charge of domination which critical theory makes against the aims of traditional theory must be assessed alongside some of the more inelegant and puzzling aspects of Marx's thought, for instance his statement on "one science," which crept into his early writings. Marx, in his own way, contributed to the entrenchment of domination in the sense that he held up positivism as the future of sociology and also that his theme of man dominating nature and leaving his "stamp" on it is a latent science-as-domination position. There is no question that Marx left himself open to these sorts of criticisms. In the Manuscripts, for instance, Marx says: "natural science will in time incorporate into itself the science of man, just as the science of man will incorporate into itself natural science: there will be one science."[59] Fred Dallmayr, in interpreting

130

Habermas' criticism of Marx, argues that Marx ultimately submerged communicative interaction in instrumental labor, thus inviting a positivist interpretation and reductionism of his arguments.[60] If Dallmayr is correct, then it can be argued that Marx did foresee, even if he was reluctant to speculate on it, that men's urge to stamp nature would eventually mean coordinated control of themselves, but, unlike Weber, he left them with the option of purposively liberating themselves as well.

In a class society such as ours, the domination of the subjectivity of the working class is a precondition of exponential growth and of what Adorno called destructive irrationality. The relationship between a condition of life and a consciousness is never clear-cut. But what we should not hastily conclude is that any lack of radical consciousness among the wretched of Canada is due to the unquestionable saneness of bourgeois social institutions. The evidence points in another direction. In this context, Marxian analysis performs its main task of demystification by developing the conceptual instruments to bring into the open the social characteristics of those properties of things which otherwise appear as objective and natural.[61] Theory should deepen our understanding of the phenomena we wish to study, and should constantly chase after those conditions or situations which through their own seeming plausibility discourage our questions and our intentions to search. In sociology, it is luminously clear to the critical mind that the process of cultural socialization is perhaps the one which most easily passes without inspection. Yet in the final analysis this process contains the truly revelatory clues regarding, not only the social construction of reality, but, specifically for our discussion here, the theory and method of socialized consciousness.

Charles H. Anderson has persuasively argued that the potency of Marxist theory to identify the major problems of the day constitute its deep and lasting strength. As a schema which seeks to locate social reality in the social relations of a group or society, it is a powerful framework for the understanding of our society because such an understanding must be grounded in a thorough comprehension of class relations. It is a theoretical framework which provides for its users indispensable pointers as to where to begin the search for knowledge and understanding.[62] Having made that point, it ought to be accentuated and made clear that the oft-repeated and naive view that Marx was "an economic determinist" is fully at odds with the focal view adopted here that people can emancipate themselves from the historical snares which are of their own making. It is not the case, as anyone who understands the dynamics of socialization realizes, that Marxian theory sacrifices man to the alien and dominant so-called "economic laws" which confront him, as it were, with cold inevitability. Instead, as Max Adler points out, man is sacrificed only as long as he has not understood the "laws" of economic condition, which are really nothing but social conditions, that is, human conditions in which men produce, exchange and consume.[63] It is part of our business to deliberately create that intellectual uneasiness which will predispose the mind toward the unexplained empirical referents of sociological theorizing. Throughout this short exposition we will endeavour to make clear that theory in sociology need not be of the formal, abstract, type before it can provide a deep understanding of human history and meaningful explanations. The frontier of understanding remains out of vision for as long as we remain uncritical or even unmindful of the ontogenetic processes through which history and humans as the subjects of that history are shaped.

We have already suggested that the faith in science ushered in with the Enlightenment ought now to be tempered by the serious possibility that we may be entering another Dark Age, computers and laser equipment in tow. The focal concern here is a simple one. We seem to have gone too far, in social and political life, in ridding our thought and action of values and moral/ethical concerns, best exemplified in the almost total scientization of politics and communication (Habermas). But this conclusion will certainly seem sensational and uncalled for by many. We can arrive at a positive point of reflection on such sensationalism only if, like Dr. Kenneth Hare, Director of the Institute of Environmental Studies at the University of Toronto, we realize that "for 99.9 percent of all the troubles that confront society in which science plays a part, there is no scientific answer and value judgments must play a much larger role than science."[64] Interestingly, more and more philosophers, sociologists and historians seem to be moving to the position that perhaps values are just as fundamental as facts, or even more so; and that, perhaps, there is no clear distinction between facts and values.[65] If that is so, then the important thing is that these values should be the subject of open discussion, debate and analysis. In other words, the values that underscore the procedural rationality (but which are frequently denied) must become the focus of social and political evaluation, and should not be left to the experts alone, for there is no reason to think that these so-called experts have ever given the questions of rationality or values, or human survival, anything more than a whimsical, scientistic consideration.

We have now reached a stage in the discussions in this book where it is possible to state that the principal difference between a Marxian theory of society and conventional theories is that in Marx a thoroughgoing analysis of the labor process yields a phenomenology of human beings, where the others do not. In Marx, the theory states that human beings instrumentally and historically produce an objective world, which nevertheless appears alien and tyrannical. Interestingly, we can locate, in both Marx and Weber, the realization that human creations tend to become, over time, seemingly independent entities and wield a power over their creators, following what seems to be laws of their own. Weber's fundamental thrust was to analyze the Puritan ethic in search of a governing principle. This he discovered in the process of rationalization and established thereby one facet of reification: the domination of human over human and the fragmentation and destruction of subjectivity. Relationships between men and women take on the appearance of relationship between things. In Marx, the domination is also recognized, but in a much more phenomenological way. For him, the seemingly fixed and dominating arrangements appear that way because of alienation; it is the process that leads to reification. When we are alienated we experience our subordination and our powerlessness as "natural," as permanent. A second facet of reification thus emerges: the domination of things over humans, typified in the fetishism of commodities. These points are illustrated in figure 3.

In the next chapter we will engage in reflection on some aspects of modern history which we think need to be reinterpreted and reappraised.

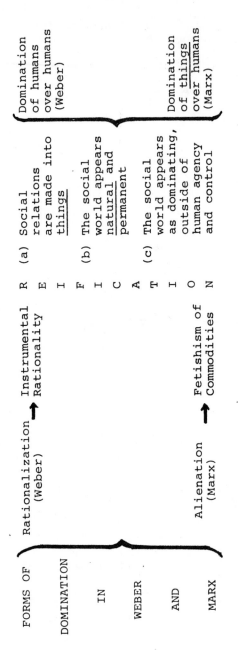

FORMS OF			
DOMINATION	Rationalization (Weber) → Instrumental Rationality	R E I F I C A T I O N	(a) Social relations are made into things
IN			(b) The social world appears natural and permanent
WEBER			
AND	Alienation (Marx) → Fetishism of Commodities		(c) The social world appears as dominating, outside of human agency and control
MARX			

} Domination of humans over humans (Weber)

} Domination of things over humans (Marx)

Marx, unlike Weber, interpreted the seemingly fixed arrangements as simply the dialectical interplay of object and subject, the subject resolutely making himself/herself, but also destroying himself phenomenologically as he mortgages his subjectivity through forced labor. In Marx's paradigm, the arrangements, as humanely created, are historically transient and rationally controllable.

FIGURE 3: Forms of domination in Weber and Marx

134

NOTES

1. Weber, 1947, p. 337; 1948, p. 25; 1954, pp. 335-37; Bendix, 1960, pp. 430-35.

2. Weber, 1954, p. 223; 1948, p. 229.

3. Giddens, 1971, pp. 183-4.

4. See, e.g., Lowith, 1972; also Bendix, 1960, p. 421 et passim; Blau, 1956, 1975; Blau and Scott, 1962; Selznick, 1943; Sills, 1957. One of the most interesting critical evaluations of Weber's thesis is found in Israel's important work (1971). In analyzing bureaucratization as a reifying process, Israel points out that for clarity of analysis it is important to distinguish at least four usages of bureaucracy: (a) bureaucracy referring to the social and administrative structure of organizations, (b) bureaucracy as a system of values, (c) bureaucracy referring to the people who are in charge of or hold power in those organizations or social systems having bureaucratic structure, and (d) bureaucracy referring to the ways in which bureaucratic organizations function (1971, pp. 322-23). It is manifestly obvious that the flurry of "criticisms" which developed in the 1950s and 1960 around Weber's thesis of the bureaucratization process concentrated primarily on the "function" usage, while soft-pedalling the larger reifying process whereby the domination of things over humans became the negative (according to certain value premises) hallmark of the process. For other critical assessments, see Allen, 1975; and Meszaros, 1972.

5. Weber, 1954, p. 329; 1948, p. 133.

6. Weber, 1930, p. 17.

7. Ibid., p. 174.

8. Ibid., p. 128. Also see Weber's "science as a vocation" in Weber, 1948, and the editors' remarks, pp. 51-52, 73-74; cf. Parsons, 1937, pp. 673-77.

9. Weber, 1930, pp. 17, 64.

10. _Ibid._, p. 25.

11. Weber, 1947, p. 123.

12. Weber, 1954, p. 350; 1948, p. 215.

13. Parsons, 1937, p. 533.

14. Dreitzel, 1972, p. 178.

15. See, e.g., Gonick, 1975; and Anderson, 1974.

16. On Weber's methodology see Parsons, 1937; Soloman, 1934; and Andreski, 1964.

17. Habermas, 1968a, pp. 82-92; 1968b, pp. 306-17.

18. Marcuse, 1968, pp. 201-226; and see, also, Marcuse, 1964, especially chapter 6; cf. Shapiro, 1970, p. 181.

19. See Nicolaus, 1972, p. 311; and Wellmer, 1971, p. 130.

20. See, especially Marcuse, 1964, pp. 166-67; Agger, 1975, p. 188; and 1976, pp. 166-67, 173.

21. Marcuse, 1970, p. 12, for extensions and critical appraisals of the domination theme see, among much else, Schroyer, 1970, 1973; Leiss, 1974, esp. part II; and Rose and Rose, 1976.

22. See Marx, 1964, pp. 72-73; and Elliott Leyton, _Dying Hard_, Toronto, McClelland & Stewart, 1975.

23. Marcuse, 1969, pp. 31ff; 1972, p. 39; and Habermas, 1968b, pp. 32-33.

24. Becker and Horowitz, 1972; and G. Radnitzky, _Contemporary Schools of Metascience_, Chicago, Henry Regneny, 1973.

25. Baran, 1969, pp. 92-96, and pp. 102-103.

26. See Dreitzel, 1972, p. 176.

27. See Ingleby, 1972; Rose and Rose, 1976, among others.

28. See the illuminating essay by Resler and Walton, in Armistead, 1974, pp. 282-93.

29. Rose and Rose, 1976, chps. 6 and 7 fully document this. See, also, on this matter, Jacoby, 1975.

30. Kline and Leiss, 1978, esp. pp. 16-17 and cf. Birnbaum, 1969, pp. 66-72.

31. Dreitzel, 1972, p. 179; and Wilson, 1976, pp. 205-30, but esp. p. 216.

32. Rex, 1974, pp. 4, 84.

33. See Horkheimer, 1974, esp. pp. 177 ff.

34. Horkheimer and Adorno, 1972, pp. 20, 24; and Mills, 1959, pp. 170, 179.

35. Giddens, 1977, p. 67.

36. See, among much else, Leiss, 1972; and Rose and Rose, 1976. Marx's own critique of the Enlightenment is, of course, encased in his well-known Third Thesis on Feuerbach.

37. Weber, 1947, pp. 338, 420-421; Weber, 1954, pp. 190-92; and Parsons, 1937, p. 533.

38. Kolko, 1959, p. 29.

39. Weber, 1930, pp. 17, 64.

40. Following Gouldner, we can define ideology as a belief system that makes pretentious and unjustified claims to scientificity, and, simultaneously draw on Offe's insights to stipulate that an ideology serves to consolidate an existing social condition with justifications derived from the status quo, as well as to defend the existing society against its own historical alternatives. These conceptions are quite consistent with the one offered at the beginning of this book. See Alvin Gouldner, 1976, p. 9; and Offe, 1976, p. 13.

41. Kolko, 1959, p. 35; and also Mészáros, 1972, pp. 35-81.

42. Weber, 1948, p. 229; 1947, pp. 89-112, 324-329; 1930, p. 50; and 1927, p. 337.

43. See "The politics of neurobiology" in Rose and Rose, 1976.

44. In this connection, see Jacoby, 1975, pp. 15-16; and Becker and Horowitz, 1972, esp. pp. 48-50; Gonick, 1975, pp. 6-7.

45. Gonick, 1975; and see also Clement, 1975. Both works must be read closely to yield the optimum fund of insights and explanation of the seemingly elusive Canadian political economy. Cf. Horkheimer, 1972, p. 67; and Schroyer, 1973.

46. Leiss, 1974b; Wilson, 1976, p. 244; Marcuse, 1964, pp. 158, 166.

47. Weber, 1948, p. 128; and also Weber, 1930, p. 29, 180-83, esp. 182.

48. Wilson, 1976, p. 209; Jacoby, 1975, p. 17.

49. Fay, 1975, pp. 57-69, but esp. p. 60; Allen, 1975, pp. 22, 119.

50. See, e.g., Homans, 1967, p. 107; Turk, 1969, p. 57; and Porter, 1975a, p. x. But Meszaros points out that "for the time being" usually becomes for good, by virtue of the systematic avoidance of the question of when and how we are going to examine the institutional structures as not "simply given." (1972, p. 49)

51. For excellent expositions of this important concept in critical social science, see Hamilton, 1974; Giddens, 1971; Swingewood, 1975; Israel, 1971, esp. chapter 9; and Fay, 1975. The original and still widely referred to conception is in Lukacs, 1971, esp. p. 88-209.

52. See Berger & Pullberg, 1965, p. 205; and Berger and Luckmann, 1966, pp. 89-91.

53. See Jacoby, 1975, pp. 4, 157, 158.

54. Henri Lefebvre, 1969.

55. This idea derives from Professor Tom Goff, sociologist at Mt. Allison University, Sackville, New Brunswick: "Reification in theory and practice: Some comments on a relatively neglected concept." Paper read at the 1977 Atlantic Association of Sociologists and Anthropologists Meeting, Wolfville, Nova Scotia. Marcuse (1955) reminds us that against the surrender to time, the restoration of remembrance to its rights, as a vehicle of liberation, is one of the noblest tasks of thought (p. 212). Also, see Marcuse, 1968, p. 75.

56. Berger and Pullberg, op.cit.

57. Habermas, 1968b, p. 4.

58. It is important to see this claim in the light of sociology's struggle to accrue credibility for its operations. See Agger, 1975, and 1977, pp. 1-34; cf. Marcuse, 1964, pp. 158, 166.

59. 1964, p. 134.

60. Dallmayr, 1972a, pp. 83, 87. See, also Rose and Rose, 1976, esp. pp. 101-102, 107, 130.

61. Ciccotti, et al., 1976, p. 37.

62. See Anderson, 1974, p. 325 et passim.

63. For further discussion see Avineri, 1968, pp. 66-67; and Max Adler's essays in Bottomore and Goode, 1978, p. 57 ff.

64. University Affairs, September, 1978, p. 9.

65. Margaret J. Osler, "Apocryphal knowledge: misuse of science," in Marsha P. Hansen, et al, (eds.), Science, Pseudo-Science and Society, Waterloo: Wilfrid Laurier University Press, 1980, p. 285.

CHAPTER VI

FROM REIFICATION TO UNDERSTANDING

So far we have seen that there is a persistent Marcusian thesis, in One Dimensional Man, that advanced industrial society, which is premised on Weberian formal rationality, is irrational because the accumulated wealth of that society could be effectively used, but is not so used, to pacify the struggle for existence. Instead, it perpetuates that struggle, principally because the ideology of private accumulation ensures that the established system of production is one of planned obsolescence. It is possible, Marcuse argues, given our professed state of knowledge, to calculate rationally the necessary labor required to maintain an adequate standard of living for all. Based upon these calculations, men and women could be relieved from having to spend so much of their human energy and collective resources solely in the productive process. To the extent that the human capabilities are present within advanced industrial society, but are not realized, there is irrationality. If the existing technology were appropriately managed, it could provide the material preconditions for the elimination of unnecessary labor, could make possible a more creative and liberated existence. So formal rationality may be the most efficient way of getting things done. The question is: are these things being done in such a way as to achieve both objective and subjective maximization within advanced capitalism? In this regard, Paul Baran has forcefully argued that what is frequently and casually called the strength of monopoly capitalism is its power to overproduce for consumption in the private sector, for given levels of class income, while under-producing or misproducing in the public sector, as determined by the liberal ideology and the power of corporate interests.[1]

This whole business of overproduction is, of course, one of the unacknowledged supreme ironies or negativity in capitalist structures, a negation of rationality in two senses. Firstly, the entrepreneur, according to standard economic theory, is supposed to be a smart person, one who has a sound, even "perfect" knowledge of the market, one who is supposed to run a business with the aid of accurate planning, sound calculation and sober thinking. Yet he/she over-produces. Secondly, however, because of the profit motive, it is important to overproduce, <u>just in case</u> the demand can be whipped up to consume as much as possible. Often, then, production is in excess of what the market can or will absorb. On the one hand that production is not congruent with "rational" planning; on the other, overproducing without a <u>known</u> demand is wasteful and non-rational. One can see <u>why</u>, in many places in Marx's works, but especially in the third volume of <u>Capital</u>, he argued that the capitalist mode of production is generally, despite all its niggardliness, altogether too prodigal with its human material, just as conversely, thanks to its method of distribution of products through commerce and manner of competition, it is very prodigal with its material means, and loses for society what it gains for the individual capitalist.[2] We wish to reflect on this thesis in this chapter.

What Can We Observe (Or Know) About Modern Society

The anarchy of production of which Marx spoke, carries the possibility of crisis as an inherent feature of the structure of capitalism. Some of this is demonstrated in organized capitalism with its accompanying highly sophisticated worker psychology and manipulative interests. The latter exploit personal conflicts, mainly through advertising, create or awaken purely artificial needs,[3] and thereby lend sustenance and longevity to a particular social arrangement.[4] But, as Baran says, the cancerous malaise of monopoly capitalism is not that it happens to squander a large part of its resources on the production of means of destruction, that it happens to allow corporations to engage in liminal and subliminal advertising, in peddling adulterated products and inundating human life with moronizing entertainment, commercialized religion and base "culture." The malaise of the system which renders it a formidable obstacle to human advancement is that all this is not an unconscious assortment of fortuitously-appearing attributes of the capitalist order; this <u>modus operandi</u> is the very basis of its existence and viability.[5]

Herein lies the paradox which so many political economists and critical sociologists have identified. The corporate economy promotes a highly rationalized, that is, profit-maximizing, form of production, bureaucratic administration and market control, at the same time as it "squanders human lives or living labor, blood and flesh, nerve and brain."[6] The irrationality of the whole comes out in what must be conceptualized as capitalist waste: in the fact, for example, that "distribution costs" now make up a greater portion of the price of a commodity than the actual manufacturing cost.[7] The clue to understanding this paradox is that the "efficiency" which serves to justify contemporary technocratic society is apparent rather than real. The idea of instrumental efficiency and the seemingly neutral administration of society, by experts, the crowning height of modern industrial society, carries some very important implications for social theory. For one thing, this picture clouds the structural understanding of modern capitalism; for another, as we argued above, it depoliticizes political life. Finally, the rationality which undergirds this socio-political order transposes all kinds of crises including legitimation crises, into "rationality crises" that confront us in an epiphenomenal way, as something alien, even mysterious and impenetrable.

It is therefore an appropriate point to ask whether we understand, or even want to understand, the values, assumptions and scheme of priority associated with capitalist societies today. If we claim under-standing, it would have to be admitted that we have no interest in social change, for few would deny that the day-to-day operation of capitalism as a structure of social relations, fails to meet human needs or to satisfy human hopes in freedom from unnecessary constraints. If, on the other hand, we plead ignorance, we are forced to ask how we could expect Marx to have predicted or even understood these same relations at the time that he was carrying out his analysis. And yet he accomplished both.

Part of the problem of understanding modern capitalism stems from our inability to view it as a type of relationship, which, by definition, can only survive if it grows and expands - at all costs. Most of us are caught up in this growth syndrome, yet few of us see any connection between our own life-world and that of the larger structural pattern of which we are a part. As capitalism grows, it changes shape, foci and justificatory ideology. Too many critics of Marx fail to recognize these facts, and far too many even vaguely grasp the many ways in which capitalism is still contradiction-in-process. We might have gone from

competitive market capitalism to <u>monopoly</u> capitalism
characterized most plainly by a consumption pattern
that is "colonized by distorted needs," as well as by a
"gradual scientization of capitalist accumulation
process," by the scientization of social relations (and
the concomitant stifling of critical reflection), by
the disguise of the political process and finally by a
drift towards cultural crisis.[8] But the dialectic of
discontinuity is still discernable, except that there
is, now, unlike the earlier phases of capitalist
development, greater proficiency at cultural and
political manipulation. All of these fundamental
changes carry implications that bear directly on our
efforts to understand modern society. With regards to
the role of social theory, they are challenges.

The theoretical probe of critical theory takes on
added meaning when the multiple changes within
capitalism are grasped at the structural level, a level,
for instance, which conceives of Canada as a society
which, because it is capitalist, has its own made-at-
home hinterland. Living and working in these hinterlands gives one the rare opportunity to recognize a
number of obscure issues, for example, the dogged
commitment to the liberal ideology of <u>economic
expansion</u> even at the expense of cultural terrorism, a
focus typified in the mandate of the Department of
Regional and Economic Expansion (or DREE). DREE's
manifest aims are almost, <u>prima facie</u>, beyond reproach,
for DREE seeks to iron-out regional disparities and to
make all Canadians equal as far as the benefits of free
enterprize are concerned. But yet the illusion escapes
our total grasp. Whether measured diurnally, or
annually, or by decades, these hinterlands remain that:
<u>internal</u> hinterlands which are the markets and
laboratories for the "developed" and "overdeveloped"
regions; hinterlands on which to dump surplus products
and shoddy third-rate goods.

Economic expansion <u>per se</u> does not "naturally"
narrow the divisions between class, or lessen economic
inequalities. The evidence in Canada shows quite
convincingly that the pattern of income distribution in
the society has remained remarkably constant, inspite
of DREE or anything else of the same genre. The notion
that somehow technological development and economic
expansion automatically smooths class differences, is,
quite simply, a myth. Myths are very comforting, but
they do not explain concrete reality. The profound

intent of the unity between state and "private industry" seems far removed from equalization. Indeed, given the avowed degree of understanding and expertise contained in the two elements, equalization and the rational organization of social life in the hinterlands should be easy. Yet both remain only a distant possibility. Undergirding the scandal of Maritime unemployment and Maritime prices of everyday commodities, are many unexplained aspects of the "market system," hidden premises of capitalist production and distribution, and non-debatable privatized rationale and ends. Orthodox sociology's theoretical weakness consists of its unwillingness to make these kinds of puzzles the centre of its enquiries into modern society. Consequently, sociology has not always delivered the kind of macro-understanding that this stage of history demands. It is not that that understanding is unreachable. It is, rather, that we still conceive of epistemological anxiety as a greater evil than the articulation of comforting ideologies, even if these ideologies are at odds with concrete reality. This is why everyone seems so obsessed with economic expansion. This is why the poor (especially in the hinterlands) have been studied and studied and rediscovered in each generation. But, clearly, poverty has not declined. Indeed, one can go so far as to suggest that we will never understand poverty by studying the poor themselves. At some point, if we want to generate critical understanding, the liberal ideology of free enterprize, individualism, equality of opportunity, supply and demand, will have to become a key topic for critical analysis.

Marx had suggested that in the evolution of capitalism the rate of profit will tend to fall. But, (and this is the important point) the mass of profit will rise, and both the rate and the volume of surplus must rise. This swelling surplus is precisely what helps to make for the flexibility of capitalism. Nicolaus articulates the complexity of this process in his "hypothesis" that the possibility of a rebellion among the working class varies inversely with the rate of exploitation. That is, the higher the rate of exploitation, the bigger the margin of surplus controlled by the capitalist class and hence the easier it is to safely grant wage demands. And this in no way hinders the accumulation of capital. The bigger the margin of surplus, the more easily can labor demands be satisfied, and hence the less threat they present to the entire system. This hypothesis, of course, is to be found in Marx, in his discussion of the rate of surplus value, in volume 3 of Capital.[9] Furthermore, however, such surplus enables the capitalist class to create a class of people who are not productive workers, but who perform services for the capitalist class as a whole. Such a class of unproductive workers fulfills the functions of distribution and marketing, generally keeping track of and glorifying the swelling surplus. It has to be significant, then, that in a period of declining university enrolment (and population) schools and faculties of "business" and "business administration" are experiencing a veritable boom. The process of the accumulation of surplus profit may indeed entail some important social and political numbness. We do know that it enables the capitalist structure to face workers' demands for higher wages with an unprecedented degree of flexibility. That much we know from our analysis of modern industrial capitalism and from our historical studies of this period.

But it is too easy to conclude from the apparent passivity of the worker under capitalism that they thereby share the benefits of technological society, or that they are in fact totally served by the system. They have not rebelled in earnest because their past has always been a little worse that their present, and their future has promised to be a little better yet.[10] The proletariat in the advanced industrial countries have not developed in the way anticipated by Marx, although we would contend that the structural definition of the proletariat as the "universal class" is still valid. That is to say, the laboring class must still be conceptualized as wage-laborer, (although there can be no "just" price for labor) and as the class which endures in the most concentrated form the suffering imposed by history upon the whole of humanity. Its suffering and dehumanization makes it the paradigm for the human condition at large. This point, made by Lukacs more than half a century ago, still seems applicable today, although there have been trenchant criticisms of it. Whatever reservations we might have about Lukacs' theory, since he was not able to account theoretically for the empirical absence of an insurgent working class who were supposed to carry out their historical mission of their own liberation, that theory was nevertheless instrumental in leading to a recovery, in the 1920s, of the philosophical dimension of Marxism. As we pointed out above, this dimension had suffered greatly at the exegetical and editorial hands of Engels, and of orthodox Marxists of the Second and Third Internationals.

A second fundamental aspect of late capitalism concerns the extent of state intervention. As Habermas and others have been at pains to point out, the modern State now actively intervenes in the economy and attempts through monetary and fiscal controls to stabilize the "free market," thereby openly undermining the still adhered-to laissez-faire philosophy, while at the same time forestalling any impending terminal crisis of the capitalist system. Such intervention raises some serious questions regarding the nature and scope of political participation and decision-making: to quote Habermas, "politics is no longer a phenomenon of the superstructure." Because the State itself is its own political legitimizing force, it is accurate to say that what is now the focal point of concern is the "crisis" of legitimation, a crisis which has its roots in the collapse of liberalism which once elicited mass belief in the rationality of the social system. In short, the economic crises, once endemic to an earlier phase of capitalism, have been displaced by a crisis legitimacy. There is still contradiction and negativity; only, it moves from the sphere of the economy (where it is managed) to the political and cultural spheres. We know from the evidence that State intervention notwithstanding, economic crises and contradictions of all kinds persist, in Canada as in other advanced capitalist societies: from chronic unemployment to unprecedented high interest rates, to the collapse of once-solid enterprizes such as Chrysler or Massey-Ferguson, and the stupidity of overproduction, mentioned earlier.

State intervention into the working of capitalist social structures has only partially stabilized economic conditions that are inherently crisis-ridden, but over and above that, such intervention does not seek to eliminate the decisive irrationality inherent in capitalism. Thus the intervention does not necessarily consider the structural tendencies toward crisis; it has not eliminated crises and contradictions, only displaced them. Thus, it serves to transform class struggle into administrative regulation, or, as Schroyer puts it: "the costs of maintaining private enterprize are pushed directly onto the consumer and taxpayer." The Welfare State, indeed, has not

abolished the conditions of alienation and exploitation
- it has simply mystified them.[11] And if the material
conditions of life on the whole have improved, the work
position of men and women has become all the worse -
more and more subject to exploitation by personal and
impersonal forces which make them helpless and their
work "meaningless." Habermas' contention that Marx's
labor theory of value is obsolete and must therefore be
transcended or supplemented, is based on the premise
that it is not _labor_ which is the major source of
wealth in modern society, but rather science and
technology. But this is a grossly misleading and
regressive argument which loses sight of the fact of
the fundamental tyranny of work (or labor) [even] in
the industrialized world, even if such work is subject
to the process of capitalist de-skilling, a process
vividly portrayed in Harry Braverman's _Labor and
Monopoly Capital_.

There are two sets of arguments which cut across
this idea, and in essence demolish Habermas' thesis.
The first is contained in the brilliant exposition of
the political economist James Becker who reasons that
however social life is to continue, the labor theory of
value must go hand in hand with it, for in its broadest
aspect the labor theory proposes that the social
activity devoted to reproduction of the material means
of life provides critical support for the sustenance of
all other varieties of social activity. The labor
theory, Becker points out, constitutes that theoretical
first premise that has its roots in social life, that
premise being that the power of productive labor both
sustains and requires sustenance. This is the touchstone from which the labor theory departs and to which
it returns.[12] Becker's answer to Habermas is extremely
complex and takes the reader into deep-water economics
(even though the author insists that his is a
compendium of elementary principles, a sketch rather
than a portrait). In any event, for those who lack the
skill or the penchant for the sophistication of the
economic analysis offered, the theoretical gist of the
labor theory is that it is so fundamental to Marxian
political economy that all of the other branches of
Marxian science - its sociology, politics, philosophy,
social psychology, and all else rests. As one extends
the theoretical structure from labor value premises to
contemporary history, the theory, instead of breaking
down, becomes a steadily more powerful instrument for
probing into the secrets of the present order, into its

structure of political as well as economic power.[13]

The second rebuttal of Habermas's mischievous thesis points out that, technological developments aside, labor still occupies a central place in the economic life of contemporary capitalism, and that "living labor" remains more than ever the sole source of surplus value, and a key source of profit. Moreover, capitalism is still based on exploitativelabor. But what stands out is the fact that industrial labor in the broadest sense of the word is still the kernel of the modern economy's structure. As Ernest Mandel has remarked, one has only to observe how billion-dollar corporations haggle and shout like fishmongers over a 50-cent wage here, and 2 hours off the work-week there, to see that whatever sociologists might argue, the hard facts of contemporary life conform to Marx's thesis, namely that capitalism's unlimited appetite for profits is an unlimited appetite for human surplus labor, for hours and minutes of unpaid labor.[14] Capitalism thrives in the sacrificial lands of the Third World on abundant cheap human labor. This is what multi-national corporations gain from going multi-national rather than remaining uni-national. Significantly, too, one should note that the great majority of the struggles that characterize modern Canada are struggles between labor and capital. Such strifes show no sign of abating in the near future, in spite of technology.

Those who question Marx's proposition that human labor is the sole source of surplus, and argue instead that science and technology are today the key forces of production and wealth, conveniently forget that technology is a human product, and that science is a social, that is, human enterprize. These modern developments have moved to control labor, not to eliminate it, or to lessen its import in the production process. Habermas's claim that Marx's critique of political economy must be quickly transcended is also a claim that Marxism is perhaps not critical enough because it lacks an adequate concept of reflection. But, as O'Neill rightly points out, Marx's critique of classical political economy is methodologically in no way below the level of reflective critical theory.[15]

The Bearing of Piecemeal Understanding on Compliance in Society

The reader should not conclude that because Marx

assumed that the industrial worker is the potential
bearer of a higher form of social organization, he/she
would inevitably be revolutionary. Marx thought that
from his analysis of the social processes, he had
discovered such a rebellious potential. But he did not
impose this insight upon history.[16] The problem of the
relationship between existence and consciousness is
much more complex than that. The conceptualization of
the proletariat as the universal class is taken to be
the theoretical expression of the "class" struggle for
emancipation. But there is no isomorphism between a
condition of life, and protest and/or revolution, in a
situation where the subjectivity and the spontaneity of
a population are manipulated as they are under
instrumental capitalism. It is clearly a fallacy to
think that simply giving the worker a higher price for
his labor-power solves the problem of alienation, or
necessarily helps the worker to adjust to his situation.
Alienation and the factors that generate it cannot be
structurally siphoned off once and for all, but must
change simultaneously with the entire work process.

Similarly, as it is often presented, theory alone
cannot change the world, least of all when theory does
not seek to understand the world. Agger is essentially
correct when he says that "the working class will not
awaken to their revolutionary potential by reading
Capital or One Dimensional Man," or any other
theoretical work for that matter, but neither will they
necessarily revolt or act constructively to change
society because of their subjectively experienced
exploitation and unhappiness, or because "their current
lives are no longer bearable."[17] That the relation
between theory and struggle or between knowledge and
change is not that simple and decisive is borne out by
history. It seems abundantly clear that sociology has
not provided the kind of conceptual leverage that would
show that the fundamental vehicle which imparts
knowledge, namely, language, is, in all societies
context-laden and hence easily reified, although
perhaps only up to the point where theoretical grasp is
precluded.

Understanding cannot be formalized in a totally
context-free language; therefore, in phenomenological
terms, the language which justifies and defends the
established order, as revealed, for instance, in mass
advertising, serves essentially to conceal rather than
to reveal meanings and symbols, although it is commonly

recognized that the medium is "public" language. It is no doubt for these reasons that John O'Neill argues that so-called "knowledge" alone does not bring about or even encourage social change: critical reflection can never be arrived at by reading texts in the ordinary sense; what is needed is "phenomenological pedagogic practice."[18] Such a practice, which is to be informed by theoretical insights, does not fall solely in the lap of intellectuals, for as we have sought to show throughout, some theoretical perspectives, by refraining from asking certain questions, can never hope to arrive at certain answers about social structure. Consequently, that practice too, is problematic. There is no clear-cut evidence that everyday practice of the class struggle, or experienced misery, necessarily lead to concerted revolt. So while theoretical insights are crucial, and should be sought, they do not <u>guarantee</u> action geared at social change.

There is no truly convincing evidence in recent history to support the related contention that economic deprivation, political repression, or "depressions" in themselves lead to a rise of revolutionary activity or an increase in anger and resistance among the objectively disprivileged classes in modern society. On the contrary, one can propose the perfectly valid hypothesis that workers and exploited classes in the industrialized world tend to become profoundly conservative under increasing <u>relative</u> material well-being.

In the light of these reflections, it is inaccurate to think that "subjectively experienced exploitation" could alone revolutionize consciousness. The <u>major</u> factor which a theory of modern society must incorporate into its scheme, is the attribution of what Mills terms "private troubles" to the larger system processes. In other words, for the masses to attribute their particular woes to the social system, they must be broadly convinced that the interests of the powerful groups in society are, most often than not, at variance with those of society in general, and of their own class in particular. The corporate rape of the environment in the last half a century contains sufficient evidence that particularized interest has always taken priority over public or social interests, even if we are often asked to believe otherwise. The great majority who toil under capitalism are quite unable to perceive or conceive of the possibility of a

different social order. To the extent that they are
entrapped by the standard liberal ideology, they are
not predisposed to develop creative consciousness, or
critical reflection on the state of modern society.
Hence there is no insight into the actual working of
capitalist social formations. Most certainly, a total
grasp of how one aspect of society interlocks with the
other is absent. The "affluent" populations are not
able, in short, to make the necessary connections
between the different spheres of social existence.

Marx, as well as Lukacs after him, pointed to the
important fact that what makes for the ideological
ballast of much of social science is the systematic
ignorance of a concept of historical totality. As we
have seen, the lack of such a concept is a precondition
for reified consciousness. Besides, the lack of such a
concept occludes the unity of theory and practice, for
that unity is possible only when a class effects a
double understanding: that of itself as the living
stuff of history, and of the society as a whole, of
which it is a part. The atomization and fragmentation
of life and thought in this historical period
constitute the greatest obstacle to the realization of
radical consciousness. Besides, as we have said, in
advanced capitalist societies the satisfaction of
material needs made possible by economic growth, and
the ideology of steadily expanding consumption of goods
and services, serve to effectively depoliticize the
greater portion of the population, as opiates
distracting people from a critical understanding of
themselves and their society. This thesis carries some
important sociological implications both for the
process of cultural socialization in our society and
for the futile future of protest as a potential
political resource. The blow to the counter-cultural
movements of the 1960s, for instance, was part of a
familiar occlusion of alternative life styles and
values.

John Anson Warner provides an excellent assessment
of this development when he reminded us that the system
has demonstrated that it is capable of draining the
meaning out of many forms of symbolic protest, and
gutting counter-cultural life styles of their radical
content in order to absorb them into "normal" youth
culture and the norms of organizational society. Even
in a political sense, the system has proven that it can
take radical slogans and employ them for the most

conservative purposes.[19] The collective imagery which makes possible the integration of modern working class populations may not always seem logical or meaningful to critical minds, but at least they typically remove from public debate any topic which may be critical of the political status quo. Conformity to a political system that does not itself question collective imageries is best described in terms of "structured consensus," that is, one reached by the political elites and passed down to the public who responds as an acclamatory agent only.[20] Protest no longer seems a viable resource in such contexts. Indeed, the layperson who protests against the dictates of the political and technical experts risks the charge of anti-intellectualism; and one might even be charged with revolting against reason itself. As Marcuse has observed, to entertain the idea of an alternative to capitalist society could easily appear ridiculous, given that the thoroughly sophisticated ideology of capitalism seems, to most, preeminently rational and praiseworthy on all accounts.

But these claims should not lead us into believing that, after all, there are no good reasons for developing a critical spirit. In effect, as Habermas observes, it is one of the major paradoxes of late capitalism that it creates

> impediments to communication which
> make a fiction of the reciprocal
> imputation of accountability
> simultaneously support the belief
> in legitimacy which sustains the
> fiction and prevents its being
> exposed.[21]

It is the many changed aspects within late capitalism that should concern our critical efforts. If we are to fully understand modern society, it seems incumbent on us to bring under close scrutiny those very processes that work to prevent the fictions from being discovered. It is on this count that the work of Habermas is so path-breaking and, in the final analysis, potentially emancipatory.

In summarizing this part of the discussion, we want to reiterate a number of important points that bear directly on our structural understanding of "late capitalism." First, there is the uncomfortable realization, reflected in the ideas of critical theory, that the technology and rationality of the modern era have been turned into a powerful means of ideological domination. This realization is given explicit formulation in the works of Habermas, whose discussions point to several far-reaching social, cultural and political implications. Insofar as this domination transpires under the auspices of capitalist social relations, it is not easily recognized, for capitalism does not reveal the social relations on which it rests. This concealment is inextricably bound up with ideological domination, which is our second point. A little-understood form of ideological domination is now endemic in current modes of social and political life.

The domination with which we are here concerned is the type that smothers creative consciousness at the same time as it incubates reification. Given these considerations, it is clear to see how, among the other developments within modern capitalism, is its finesse in integrating and engulfing all consumers into its ethos without much difficulty. Given, too, Habermas's understanding of the developments within late capitalism, it is extraordinarily strange that he should think that ordinary people can think their way to emancipatory truth. It is a little doubtful if the average citizen thinks very much at all, never mind thinking critically about the superficial niceties of modern consumerism. How, then, is emancipatory thinking possible in modern society, when every organ of civil society labors to cloud the issues, to occlude criticism, to misdirect the anger and to produce resignation and insouciance? And where do we begin to cultivate this consciousness? In the nursery, in the university classroom, in the market place, or at the barricades? These are questions which any worthwhile substantive theory of liberation must confront, deeply conscious of the ways in which the legitimation process in modern capitalist societies is reified. The fact that the dominant ideology becomes rooted in the consciousness of the exploited majority means that they come to regard the current structure as serving not just the elite, but as being in their best interest as well. Symbolic misrepresentation creates further problems in critical understanding.

Passivity, Reification & The
Politics of Miscommunication

The range and types of factors surrounding passivity and compliance in a liberal democracy, such as Canada, are no doubt very complex. But in the light of the previous discussion and observation about how the cultural apparatus of capitalist societies works, a major hypothesis emerges concerning the institutionalization of powerlessness by the dual process of the distortion of communication, and the spurious equation of dominant interests with the interests of the population as a whole. By dominant interest is meant those shared and propagated by the powerful in society (variously termed "power elite," "corporate elite," or "ruling class"). A suggestive hypothesis is given by Marx who, more than a century ago, saw that the gate-keepers of knowledge were always those who define themselves, or are defined as, in Marx's time ruling class; in our time, the corporate elite, which, for all its apparent abstractness, is explicable in terms of identifiable groups and their value premises. The issue is whether we should completely trust that powerful group or, alternatively, explore and examine its interests, intentions and professed goodwill for possible distortions which may reside in the highly processed media content, taken for granted.

The phenomenon of distorted communication has deeply concerned critical theorists, and one of the most illuminating discussions of it is that offered by Mueller, on which we shall rely.[22] First, he defines distorted communication as all forms of restricted and prejudiced communication that by their nature inhibit a full discussion of problems, issues and ideas that have public relevance. Second, he offers three major forms of distorted communication, all of which interfere with open political communication, since they all <u>distort</u> and hence preclude the articulation of demands as well as our unobstructed discussion of specific issues.

<u>Directed</u> distorted communication results from governmental policy to structure language communication, demonstrative of the way language is used in political debate to conceal biases, priorities and value commitments. Government spokespersons, for instance, constantly tell us that the great evil of our time - inflation - is due to people's unreasonable

expectations of greater incomes, better and more commodities, but is not a function of the very nature of capitalism's exponential imperatives. We are consciously and carefully socialized into having many and high expectations (as anyone who ponders our advertising empires will recognize); yet we are somehow led to believe that our personal whims and "rising expectations" directly breed inflation, and by association, unemployment. The logic is elusive. In deep retrospect, it is crucial that we situate the phenomenon of accelerated inflation to the long term metamorphosis of industrial societies. The psychology of inflation has been preached ad nauseam - it forms the favorite sermon of our politicians. The sociology of inflation is never mentioned. This they are authorized to deny, which means that the whole syndrome of exponential growth, unlimited "investment," increased production, cultivated consumer demands and endless profit-making are never examined. The larger structure of social relations which could be expected to provide clues to the understanding of the whole, remains hidden from view, and politicians, academics and by cultural osmosis the general public, come to speak glibly of "getting the country moving again," or "getting the economy back on its feet." To sentimentalize in this fashion is to structure not simply communication but consciousness as well. In spheres where the profit motive does not reign supreme - as for example, hospital services, we face a rather different, but no less significant a blockage, as Ivan Illich's probe into limits to medicine clearly illustrates.

The distortion of communication in a mass society that is also class-based, cannot be divorced from the widespread, but little understood, practice whereby the ruling class is able to impose its own ideology and interpretation of social life on the rest of the population. Canadian manifestation of this is nowhere better illustrated than in the early history of the Cooperative Commonwealth Federation (CCF), especially well documented by Gerald L. Caplan.[23] Caplan brilliantly demolished the myth that radicalism flourishes in times of economic hardship and pointed out that in the 1932-1945 period the Ontario experience of the CCF was effectively nullified by an unmistakable stigmatizing of the CCF as a ghoulish communist conspiracy, and by the systematic distortion and mis-representation of its ideas by a powerful and well-run

propaganda machine financed by a ruling class dedicated
to the virtues of private enterprize. The war against
socialism which was waged against the CCF nation-wide,
succeeded not because the cause of the CCF was not
worthwhile, but quite simply because the ideological
hegemony of the anti-socialist organizations was
synonymous with the control of the principal
communication media. The message and remarks of the
new party were repeatedly distorted, and when the
distortions were eventually mailed to "every postal
address in Canada" the situation resembled one where
the ruling ideas of that period were those of the
ruling class. The ruling ideas were necessarily
convincing, but distortive.

The second type of distorted communication,
arrested communication, relates to the limited capacity
of individuals or groups to engage in political
communication, because the nature of their linguistic
environment inhibits such communication. This is a
problem of linguistic codes. The language of most
political debates assumes an elaborated code, a precise
meaning of political concepts, and a vocabulary
sufficient to decipher political rhetoric. But yet a
large proportion of our population have only a
restricted linguistic code, in which the meanings of
common political terms are not necessarily understood.
It must be one of the supreme ironies of our times that
while we boast of a high level of literacy and other
advancements we require, more than ever before, armies
of lawyers, tax consultants, and other specialists to
interpret for us, at high cost, some of our most
fundamental social, economic, and political trans-
actions. The importance and status of such specialists
is a function of our general incapacity (rather than
inability) to meaningfully engage in economic and
political communication.

Finally, constrained distorted communication is
the type which is easily recognized in modern society,
where the corporate presence is unmistakable.
Constrained communication involves successful attempts
by private and governmental groups to structure and
limit public communication in order that their
interests (perhaps joint) prevail. A perfectly good
example of this concerns the way government departments
hide behind the screen of "confidentiality" or "secrecy"
on issues that are obviously of public interest. Robert
Cooper, the former Canadian Broadcasting Corporation's

Ombudsman, once related at a seminar at the University of Prince Edward Island that a few years ago a Federal Department discovered that a particular fast-food chain in Canada (perhaps the biggest) was lax with respect to the control of bacteria in its food - a situation clearly of national and public importance. When the Ombudsman department tried to find out which company was at fault, the reply was that the Department could not divulge such information, as people would lose trust both in the Department and the Federal government. In the meantime, consumers, no wiser for the discovery, continued to buy and consume (unknown to them, but known to the private party and the government) tainted hamburgers or milkshakes. We are bound to ask: whose health and welfare ...? The death of the public sphere is also, simultaneously, the death of liberal democracy; and one cannot help wondering why the Ombudsman's department of the CBC has been disbanded.

Mueller argues that by definition science and technology, insofar as they operate as paraideology, that is, as ideology without a normative ingredient, do not provide ethical standards of conduct, nor offer any transcendent goals that could motivate the population politically.[24] Used as the sole basis for governmental decision-making, such a paraideology cannot be expected to fulfill the spiritual and moral needs of modern publics, to provide guidelines for political activity, or relate to any dimension beyond the daily "consumerism" of the period. In fact, the apparent paradox of the situation is that the relative affluence of the industrial worker of the modern period, together with the social compensations which come from the Welfare State, serve to veil the political nature of many of our problems. It took a very long time, for instance, for Canadians to become even mildly critical of industrial pollution and the rape of the environment. The certainty of a weekly pay check was always more important than the probability that someone working in, say, the asbestos mine would die young, unnecessarily, from a disease associated with bringing that product to market.

The level of political consciousness in Canada, as in many industrial countries, is in inverse proportion to the physical affluence of the society, and it is easy to generalize from that relationship to the one that in the affluent society there is generally no need for protest or political activism. Yet the issue is more complex than that. One can hypothesize that only a small handful of Canadians understand anything about international finance although, presumably, our lives are inextricably tied in with it. Who understands what it means when the dollar "slips" to 85¢ U.S., or what it means to borrow money on the Open Market, or that "advances" lead "declines" on the Toronto Stock Exchange? And how many care? And yet, given the centrality of the exchange rationality in our lives, one would expect that most of us would have acquired that knowledge as easily and as deliberately as we learn to drive. As long as public issues (such as unemployment) are not given political interpretation, for so long do they remain below the level of informed debate and appraisal.

It cannot be said that the political systems of capitalist societies (such as Canada) stabilize themselves on the basis of political education or value consensus, for the evidence does not support that position. Rather, the sheer absence of meaningful information provides its own type of compliance. The well-known phrase that "you can't beat the system" is often more a confession that one does not understand the system, rather than an expression of certain defeat in a duel. The choreographed fascination with the commodity (mindless consumerism), together with the structural impediments to communication, and indeed the hopeless fragmentation of knowledge, are all different aspects of the same instrumental rationality which is the hub of modern capitalism. The legitimation of this state of affairs according to spurious criteria of efficiency and exponential growth, pushes normative or ethical factors of social life to the very margin of, if not completely outside, political debate. The belief that social problems can be solved purely technically, without appealing to normative or political values, is a strong one which is pointedly relevant to this discussion. Such a stance effectively depoliticizes the masses, and propels decision-making as well as social and economic organization outside the realm of values and moral choice. In short, the shuttle is from one type of rationality to the other, without any true awareness of the far-reaching implications.

The Hidden Value Component of
Substantive Rationality

We have already suggested that rationality is double-edged, for on the one hand there is the procedural (or computational) rationality with its emphasis on means; and on the other there is substantive rationality which weighs the pros and cons of the pursuit of procedural rationality. At least, in theory, this is what is supposed to happen. It is quite easy to see, however, that this distinction can only be kept at the conceptual level. At the empirical level we are bound to connect the two, for it is manifestly impossible to seek to manipulate nature and achieve mastery over the flesh, without at the same time considering the ends of such pursuit. Often, however, we do not know as a matter of course what ends propel given courses of action and, to make matters worse, sociologists find it convenient not to ask too many questions about the values inherent in substantive rationality, on the premise that it is impossible to present a system of values which is not arbitrary. That argument is, needless to say, shallow, for values by definition are neither true or false - they simply are. And whether we recognize it or not, the decisions of politicians and other "experts" who work in the social spheres are made on the basis on some value commitments; substantive rationality is value-laden. Does anyone suppose, for instance, that the famous cost-benefit analyses of economic theory are without a normative gut? Surely, the overriding question must be: for whom is the social policy or project a cost, and for whom is it a benefit? Does the cost, and the benefit, accrue to the same group(s), class(es) or individual(s)? And are the inherent values made explicit? Values are always at the heart of political decisions if those decisions are at all political in the true sense. The important socio-logical concern ought to be to determine how and why we have agreed on certain values, and whether by virtue of that agreement we do not also serve notice that at any time we can criticize them. To a large extent, nowadays, we can only plead ignorance of a vast array of topics that are ostensibly public. If, in the pursuit and perfectability of procedural rationality, we "forget" that ends are being served, that is not to say that such rationality is thereby value-free and neutral, or even unquestionably benevolent.

In the current period, formal rationality has eclipsed substantive rationality; that is, concern with the rules and with <u>domination</u> for its own sake effectively precludes adequate consideration of the <u>ends</u> sought. We have seen that Weber, for his part, <u>did</u> not believe in the possibility of the transcendence of modern industrial society, neither did he look for structural possibilities or hidden dynamics pointing to radical change. Essentially, the historical emergence of a rationalized modern world results, for him, in the resigned impossibility of collective subjectivity.

Any judgment regarding substantive rationality must, in the final analysis, draw upon value judgments and normative evaluation, even if, as is customary in the context of modern politics, the judgments are not publicly debated or weighed or gauged, but are simply imposed "from above." So-called neutrality in politics is as hypocritical as claims to value freedom in sociological work, and it is in the processes of "overformalization" in sociology and the "scientization" of politics that we jettison the value and normative aspects of modern day existence. In both cases, the ends are sacrificed for the means; in both cases we carelessly take the assumptions of the powerful uncritically.

The scientization of politics - handing over the process to the "experts" - is a relatively new and awesome development of late capitalism, and one which contributes to the entrenchment of reified consciousness on the part of the great mass of the population. The common acceptance of the institutionalization of expertise is strangely paradoxical. <u>Prima facie</u>, this development <u>seems</u> desirable, but on the other hand it can serve as a straight-jacket that suffocates reason. It is not necessarily a substitute for self-direction and social responsibility. Nor can it be assumed that "rational calculability" can be equated with human freedom or humanness. As C. Wright Mills long reminded us, the fact that the techniques and rationalities of science are given central place in a society does not mean that men live reasonably and without myth; technological or bureaucratic rationality is not a grand summation of the individual will and capacity to reason. In modern society, thanks to entrenched "expertise," there is uncritical widespread acceptance of many forms of destructive irrationality and a concomitant denial of democratic

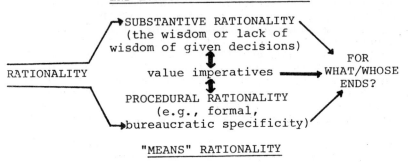

"END-EVALUATION" RATIONALITY:

SUBSTANTIVE RATIONALITY
(the wisdom or lack of
wisdom of given decisions)

RATIONALITY   value imperatives ⟶ FOR
                                         WHAT/WHOSE
                                         ENDS?

PROCEDURAL RATIONALITY
(e.g., formal,
bureaucratic specificity)

"MEANS" RATIONALITY

FIGURE 4: The two rationalities
           in Weber's thesis

decision making. This is not, however, a sufficient
basis for the questionable assertion that a certain
degree of reification is the price which has to be
paid for objective knowledge.[25] As Lukacs points out,
following Marx's observation on the same subject,
reification was not a feature of modern society in
general, but of a particular type of modern society
dominated by the exchange rationality of the market
such as is characteristic of capitalist society.

Against Thorstein Veblen, who, in his The Theory
of the Leisure Class and other essays, thought that the
fetishism of commodities lay in their prestige value,
and that reification does not therefore reflect the
thinghood of commodities, we contend that it is
precisely the paradox of thinghood's ability to
mesmerize (in the market) which is the essential
problem. If Veblen is right, how else can we explain
the mindless alacrity with which the modern consumer
buys junk? Surely, not because of prestige or snob
value, but because of a highly complex mechanism which
few social scientists have bothered to critically
reflect upon. At the very centre of this mechanism
lies the fact that in modern "consumer society" the
only rationale for production is often that, even if
the product is planned to be obsolete in a few days,
many persons can be induced to believe that they really
want and need the newest offering of commodities in the
marketplace. The outstanding complexity of the ethos

162

that propels the production for profit-accumulation-consumption sequence in modern capitalist society is never the serious topic it should be for teachers and students, as Gonick so carefully points out. The political economy of this state of affairs is given as treacle to students in the social sciences without the slightest encouragement to critically review the underlying assumptions of the "marvellous delights of the competitive economy, of supply and demand, and marginal productivity." What we have termed the treacle approach does nothing to help us understand the motions of the modern economy.

It is the prime motive of production under private enterprize that the profit-propelled growth ethic which accumulates commodities be followed by continuous and rising consumption. Consumption is itself an escape from, and a compensation for, the tyrannical and oppressive nature of work which, under present arrangements, does not fulfill its potentiality as the single most fertile outlet for initiative, individuality and creativity. "That potentiality having been snatched away from us," we turn to other outlets to realize these human goals, being liberally helped along by sponsors of culture. Advertizing is the vehicle par excellence of the sponsors who want us to forget: "the corporation does not simply sell consumer goods. It sells means of forgetting, means of distraction." In this complex, subtle, yet eagerly obscured set of relations, we are forced to view the super-consumer not simply as the creation of Madison Avenue, but as the living other side of the coin of the alienated worker.[26]

At this stage, domination over nature and men, directed by the ruling class becomes internalized in the psychic process of individuals; and it is self-destructive because the compulsive character of consumption and behavior destroys personal autonomy and negates the long and difficult effort to win liberation from that experience of external compulsion which marked the original relationship between humanity and nature.[27] Veblen's theory overlooked the "mystery" of the universal hegemony of exchange, whereby all personal and social relations among individuals are mediated through material objects. This is the capstone of reification; as a pacifier, "older values are subtly employed to allay the guilt that might otherwise arise from spontaneous and reckless indulgence.[28] On

163

critical theory's own premise that knowledge is never neutral but often _ideological_, the critique of ideology and the critique of knowledge are charted as prime concerns of a truly human science.

As Weber was no doubt aware, the scientization of modern politics and the general bureaucratization of modern society requires that people not question the contents of administrative decisions and imperative commands, but instead concern themselves only with the accomplishment of tasks set for them.[29] But to eliminate questioning of the ends of society, or of those interests that govern society, is to reify, and for so long as we are being tempted not to question the ends of society, for so long will our role as critical students of society be assured. It may very well be, then, that one of the ironies of critical theory in the 1970s is that although it is barely alive in Germany, its birthplace, it is alive and well in the English-speaking world.[30] But even this late arrival is to be welcomed. Critical theory resists social amnesia and seeks to be a de-reifying force: its principal _raison d'être_ is a critique of ideology and para-ideology.

To the extent that sociology still flirts with, and feeds on existing reifications, critical theory's role is sharply defined. The scientific value of the ideas of the European critical theorists (the Frankfurt School) lies in the fact that they have delineated the inhuman and questionable aspects of the prevailing system of reified domination. They have, besides, accentuated how the stranglehold of a "scientized" domination serves to prolong reified consciousness. If nothing else, the theory of culture developed by the Frankfurt School demonstrated how powerful, and subtle, is the spell of domination in bourgeois society, and how the experience of domination, as the "slime of history," effects its historical transmission without fear of an ombudsman demanding clarification of the working assumptions of bourgeois rationality. They have fostered a theoretical endeavour, culminating in an intellectual synthesis which does justice to the original purpose of critical theory. Equally significant is the fact that they have pioneered explorations of the ways in which impersonality and the ideological rationality of science have extended into and dominated political life.

The complexity of all these developments cannot be

overemphasized. In the effort to prove Marx's crisis theory inapplicable to the current situation, we should not overlook the development of other forms of crises within late capitalism which impinge on socio-political life.

John Keane has carefully shown that Habermas recognizes fully that late capitalism is still haunted by crises. However, it is imperative to grasp that these new crises are qualitatively different from those analyzed in detail by Marx. Essentially, the crisis tendency of modern society is cultural rather than economic and results, ironically, from attempts, particularly via the state apparatus, to stave off economic crisis. One dimension of this tendency is political in character. In late capitalism, the state plays a relatively autonomous, absolutely crucial role of organizing the capitalist process.[31] We have already suggested that state intervention has its unrecognizable ramifications for politics, economics, cultural socialization, and ideological husbandry. But it is in looking at what Keane calls the "relative autonomy" of the state that we fully grasp how, in fact, it not only safeguards the production process, but also intervenes in that process, playing a key role in scientific and technological research, the recruitment and training of non-reflective workers, and in overall planning. As a capitalist state, it attempts to ensure the continuity of the accumulation process and the legitimation of the existing order.[32] In short, extension of state planning, the scientization of politics, the control of the cultural institutions, are all aimed at crisis management. Besides, however, such unabashed intervention implies the "suspension" of popular participation in policy formation. A theory that will provide explanation and clarification rather than mystification must earmark precisely these areas for further, more attentive discussion and evaluation.

This chapter has attempted to dramatize, in a tentative way, that the problem of history is the problem of consciousness, and that that problem can only be understood against the background of the more pervasive and entrenched experience of cultural domination as this transpires under the auspices of capitalist values and claims to "rationality." In all of the social sciences, the fundamental problem remains how to bring the contradictions of bourgeois society to the level of consciousness and how to begin to puncture

the articulate reductionist dogmas of established
social science. It seems clear that until we develop
critical analyses which point to the ways in which our
"understanding," produced by our own institutions and
normative systems, is <u>systematically</u> distorted, talk of
raising consciousness must necessarily be misplaced and
pointless.

Writing from within Europe, Habermas has
persuasively argued that a theory of modern society
must move beyond the critique of political economy to
take full account both of the increased state intervention in the modern "welfare state," and of the
growth of science and technology as the leading
productive force and ideological matrix. Specifically,
he has in mind a drastic overhauling of Marx's
historical materialism sufficient to illuminate the
distortions which occur in communicative praxis, and of
the repressive constraints which serve to amputate or
block the self-understanding of society. But it is
perhaps fair to say that in North America we are still
at the stage of trying (belatedly) to sketch the role
of modern science and technology (indivisible as they
are) in terms of their guiding principles of
accumulation, profit and domination. We have only just
given a wavering beck to critical analysis, and much of
it still lingers at the periphery of North American
academia. Only after we have mastered the critique of
political economy can we fruitfully move to the higher
level of reflective critical theory of the type
proposed by Habermas, in which the understanding of the
institutional framework of society, as the very
incubator of reified consciousness, would be grounded
in a metatheory of language and metatheory of symbolic
communication.

In view of the developed concern, thus far,
regarding reified consciousness, it will be of great
interest to examine next one particular facet of
Canadian theoretical understanding, in order to discern
at what level some confusion, reification and/or
conscious omission obtain. The topic to be discussed
is, we feel, particularly important, for the theorists
who are involved in this sphere - socio-cultural
pluralism - seem to have some hesitant agreement on
substantive points. There seems to be some general
agreement, for instance, that ethnic diversity and the
relations between ethnic groups are a common structural
feature of modern cosmopolitan societies. These

166

relationships carry immense implications for "race relations" so called, for conventional models of social stratification, for the sociology of conflict, and finally for the role of political coercion in culturally heterogenous societies. Let us proceed to examine that area and some of its current conceptual problems in the Canadian context.

NOTES

1. Baran, 1969, p. xix.

2. Marx, 1971b, pp. 86-87.

3. Ibid., xxii. Baran goes on to point out that "in the absence of any alternative to the Protestant Ethic, the individual's non-work time (not "leisure") is invaded by a quantitative ethic of wants, which seduced him into cooperating with the alienation of his conscious sensibilities at work in order to satisfy a fantasy of wants conjured up in the "privacy" of the home." See, also Clement, 1975, p. 281.

4. Connerton, 1976, pp. 24, 25.

5. See, among much else, Rose and Rose, 1976; Baran, 1969, pp. 100-102; Kline and Leiss, 1978.

6. Marx, 1971a, p. 88.

7. Nicolaus, 1971, p. 11.

8. Keane, 1975b, pp. 83-85.

9. Marx, 1971b; and in addition, see, especially, Nicolaus, 1967, pp. 44-46; idem; 1971, pp. 7-8; cf. Leiss, 1974, p. 331; and Marx, n.d., p. 209.

10. Nicolaus, 1971, pp. 7-8.

11. Supek, 1977, p. 80; and Schroyer, 1973, p. 237.

12. Becker, 1977, esp. pp. 1-37 and 93 ff.

13. Ibid., p. 8. Becker points out that the Marxian political economy is superior to the standard treatises on economics because at least "it is capable of defining operationally useful goals that are within our powers of realization." Conventional textbooks in economics, on the other hand (such as Paul Samuelson's multiple edition best-seller), offer "strange and yawning gaps in their discourse." While they pay great attention to "theoretical mechanics," they choose to ignore the role of economic circumstance in relation to larger issues such as war, civil unrest, social

inequality and political, racial, religious and sexual repressions ... and other issues. (pp. 9-10).

14. "Workers and Permanent Revolution," in Fischer, 1971, pp. 174 ff; Walton and Hall, n.d.; and also Agger, 1975, p. 196.

15. O'Neill, n.d., p. 84.

16. Lichtheim, 1974, p. 75.

17. Agger, 1977, p. 22.

18. O'Neill, 1976, p. 9; and O'Neill, n.d., p. 73.

19. Cited in Anderson, 1974, p. 305. Also see Habermas, 1968a, p. 112.

20. Mueller, 1973, p. 92; and Dallmayr, 1972a, p. 81.

21. Cited in Keane, op.cit., p. 94.

22. Mueller, 1973, esp. chp. 1.

23. Caplan, 1963, pp. 93-121.

24. Mueller, 1973, pp. 109-11.

25. Markovic, 1972, p. 30.

26. Gonick, 1975, pp. 6-9, et.passim.; and Clement, 1975.

27. Leiss, 1974b, p. xvii; and 1974a, p. 334.

28. Ibid.

29. Mueller, op.cit., p. 178; and also Agger, 1975, p. 11.

30. Piccone, 1976, p. 91.

31. This discussion owes much to Professor John Keane, to whom the author is most grateful for the very rewarding exchange of ideas on the subject. For luminous and deep insights into political economy, see Keane, 1975a, 1975b, 1978.

32. <u>Ibid</u>.

CHAPTER VII

TOWARDS THE CONCEPTUAL UNDERSTANDING OF
SOCIO-CULTURAL PLURALISM IN CANADA*

Definition of the Problem

The aim of this chapter is to present some preliminary ideas that can be incorporated into a conceptual understanding of a neglected area in Canadian sociology. Despite some recent claims that this thesis has been presented "hundreds of times" there are some very important areas of confusion which demand another look.

The idea of a plural society, taken to mean not any and all examples of heterogeneous societies, but, specifically, culturally composite societies where there is no one set of basic institutions serving all ethnic/racial groups, has come to occupy an important place in modern sociological analyses. A growing number of contemporary sociologists and anthropologists seem to agree, as van den Berghe has expressed it, that the analysis of pluralism is a somewhat new vantage point from which to approach the comparative study of whole societies and more specifically a conceptual framework for the understanding of complex heterogeneous societies.[1] Still others argue that the area of race relations in plural societies is one which is of crucial and strategic importance for sociological theory, since it may well be that a clearer picture of the workings of plural societies might serve to illuminate some of the problems of Western industrialized societies better than can be done by the model of an integrated social system.[2] Yet, Canadian sociologists have given very little formal attention to this theoretical model in their effort to understand the Canadian "mosaic." More specifically, two key reasons for the inattention suggest themselves: one, because of the confusion in the literature as to the meaning of pluralism, and hence ambivalence with respect to how a pluralist framework can be applied to the understanding of Canadian society; and two, because presumably certain ideological factors serve as roadblocks to the application of the model to Canada.

*Reprinted by permission of Human Mosaic. This chapter is a revision of an article originally appearing in Human Mosaic 11 (1): 45-59, Spring, 1977.

Overview of the Literature on Pluralism

(a) J.S. Furnivall and his critics

The sociological interest in the idea of social
and cultural pluralism dates back to the work of J.S.
Furnivall, a Dutch economist with wide experience in
administrative matters in the colonial Far East. In
his important work Colonial Policy and Practice, first
published in 1948, Furnivall drew attention to the
importance of a plural model in his explanation of
social relations in a colonial society. His definition
of a plural society as one lacking a social Will, but
yet having some sort of contract Will, is contained in
a deceptively simple passage which laconically pin-
pointed the properties of the plural framework as one
where a medley of racial and cultural groups, whilst
living side by side and within the same political unit,
"mix but do not combine." Furnivall observed that in
Burma, as in Java, probably the first thing that
strikes the visitor is the medley of peoples - European,
Chinese, Indian and native. It is in the strictest
sense a medley, for they mix but do not combine. Each
group holds by its own religion, 'its own culture and
language, its own ideas and ways. As individuals they
meet, but only in the market place, in buying and
selling. There is a plural society. Even in the
economic sphere, there is a division of labor along
racial lines. Furnivall further remarked that the
plural society was like a "business partnership" in
which the social Will linking the sections does not
extend beyond their common economic interest. As a
business partnership, its function is solely economic,
so much so that even in a matter as vital to the whole
community as defence against aggression, the people
were reluctant to pay the necessary price.[3] Furnivall
rightly pointed out that whilst all forms of society
can be characterized by many sorts of conflict
situations, in the colonial Far East, the conflicts
were deliberately and effectively monitored along
racial lines.[4] Unlike Far Eastern societies, Canada's
division of labor is not along racial lines; nevertheless, Canada is a "segemented" society in the plural
sense, comprised of a multiplicity of culturally
identifiable, and in many respects "non-combining,"
units: racial and ethnic, even linguistic groups.

Since the initial work of Furnivall, the idea of
pluralism as an approach to the study of multi-ethnic

or heterogeneous societies has been fully utilized by sociologists and anthropologists as a crucial tool for the understanding of structure and process in colonial societies. Specifically, scholars of African and Caribbean societies have given the concept its most elaborate refinements and application in the study of social relations in these regions. Amongst these scholars, the works of M.G. Smith, Leo Kuper, Pierre L. van den Berghe, Raymond T. Smith, Leo Despres and Richard Schermerhorn are of particular importance. While a detailed discussion of their many and complex works would be inappropriate here, we would nevertheless refer the reader to their sources.[5]

For the purposes of this chapter, we wish to indicate that between them, these authors may well have shaped out what is one of the most important perspectives for understanding modern cosmopolitan societies. While critically extending and revising Furnivall's original formulations, these scholars have also accepted the essential thesis that societies are pluralistic in so far as they are segmented into corporate groups that frequently, although not necessarily, have different cultures or subcultures. Also, they are pluralistic in so far as their social structure is compartmentalized into analogous, parallel, non-complementary but distinguishable sets of institutions through which they were welded together into one "society" by the dominant section. In seeking to make sharp a distinction between social and cultural pluralism, van den Berghe argues that cultural pluralism of ethnic groups cannot exist without institutional duplication and hence without social pluralism; that is, any form of cultural pluralism has a structural facet which can be treated as social pluralism. The distinction is significant. From a sociological point of view race complicates the matter, in so far as racial divisions can be conceived as a very special instance of structural or social pluralism, as distinguished from ethnic divisions which are a case of cultural pluralism.[6] Both types, of course, have various dimensions which van den Berghe explicates. Both Raymond T. Smith[7] and Leo Despres[8] read into this observation the implication that in so far as the cultural sections of a society are integrated by an overall institutional system which is capable of containing and controlling the differences between them, this continuity ultimately depends on consensus.[9]

173

But, as we shall stress below, plural societies may "cohere" on bases other than value consensus. As a critical response to the position of M.G. Smith and Furnivall which posits built-in cleavages in plural systems, Leo Kuper[10] contends that the correlation between pluralism and conflict is not as direct or linear as M.G. Smith and Furnivall believed. In essence, he argues, one should be skeptical of the idea of a universal class struggle which he seems to think is implicit in Furnivall's model.[11] Finally, we see in Schermerhorn's work an attempt to synthesize a wide range of historical conditions that generate plural situations. Schermerhorn (1970) agrees that the very nature of plural societies produces a potential for conflict, but he also maintains that it is not the pluralist or non-pluralist nature of a society, but the congruence of the collective goals of minority versus majority, which shapes ethnic relations,[12] and that the great bulk of ethnic group formations attain subordinate status as a result of coercive subjugation by dominant groups. It should also be mentioned, finally, that renewed and vigorous interest in the phenomena discussed in the above review is highly visible in the very recent literature.[13]

The foregoing overview, necessarily synoptic, reveals the concern of socio-cultural pluralism. This perspective, we submit, promises great insight into, and systematic understanding of, social relations in a complex culturally composite society such as modern Canada. But, Canadian sociologists do not readily utilize the ideas of the cultural pluralists, and seldom refer to the excellent literature on the subject in looking at the Canadian situation. A notable exception is Donald Baker[14] who accurately points out that although the model was initially used to describe developing countries in Africa, Asia and the Caribbean, with some modification it is applicable to the Canadian situation. The key to the utility of this model is that it focuses on power relationships and cleavages caused by the presence of diverse cultural, ethnic and racial groups. Sure, there is a long line of Canadian sociologists whose primary and deep concern is the analysis of the plural situation in Canada. But there seems to be some serious confusions and misunderstanding on the part of some sociologists regarding which version of pluralism distinctly addresses the subject of multi-ethnic relations. As we shall shortly show, there is a version of pluralism which does not

174

focus directly on the same set of factors that interest the cultural pluralists. The two versions have often been confused.

Attention should also be drawn to the very unnecessary and cavalier way in which some sociologists treat important concepts in the study of ethnic relations such as the concept of "minority." Two sociologists, writing on the subject in the context of ethnic relations analysis, clearly succeed in giving the impression that the opposite of minority is majority,[15] and that the demographic count is what makes the difference. Certainly not. The opposite of minority is dominant, and this distinction turns on an axis of power: the minority is the group or groups having less power relative to other group or groups, regardless of numerical count. The key intervening variable is power-relations. As Smith put it tersely: the dominant social section of culturally split societies is simply the section that controls the apparatus of power and force, and this is the basis of the status hierarchies that characterize pluralism.[16] After considering these sorts of analytic short-falls, together with the confusion surrounding two common uses of pluralism, it will become somewhat clearer why the model of the cultural pluralists has not received the kind of attention it deserves in the Canadian experience. Before we discuss some of the alleged confusions, let us comment briefly on the non-cultural version of pluralism.

(b) The "political" pluralism approach

In the social science literature, there is another conception of pluralism which departs fundamentally from Furnivall's paradigm, and those who followed him, a conception which, in fact, does not derive from Furnivall's thesis at all. Such an approach is found mainly in the works of American political scientists.[17] The conception of "pluralism" as adumbrated by these theorists is one that equates pluralism with democracy. The corollary of this view is that "elitist" political systems, or "totalitarian" regimes are not pluralistic.[18] Todd Gitlin refers to this perspective as "local pluralism";[19] it is what we will term political pluralism. Central to this view of pluralism is the notion that "western liberal democracies" are pluralistic, in the sense that power is shared or democratically distributed amongst several competing

175

groups. No one group, or alliance of a few groups, it is claimed, can successfully impose itself on the rest.20

The major difficulties with this conception of pluralism are not hard to discern. Most certainly it does not account for the empirical instances where large segments of society are powerless on some fundamental issues, within political "pluralist regimes." In the haste to show that in the U.S. power is shared, the local pluralists ignore the social and cultural dimensions of power. Even if one accepts the dubious assumption that power is shared in the way they claimed, if it is shared between "interest groups" from one ethnic group, then we are not addressing the same set of issues as the cultural pluralists.

Gitlin seems to capture the thrust of what he calls the "misleading apotheosis" of this approach when he writes:

> Implicit in local pluralism is the definite feeling that in a qualitative way things are as they should be. Because power is "slack," anyone with grievances to bring to bear against the system - as long as he regards the system as legitimate in its broad outline - can organize a pressure group that clashes with others in the political arena and emerges, presumably, with some part of its loaf firmly in hand... Because there is no power elite, anyone can exert power by careful accumulation and application of resources, as long as he plays the game according to the rules.21

No further comment is necessary in order to dramatize that the idea of "local pluralism" does not address the same question as socio-cultural pluralism, and is not likely to shed much light on the dynamics of multi-ethnic social relations. It is doubtful if local pluralism is a theory of participatory democracy. However, this contention is perhaps best left to political scientists to resolve. Our purpose here is not to discuss this school of pluralism; suffice it

to point out that this conception is useless for
helping our understanding of ethnic relations in the
multi-cultural, multi-ethnic context of Canadian
society.

The distinction which we make here between the two
conceptions of pluralism is not to be taken as an "all-
or-nothing" approach. The focus, however, on the
"sharing-of-power" ideas as a way of explaining
competing ethnic/cultural groups in Canada, inhibits
our understanding of Canadian political practice,
principally because of the operative assumption that
instead of there being a hierarchy of power there is a
horizontal relationship of power between equal units.
The cultural pluralist model, on the other hand, first
of all recognizes the inequality between the cultural
units. It then seeks to recognize that, superimposed
on that situation, is the controlling power-relations
of a particular group. While we do not need a plural
framework to analyze power in society, in the Canadian
context such a framework is particularly useful in
drawing out the important empirical fact that in
culturally plural societies it is the dominance of one
group over the others moreso than any synchronization
of disparate values that make social harmony possible.

As with any theoretical tradition in sociology
there are different variants of the two approaches
described here. But the basic dichotomy holds, in the
sense that one group operates on distinctly political
axis, concentrating on whether or not different
interest groups in society share the resources of power
among themselves. This has its own built-in myths.
The other perspective, which we have termed the
Furnivallian, focuses specifically on the ethnic or
or racial medley that characterizes some societies, and
on the cultural and political implications of this
situation.

The Problem of Understanding
Canadian Pluralism

We must now focus our attention on the fact that
much of the discussion of Canadian pluralism has been
based on the misleading apotheosis of political
pluralism. I am not therefore so much concerned with
showing how the theoretical model of socio-cultural
pluralism could explain various processes in Canadian
society, as with formulating a critique of the existing

Canadian sociological approach to the question of pluralism. Such a critique is a logical and theoretical precondition for any subsequent application of the idea of socio-cultural pluralism to Canadian society.

In presenting this analysis, it will also be argued that the sociology of knowledge perspective is fundamental for shedding light on the "reluctance" of Canadian sociologists to register socio-cultural pluralism in the Canadian consciousness. It is my general thesis that the reasons for this reluctance are no doubt complex, but that they are understandable, not to say acceptable, when viewed against the background of the discussion of Canadian sociology as undertaken in Chapter 3 of this book. In the pursuit of positivism, Canadian sociology has all but abandoned the goal of creating a critical theory of society, thereby rejecting the main task of the sociology of knowledge, namely, the critical analysis of reigning ideologies and of reified accounts of social arrangements. In Canada, one can agree with Despres that a cursory review of the literature leaves the general impression that anthropologists, not to mention social scientists, have not built very carefully upon the accumulated knowledge of their predecessors. As he concludes, ethnic combinations are clearly strategic in the study of social and cultural pluralism, even if the concept of ethnicity has not received a great deal of analytic refinement in the literature pertaining to plural societies.[22]

Now, if the claim is upheld that Canada is a plural society,[23] then by definition certain structural characteristics are present (whether we recognize them or not) at the different levels of social organization. For example, at the level of the corporate group in a typical plural society, there is asymmetry in the distribution of power, heavy reliance on coercion as opposed to value consensus as the social bond, and rigid stratification based on ascriptive role and status allocation.[24] Similarly, at the level of institutions, a plural society is typified by cleavages between relatively autonomous structures; and at the level of values in such situations, if each cultural group is encouraged to maintain its own value system (as ethnic groups in Canada are), we are likely to find lack of value consensus, and perhaps discrepant interpretation of what common values the groups do share.[25] Also, plural societies, as opposed to cultural heterogeneity, consist in the coexistence of incompatible institutional systems, and depend for their maintenance on the regulation of intersectional relations by one or other of the component cultural sections. In spite of these institutional divergences in Canada (in kinship patterns, religion and language, for instance) there is one set of governmental institutions which serves to weld together an overall liveable political state. In effect, people have a certain amount of room for believing what they please in a plural society, but they will have to socialize their children into, and encourage adherence to, a particular symbolic realm that defines the nation-state.

Belonging to different cultures, of course, does not necessarily entail lack of value consensus. In any given situation, in spite of ethnic/cultural hetero-geneity some degree of consensus will tend to congeal around certain, perhaps abstract, values defined as "universalistic" (such as "freedom" or "brotherly love") and almost certainly around a commitment to the receiving or "host" society as a legitimate political unit. But strong cultural ties between old and new country of residence tend to bring about and support structural segmentation, especially reflected in such institutions as the family, voluntary organizations and religion, and ordinarily we would expect some initial conflict or intolerance. If the tolerance is weak or non-existent, the possibility of overt conflict becomes real. This experience has been documented in the United Kingdom, involving West Indians, who, in any event, share British values and customs.[26] The segmentation persists, as van den Berghe points out[27] as "sheer institutional duplication," as opposed to functional differentiation and specialization.

It would no doubt be interesting to analyze the key role(s) that these culturally duplicated havens play for groups such as newly arrived immigrants, but we must confine our discussion to explicating the central point of their relevance for value consensus. As culturally specific institutional duplication, they are potential areas of conflict with the host society's value system, and may well serve to inhibit under-standing and tolerance between the groups. Porter argues that the development of ethnic communities as psychic shelters can perpetuate ethnic stratification. That may very well be so, but it is certainly not the

whole story. Whether or not an ethnic group is able to
break out of its ethnic/cultural community and into the
"wider society" depends to a large extent on the
attitudes and beliefs of the politically dominant
groups which typically control the apparatus of power
as well as access to opportunity and reward structures.

But, we must also remark that the commonality of
culture or value, or similarity of ethos (cultural
congruence for Schermerhorn) does not necessarily make
for harmony either, or guarantee the acceptance of a
minority group. As has already been shown elsewhere,
the experience of racism easily complicates the race-
relation situation, where one would normally expect
harmony due to value and cultural congruence.[28] What
one can say of cultural heterogeneity and segmentation,
where they exist, is that such structuring could
conceivably facilitate effective domination of a
cultural minority. In this way, (paradoxically)
structural segmentation may make for a greater degree
of societal stability than in those cases where the
segments are welded (for whatever reason) into a
monolithic opposition. Seen in this light, the idea of
socio-cultural pluralism is not inconsistent with the
generalized view of consensus in liberal democracies
where, in fact, the political process is typified as
the art of playing off one contending group against
another. This is the thesis of political pluralists.

Perhaps we can easily illustrate this point by
citing Quebec's experience. Porter tells us that
French Canadians have been denied much of the
opportunity and had carried a good deal of the cost of
Canada's take-off as an industrial society.
Ideologically speaking, then, the question which might
have been posed by those depriving Quebec of pay-offs
was "how best to induce acquiescence of foreign (or
colonial) rule, without prejudice to the economic
viability of the domination"? One pragmatic answer was
the strategy divide et impera. One may well consider
several interpretations of this historical experience.
But from a sociology of knowledge perspective this
strategy does not mean, as Ossenberg seems to think,
"recognition of the traditional authority figures in
the subordinate group." Indeed, if anything, the
efficacy of this strategy, in the case of Quebec, lends
itself to an explanation of why French Canadians have
historically been divided among themselves.[29]

180

The assertion that Canada is a plural society in the socio-cultural sense makes it extremely difficult to escape the conclusion that it is a society in which there is a high degree of political coercion, ascriptive stratification and deep-rooted, continuous value conflict reflecting opposing world-views. These preliminary assertions form a firm base for the construction of empirical hypotheses about Canadian society. Hiller has, in fact, correctly observed that Canadian society is based on the rigid, ascribed criteria of race, language and ethnic traditions rather than on achieved criteria. This is a very important point. In terms of our model, inequalities in power, wealth, prestige and opportunity depend on one's ethnic and linguistic background - the independent variables in the overall situation. Given, too, the traditionally low level of tolerance associated with ascriptive stratification, Canadians are not nearly as tolerant of other cultures as they perhaps believe they are. Both historical and contemporary evidence seems to support this idea. As Jones has noted, Canada's commitment to cultural pluralism may have led to a greater tolerance towards certain ethnic groups.[30] However, the hostility expressed toward Hutterites and Doukhobors in Western Canada suggests that the expression of values or adherence to customs markedly different from the dominant Canadian values and customs is likely to arouse strong opposition. But then Jones goes on to say that the pressure towards conformity which Canadians face is not to conform to the values and customs of the British, but to the secular values and customs which are becoming common to all industrialized societies. This is a rather astonishing statement indeed, especially because Jones does not say precisely what these values and customs are. He does say that they are or derive from a complex relationship between technological development, science, the values which underlie technological and scientific development - a vague and clumsy idea.

Are we to believe then that ethnic background and cultural traditions notwithstanding, and official encouragement of multiculturalism notwithstanding, all Canadians will sooner or later come under the homogenizing spell and eventual moulding of the "secular values and customs" of industrialized society? In terms of values and customs will we then be just like the Japanese, the West Germans, the Americans, the Swedes, and so on? Are we all doomed to have our

cherished ethnic values smoothed out by industrial
society. There is, if nothing else, an unnecessary
confusion in this thesis. Either there are dominant
Canadian values or there are not. If there are, on
which ethnic group are they based? If there are not,
we must assume that all the multiple groups in Canada
have an equal impact in all things cultural. And that
does not fit the empirical reality. In plural
situations, power is a resource in unequally
distributed among the plural units, who then have to
bargain for what they regard as their "fair share."
Such competing groups usually have to demonstrate the
merits of their cause. No doubt this is one purpose
which "multi-cultural" festivals serve.

    Assigning all the plural qualities to Canadian
society may well elicit strong reaction from
sociologists, or more precisely, a denial that these
qualities accurately depict Canadian society. Indeed,
this is the very reasoning we have from Rossides who,
in his discussion of "the Liberal Nation State"
(Canada) insists that such a state operates on:

> specialized institutional structures
> based on two central ideas, the free
> market and free elections; a class
> system on inequality in which social
> benefits are distributed according
> to performance by individuals in the
> struggle against nature and in the
> rational management of society and
> not according to birth or religion
> or race.[31]

    This is a remarkable defense of the liberal nation
state. The trouble with such a defence is that it is
totally inconsistent with the analyses of John Porter
and others who have found in their empirical studies
that ethnicity has always been used in Canada "to sort
people out for social purposes."[32] In a similar
fashion, Ossenberg is willing to admit that Canada is a
plural society "in almost every sense of the term." He
is not willing, however, to assign all the known
characteristics of the plural society to Canada. As he
put it, "it would be tempting to apply most of the
observations of plural society to Canadian dualism but
there are too many complications to do so directly."
Ossenberg pleads that "pluralism poses many social
evils which, if not corrected, may contribute to the

destruction of an entire society."[33]

Clearly, any denial of the defining characteristics of the plural society (in the multi-ethnic sense) can only mean reduction in pluralism, in which case we are thrown back to the "melting pot" idea. But this is also strongly denied as a quality of Canadian society. We will quote Rossides again:

> It is well known that in her accommodation of diverse ethnic groups, Canada is more a mosaic than a melting pot... her provinces become experimental laboratories; her ethnic groups become repositories of personalized values; her interest-reform-charitable-fraternal groups identify problems, pioneer new approaches, and resist oligarchical bureaucratic coordination.[34]

This diversity, Rossides feels, must be thought of as Canada's distinct "asset." He fails to recognize the contradiction in his own argument, where the "specialized institutional structures" as the core of "liberal nation states" serve precisely to facilitate strong (perhaps coercive) bureaucratic coordination of the multiple elements in the society. Implicit here is a built-in (if unrecognized), political coercive element orchestrated by a dominant group.

It is interesting to recognize that while both Ossenberg and Rossides are hesitant in facing up to the implications of ethnic heterogeneity in Canadian society, they arrive at their respective positions from completely different starting points; from two different conceptions of "pluralism." Herein lies an important area of confusion, for at certain points one gets the feeling that both sociologists are operating on a single conception of pluralism. On reading Ossenberg (1967) we are led to believe that the pluralism which he has in mind is social and cultural pluralism. We are led, in fact, to understand that Quebec is a plural society within a plural society, which Ossenberg calls "double pluralism." No clear benchmarks for either side of the double pluralism are given, but that becomes unnecessary when Ossenberg himself takes us to the point where he equates pluralism with "indirect" rule. At this point, clearly, he falls into the trap of the "local pluralist" where pluralism is taken to mean the sharing of power between contending parties. Thus, in his discussion of the British conquest of "New France" he claimed that "the British encouraged pluralism or indirect rule."[35] One must understand by this that the British encouraged a fissuring or sharing of power in colonial Canada as a way to keep local authority figures happy. This is where the local pluralists begin.

Rossides, on the other hand, leaves us no doubt as to what he means by pluralism in Canada. He means by it a "power structure in which no one group or combination of groups could effectively dominate the rest" - the very opposite of social and cultural pluralism. Of course, Rossides does not stop here. He goes on to argue that out of this pluralist power structure there has emerged a culture which "for the first time in history" acknowledges that a pluralist society was not only workable and legitimate, but creative and progressive.[36] In Porter's case, the discussion on pluralism is much more extraordinary. To begin with, one senses that Porter regrets the changing of Canada from a bicultural to a multi-cultural society.[37] But he further argues that ethnic pluralism is not in the best interest of the individual ethnic group or the host society; second, that the saliency of ethnic differences is a retreat from the liberal notions of the unity of mankind; and third, that one would hope that multi-culturalism will pass away, for the idea in Canada encourages the survival of cultures not appropriate for a post-industrial society. He concludes: one can almost speak of the end of culture, as some have written of the end of ideology.[38] Nothing better illustrates that the problem with the idea of pluralism in Canada is not merely one of conceptual confusion but also of ideological obfuscation.

Hiller shares in this level of confusion, or ambivalence, for on the one hand he says that pluralism means that cultural differences are allowed to exist (in Canada, and elsewhere presumably) on the basis of equality of opportunity. This is the exact opposite of what the cultural pluralists argue: the hallmark of the plural society is that, given fundamental differences in belief, values, and social organization, the monopoly of power by one cultural group or section is a necessary and sufficient pre-condition for the maintenance and regulation of the total society in its current form.[39] In short, the politically dominant group in a plural society can and does control the apparatus of power and force as well as the access to opportunity and reward structures. There is neither equality of opportunity nor equality of power amongst the competing groups. Hiller himself agrees, in the end, that equality among ethnic groups is not the norm in Canada.[40] This then must mean that there is a given group with the monopoly or greater share of power and the wherewithal to control opportunity structures and to coordinate conflicts. If in fact pluralism meant equality among ethnic or racial groups, plural societies would hardly be as prone to conflict as they definitely are. The truly plural society operates on a dominant/subordinate set of power-relations, and Canada is no exception here. The key reasons why the subordinate groups comply with the requirements of what Furnivall calls a "business partnership," are not to be found in these groups' self-satisfaction with equal opportunity. On the contrary, such compliance rests on the delicate balance of economic and political factors, as we point out below.

Finally, Hiller feels that in Canada the official policy of pluralism does not prevent processes of integration and assimilation from taking place "at a rapid rate." This claim is to be suspected. The plural framework would suggest that the goals of pluralism as a national policy in Canada, must serve to inhibit assimilation. More pointedly, if we entertain both ideals, we beg the question: integration or assimilation into what?; or into what kind of society?

The assumption that the key to race relations in Canada resides in some notion of "assimilating" the immigrants into Canadian society is not without its cultural bias.[41] Besides, it is grossly misleading to suggest that a socio-cultural pluralist model is implicit in the works of Vallee.[42] The great emphasis on assimilation does not sufficiently grasp that all we can claim for the idea of assimilation is that it is a process of adjustment to the dominant culture (a process which, under normal circumstances could take several years, and perhaps minimally a generation). If that is the case, then plural societies that accept immigrants are further characterized by a long series of modus vivendi, or a situation of truce, with the plural units. But, another, more likely answer to the question of assimilation is suggested by Elliott[43] who argues that ethnic minorities in Canada attempt to achieve one of two incompatible goals which generate conflict. They either want to survive as a distinct ethnic group, or they want to be admitted into mainstream Canadian life. If, however, there are incongruent definitions of the minority as a result of self-definition and the definition assigned by the wider society, the resultant situation would likely involve pressure to conform. In other words, minorities wishing to retain their definitions of their identity must resist social pressures favoring Anglo-Conformity.

It may well be, as Rex points out, that in metropolitan societies (as opposed to colonial societies) that are ethnically mixed, the tendency toward coercive sanctions might be substituted for a tendency toward cultural unity, value consensus and the use of normative sanctions. For Canada, however, this likelihood must be seen against the background of national immigration policy and multi-cultural ideals. We need to grasp, much more firmly than we have heretofore, the crucial point made by Richmond in his perceptive essay that Canadian immigration policy, with its emphasis upon educational and occupational qualifications will attract immigrants who, "by their very nature," are neither "assimilable" nor will they be "integrated" in the usual sense. As Richmond concludes,[44] instead of being assimilated, the immigrants will be the agents of the post-industrial revolution, responsible for mobilizing the Canadian economy and transforming its social system.

Interestingly, if we want some clear statements as to the nature of Canadian socio-cultural pluralism, we have to turn to the works of scholars in the Furnivall tradition (e.g., see Furnivall, 1939: 446; Broom, 1960: 881; Smith, 1965: 87). Considerations of pluralism such as those presented by Furnivall and Broom are vital for understanding the dynamics of ethnic relations in Canada.

But if that is so, why have Canadian sociologists paid so little attention to the idea, or even refused to admit to the plural reality with all its structural consequences? These questions clearly highlight the problem of the centrality of the sociology of knowledge to sociology. Not only does the sociology of knowledge acknowledge that ideas, idea-systems, "theories" and intellectual movements in society are based on certain existing social conditions, but it further analyzes how these same social conditions determine what knowledge will be sought, how it will be interpreted, how the conditions shape the problems to be investigated as well as how investigations will be made. Clearly, this is a revolutionary perspective. For by seeking to probe and poke into the facade of long-established idea systems, rationalizations, and the styles and method of thought that underpin social relations, the sociology of knowledge promises to debunk, or at any rate challenge, the ideological assumptions of the theories we use to explain ourselves. In other words, if there are socio-cultural factors inhibiting the development of critical self-analysis and the historical under- standing of the origins and limitations of our theories and methodological rationale, the sociology of knowledge might discover those factors. This perspective forces the social scientist to face up to the ideological and political implications of his/her work.

If there is one major difference between cultural pluralism in Canada and cultural pluralism in the classical Third World (colonial) situation, it concerns the federated nature of Canadian politics as opposed to the typical monolithic colonial state. The difference means that, in theory, there may be a greater probability that members of the different ethnic groups in Canada may be represented in politics, especially at the provincial level. This could easily give the impression that all or most groups were being catered to at that level. This would not be a possibility in the colonial situation. That, however, is as far as the difference goes. At the national level there is no clear-cut ethnic input. In both situations, whatever the degree of autonomy allowed each group with respect to its basic cultural institutions, in the end it subscribes to a common set of political institutions by which a given dominant section welds all the various sections into one political unit. The presence of a lone Metis or a West Indian or an Italian in Federal politics does not in any way undermine this thesis. This apparent difference that in Canada the composition of the group with the concentration of regulative power is likely to be "mixed" is not in fact a real difference. Anglo-Canadians are, to date, unquestionably the dominant group, not in terms of numbers, but in terms of the power they eventually display over all other hyphenated Canadians.[45]   In England, as in Canada or any other modern-day cosmopolitan society, immigrants face conflicting pressures: whether to retain and cultivate elements of the old culture, or acquire the culture of the "host" society as a prelude to assimilation into the latter. In the Canadian case this process is experienced in a highly complex fashion, for on the one hand there is the national policy which encourages ethnic diversity and retention of cultural values held by the many ethnic groups within the society. On the other hand, the subtle pressures toward Anglo-conformity together with subterranean discrimination against some of the groups, for example, Blacks, Asians and Native peoples, means, simply, that many members of these groups will continue to be in Canadian society but not of it.

When all the above considerations are weighed, it becomes clear that the plural framework may be the most accurate model for understanding modern Canada. However, by refusing to realize that the confrontation between "specialized institutional structures" and resistance to "oligarchical bureaucratic coordination" (Rossides) which is endemic in such structures are highly productive of divisive conflict, we distort our view of Canadian society. Of course, in postulating a high degree of conflict in plural societies, we are not implying that conflict is a "given," just as we cannot account for consensus as a "given." Both are products of social living; the complex processes whereby they are generated is the problem of sociological analysis. Here we are arguing that because, by definition, plural societies are characterized in part by the co-existence of autonomous but non-complementary sub-societies which do not share common values, what coherence exists cannot be fully accounted for by value consensus.[46]

In citing the South African case, van den Berghe correctly points out that South Africa is one of the world's most pluralistic societies, and members of the various ethnic groups there share no common value system. Yet the society is integrated in some ways. Crucially, what integration there is, is not based on value consensus, but on a mixture of political coercion, economic interdependence and some compliance-by-routine, the latter often being mistaken for value consensus.

Other modern writers have been equally quick to point out that not even liberal democracies are held together by value consensus. One important cross-cultural study concluded that sociologists can no longer assert that elements of voluntary deference, nationalism, and other components of normative integration in liberal democracies produce value consensus between social members and value consistency within them. Hence, "whatever 'legitimacy' liberal democracy possesses is not conferred upon it by value consensus, for this does not exist."[47] More recently, this thesis was reaffirmed by a group of British sociologists who drew upon British historical evidence to demonstrate that the stuff which actually holds modern society together and controls the subordinate classes; also, that which makes such a society conflictful and unstable, is

> what Marx referred to as "the dull
> compulsion" of economic relations,
> ...the integrative effects of the
> division of labor, [and] the coercive
> nature of law and politics.[48]

These findings in no way destroy the saliency given to dominant ideology as discussed above, and as will be discussed further. However, what they have done is to clearly and empirically establish that the institutions of conflict are in large measure what make plural societies, and class societies, prone to conflict; and this throws doubt on the comfortable assumptions of the functionalist theory of compliance. When Parsons writes that

> values take primacy in the pattern
> maintenance functioning of a social
> system [and that] the most basic
> condition of compliance is the
> internalization of a society's
> values and norms by its members,
> for such socialization underlies
> the consensus basis of a societal
> community ...[49]

he severely obscures the problem of compliance and the economic-political factors that determine how complex societies cohere. Besides, he forgets to point out that the socialization process, properly understood, is itself a highly coercive process. We have enough evidence to support the contention that dominant ideology is an important cultural instrument of class and ethnic domination. Again, the sociology of knowledge is a key point of reference for recognizing the kinds of assumptions and ideological premises that the scientist uses as part of his/her cultural definition of the situation, and it underlines the complex ways in which political economy is the primary determinant of the social framework. To summarize John Porter, people in the modern world get sorted out according to their believed-in qualities or aptitudes for different economic activities. Economic forces have created the inequalities of ethnic stratification.[50]

We have demonstrated, albeit in a schematic and preliminary fashion, that we cannot even begin to understand the dynamics of race relations in Canada until we have formulated and refined our basic conceptual tools, of which the plural framework is a potentially significant one. There has to be, also, a theory of the interpenetration, overlap and conflict between class structures and race and ethnic relations generally. Having made that point, it should not be overlooked that in spite of the modest claims made by the plural theorists of the Furnivall tradition,[51] the idea of socio-cultural pluralism has not escaped strong, substantive criticisms.[52] This is commendable and desirable for any theoretical scheme. But what the critics fail to highlight are the social processes whereby beliefs and cultural definitions typically grow out of and reflect various sorts of interests and positions of power. Such processes are the central problematic of the sociology of knowledge. Positive conclusions, nevertheless, derive from the various criticisms; thus Rex argues that the plural model offers a structural understanding of patterns of social relations between men and women and the institutions which govern them. We share his position that if our intellectual interest in studying plural or segmented society is to throw greater light upon the sociological theory of race relations, then this approach is a relevant one.

The formal study of ethnic pluralism must somehow be conceptually linked with the analysis of social inequality, and hence to social/ethnic stratification. Students of stratification must note that traditional theories which almost always assume ethnic homogeneity are not necessarily valid for explaining plural systems

190

like Canada. Ethnic phenomena might best be understood
from the point of view of stratification theory or
perhaps even more general theories of power. However,
as Despres, H. Orlando Patterson (in Glazer and
Moynihan), and Porter all attest, ethnicity and class
strata typically interpenetrate, making for two
"entangled but not coterminous" status systems. In
practice

> both systems may co-exist in complex
> ways, according to the historical,
> techno-environmental, economic and
> political parameters of the
> particular societies in which they
> are found.[53]

In Canadian society, it is not the case that the model
has been tried and is found wanting. Rather, it has
been under-utilized, perhaps for reasons which this
paper has attempted to identify. And for Canadian
sociologists to say that that sort of distinction has
received the critical theoretical attention of
political scientists and sociologists in this country
is to pronounce a falsehood, and to establish a false
sense of accomplishment. The debate amongst Canadians
on "pluralism" might indeed be an old one, as I have
been reminded on occasions, but as I have tried to show,
we may not all mean the same thing by the single term
"pluralism." It does seem that most Canadians, seeped
in the liberal democratic tradition, mean by pluralism
what de Tocqueville meant by it: the sharing of power
among competing interest groups. That is very
different from socio-cultural pluralism, although the
latter necessarily involves power relations.

Has the sociology of knowledge, another badly
neglected area in sociology, any insights to deliver
with respect to understanding the cluster of ideas
sociologists (and others) have about themselves, their
society, and other people? Let us proceed to examine
that question.

1. van den Berghe, 1967, p. 141; Rex, 1970, 1973; Despres, 1975; Kuper and Smith, 1969; Newman, 1973; Schmerhorn, 1970; Glazer and Moynihan, 1975; and Driedger, 1978.

2. Rex, 1973, p. 243.

3. See Furnivall, 1948, pp. 304-10.

4. Furnivall, op.cit., pp. 308-11; and 1946, p. 132.

5. See, inter alia, Smith, 1960, 1965, 1969; Kuper, 1969a, pp. 7-26, and 1971; van den Berghe, 1964, 1967b, 1973 and 1976; Despres, 1967, 1969, 1975; R.T. Smith, 1962.

6. van den Berghe, 1967, pp. 34, 138-39; 1964, pp. 12, 14; Smith, 1969, p. 27. It is recognized here, of course, that sociologists have developed interesting typologies of pluralism to take into account the unending fascination of heterogeneous societies. Schermerhorn, for example, has pointed to at least four uses of the concept of pluralism, and such uses obviously overlap and inter-penetrate (1970, 122 ff). We simply want to stress that our use of this concept turns on the distinctly sociological idea of culture which implies the symbolic sharing, internalization and transmission of the ingredients of institutional life - hence socio-cultural pluralism, as opposed to, say, political pluralism.

7. R.T. Smith, 1962.

8. Despres, 1964 and 1967.

9. Cf. Parsons, 1951, pp. 136-167, 326, 350-51; and 1967, pp. 8-10, 471-75, 243-251.

10. Kuper, 1969b, pp. 473-79; 1971, p. 604.

11. See Kuper, 1971, p. 595.

12. Schermerhorn, op.cit., p. 156.

13. See, e.g., Glazer and Moynihan, 1975; and van den Berghe, 1976. There is no question that the

volume by Glazer and Moynihan is important. While it lacks a definition of ethnicity, the editors recognize that in the modern world the persistence and salience of ethnic-based (as opposed to class-based) forms of social identification and conflict, will have to be addressed by social scientists - on a cross-cultural and comparative basis. In explaining the dynamics of "resource competition" in plural societies, the volume edited by Despres (1975) is noteworthy for shedding much light on the key relationships between ethnic and social class stratification.

14. Baker, 1977, p. 109.

15. Krauter and Davis, 1978, p. 14.

16. Smith, 1960, p. 772.

17. E.g., see Presthus, 1964; Kornhauser, 1959; Dahl, 1967; Eisenstadt, 1966; Shils, 1956; Lipset, 1963; and Rossides, 1968. It must be pointed out that a number of scholars have clarified the important distinction between the two notions of pluralism, e.g., Kuper and van den Berghe. But in view of the imprecise nature of this distinction in the Canadian literature, we feel it is expedient to restate the differences once more for the Canadian consciousness. Porter, for instance, acknowledges that there is much confusion in the current discussion of multi-ethnicity and multi-culturalism; but he does not offer the kind of conceptual clarification which this essay, albeit tentatively, suggests.

18. Kornhauser, 1959, pp. 40-41.

19. Gitlin, 1965, pp. 21-45.

20. Presthus, 1964, pp. 8, 10; Dahl, 1967, pp. 22-24; Rossides, 1968, pp. 154, 371; Eisenstadt, 1966, p. 65. Cf. Polsby, 1963, pp. 112-121.

21. Gitlin, 1965, p. 37; also see Clement, 1975, pp. 358-61. As Clement puts it, citing Schattschneider: "The flaw in the pluralist heaven is that the heavenly chorus sings with a strong upper class accent" ... There is little reason to assume that the existence of several

institutional bases of power necessarily lead to a "Counter-vailing" or even competitive system.

22. See Despres, 1975, p. 2.

23. See, here, Porter, 1975b, 1972; Ossenberg, 1967, 1971.

24. van den Berghe, 1967, pp. 141-44.

25. E.g., see Smith, 1960, p. 774; 1965, pp. 85-87.

26. G. Llewellyn Watson, "The Sociology of Black Nationalism: protest, identity and the concept of 'Black Power' among West Indian immigrants in Britain," unpublished D.Phil. Thesis, University of York, U.K., 1972; and idem., "Blacks in Britain as a 'scapegoat class': racism as a problem in the sociology of knowledge," Paper delivered to the 1973 Annual Conference of the Atlantic Association of Sociologists and Anthropologists, Halifax, Nova Scotia (March); and Kenneth N. Pryce, Endless Pressure, Penguin Books, 1979.

27. van den Berghe, 1964, p. 12.

28. Watson, 1975; and "Blacks in Britain as a scapegoat class."

29. Pinard, 1970, pp. 87-109; cf. Porter, 1975b, p. 267; and Ossenberg, 1971, p. 113.

30. Jones, 1971, p. 431.

31. Rossides, 1968, p. 157.

32. Porter, 1975, p. 389; and Vallee, et al., 1971, p. 150.

33. Ossenberg, 1971, p. 121, 24, and 1967, pp. 201-2, 205-6.

34. Rossides, 1968, pp. 158-159.

35. Ossenberg, 1971, p. 115.

36. Rossides, 1968, pp. 154-55.

37. Porter, 1972, p. 198; 1975, p. 268.

38. <u>Ibid.</u>, p. 303-4.

39. Smith, 1960, p. 772; 1965, p. 86.

40. Hiller, 1976, p. 182.

41. E.g., see Jansen, Lee, and Vallee in Blishen, 1971.

42. As was suggested by an anonymous reviewer of my original presentation of the argument of this chapter, when it was submitted to a Canadian journal for publication. This same reviewer recommended that the paper was to be rejected because, among other minor problems with it, "Parsons was not in the bibliography!" Does Parsons have anything significant to say about socio-cultural pluralism? Another reviewer, reacting to the same paper said quite simply that since "the pluralism thesis has been presented ... hundreds of times," the paper should not appear in <u>their</u> journal. The reader will be quite capable of deciding whether <u>socio-cultural pluralism</u> has ever been seriously <u>debated by Canadian</u> sociologists. We seem to be involved in a gigantic self-deception. Maybe the problem is that most of us simply cannot distinguish between American sociology, where socio-cultural pluralism <u>has</u> received some attention, and Canadian sociology, where the topic has not been squarely confronted. See, on America, Newman, 1973.

43. Elliott, 1971, pp. 6-7.

44. Richmond, 1969, p. 23.

45. See, e.g., Porter, 1965; and Clement, 1975.

46. See, here, van den Berghe, 1967, pp. 138-39; 1964, pp. 12-15.

47. Michael Mann, 1970. See also Mann, <u>Consciousness and Action Among the Western Working Class</u>, London, MacMillan, 1973.

48. Nicholas Abercrombie, <u>et al.</u>, <u>The Dominant Ideology Thesis</u>, London: Allen and Unwin, 1980, p. 6.

49. See Parsons, <u>Societies: Evolutionary and</u>

Comparative Perspectives, Prentice-Hall, 1966, pp. 14, 19.

50. Porter, 1972, p. 196; 1975, p. 289-91.

51. See, e.g., Katznelson, 1972, p. 51; and van den Berghe.

52. E.g., Cox, 1971, pp. 385, 398; Cross, 1968, pp. 381, 397; and 1971, p. 484; Adam, 1971, p. 20.

53. See Breton, 1974, pp. 6-11; Despres, 1975, pp. 87-117; and Porter, 1975, pp. 288-89.

CHAPTER VIII

THE SOCIOLOGY OF KNOWLEDGE AND SOCIOLOGICAL
THEORY: PROBLEMS AND PROSPECTS

The Promise of the Sociology of Knowledge

Thus far we have argued about, and illustrated, the nature of the conceptual confusion with respect to socio-cultural pluralism in Canada. Other substantive areas in sociology likewise experience confusion and shapelessness, for example the political economy approach in Canadian social science. Now we must articulate that if there are indeed certain ideological factors which inhibit sociologists from critical self-analysis and from a structural understanding of the origin of ideas, the sociology of knowledge might provide insights concerning those factors. The sociology of knowledge has long been regarded as an inherently complex and esoteric area of sociology, principally because of the epistemological problems which it introduces, but also because it tends toward a metaphysical reductionism which many sociologists would rather avoid becoming embroiled in. Yet the socio-logical literature reveals sufficiently clearly, that this is a very profound area of the discipline, and that properly grasped, the sociology of knowledge can substantively deepen our comprehension of idea-systems and enhance a critical historical understanding of human conscious creations.

Simply put, the sociology of knowledge is primarily concerned with "everything that passes for knowledge in society," and it takes as its prime aim the understanding of the relationship between the human ways of understanding and organizing knowledge in society.[1] Fundamentally, it raises questions about the nature of knowledge as a social product, both in terms of its social (structural) determinants, as well as in terms of its consequences. Its primary concern is with the origin of ideas, and not so much with their validity or "truth," even if it must, in one way or another, inevitably face the demanding problem of truth, for which there certainly are no cut-and-dried answers. Although this chapter stems from, and seeks to shed light on, some queries posed in the preceding chapter, its overall insights, and anxieties, are manifestly crucial to the whole business of producing social

197

theory - in any time period, and at any and all levels of ideas. The nightmarish questions that haunt the sociology of knowledge: "how is reliable knowledge possible?" or "who should one believe?" are not the albatross of sociologists, or critical sociologists alone. Natural scientists, theologians, philosophers as much as Sunday-school teachers ought to be reflective if not critical of the ideas which they are invariably called upon to impart as knowledge and truth.

The literature on the sociology of knowledge is vast and intricate. For this reason, many students find it difficult to pursue, although this reason cannot be a necessary and sufficient one for ignoring it. In this connection, two recent commentaries on sociological theory seem revealing. Horowitz observed that "there is a widespread belief that the sociology of knowledge is neither sociology nor knowledge"; whilst Merton noted that "the sociology of knowledge has long been regarded as a complex and esoteric subject remote from the urgent problems of contemporary social life." Both these observations are essentially correct, if embarrassing, and in themselves serve as a sad commentary on the state of sociological theory and sociological understanding.

If one examines the sociological literature, one finds that there is a real paucity of discussions on the sociology of knowledge, and of in-depth, critical analysis of the cultural process which is so closely tied to it. Thus, the British sociologist Ronald Fletcher in his mammouth two-volume work (1971) on "sociological theory" makes no mention of the sociology of knowledge, and the idea is therefore not included in the indexes. Mannheim gets one grudging sentence in the volumes, and is not, of course, included in the bibliographies. And in American sociology, as Curtis and Petras note, the problem of its absence is to be explained by reference to an overly-narrow and deterministic definition of the area itself.[2]

In the Canadian context, until fairly recently there was a pronounced neglect of structural studies, and a lack of concern for structural sociology, which, as we have said, properly understood is firmly rooted in the tradition of the sociology of knowledge. In Canadian sociology, we have for a long time been noticeably timid in explicating the structural-historical forces that have fashioned our cultural definition and concepts of society. In a word, we have been blissfully unmindful of the social genesis of the styles and method of thought that underpin and sustain social relations.

Unfortunately, then, the sociology of knowledge has remained esoteric and unexplored. Its main task, namely, that of explicating how ideas and "knowledge" in society, whether mundane or intellectual, common-sense or technical, esoteric or not, are based on certain existing social conditions, is still not eagerly pursued. Therefore, the questioning of these same conditions, and the consequences of their changes, remain non-problematic. Perhaps this is because, in a very important sense, the sociology of knowledge is potentially revolutionary, for in so far as it is involved in a debunking process, it seeks to critically question long-established idea-systems; and by probing for the rationales and purposes that underlie doctrines, theories and intellectual movements, it runs the risk of upsetting the world taken for granted.

But this is its promise and its challenge. Greater attention paid to the sociology of knowledge could, conceivably, significantly enrich our theories. To that end, we may interpret this chapter as a plea for reopening the theoretical debate on the relations between knowledge of all sorts, and social structure. The chapter introduces the student to the classical argument in the sociology of knowledge, and offers, therefore, not so much a review of the literature, but an exposure (in as straightforward a manner as possible) to the significance and utility of the sociology of knowledge to sociological theory.[3] The intent is to examine the main issues and critiques in this sector of sociology, and to introduce for debate a synthesis of the arguments surrounding the sociology of knowledge.

If one accepts that sociology is potentially a critique of society, then the sociology of knowledge should be central to its concerns, since the latter seeks to understand and interpret the basis of the ideational process whereby a critique of society is typically hamstrung. This raises further issues about the logical framework within which this book is assembled. That framework is, as we stated at the beginning, polemical, and we would hope, revealingly so. But this is not being ideological in the sense in which we have discussed that concept, although one always risks being called ideological simply by exposing the operation of idea-systems in social life. It is not possible to talk about the sociology of knowledge in a totally context-free fashion. Indeed, if as Mannheim and Stark suggest,[4] the sociology of knowledge deals with the formation of a specific world-view, while ideology deals with the deformation of world-view, then one cannot logically deal with the sociology of knowledge without in this way being considered ideological. It is to be understood that as a mode for the systematic analysis and interpretation of ideologies, world views and thought-patterns of a society, the sociology of knowledge aims at comprehending the context of its own genesis and all other bodies of ideas that pass for knowledge.

Before we proceed, it must be mentioned that the development of the sociology of knowledge does not rest solely on the ideas of Marx and Mannheim, for most of the classical sociologists including Durkheim, Weber, Simmel, Pareto, and later Schutz and Mead, contributed key insights into this problem, even if they all had different points of departure. Nevertheless, as Hamilton reminds us, at one time Mannheim's name was synonymous in the English-speaking world with sociology of knowledge. The account presented here is not to be considered exhaustive or even representative of the field. The important Reader, mentioned above (footnote 2) points out that the roots of this perspective go back to as far as Francis Bacon's Novum Organum, for Bacon is said to have been one of the earliest to urge scientists to become aware of their prejudices and the "idols that control their minds."

Clearly, the roots of the broad concerns about the relation between knowledge and social structure reach back into the dark abyss of western thought. Peter Hamilton, for example, has suggested in his eminently readable book on the classical argument in the sociology of knowledge, that whatever the faults of the eighteenth century philosophers might have been, "when their gaze was directed towards scientific analysis of society" they characteristically produced a sociology of ideas and values. The critical thinkers of the Enlightenment, he points out, were concerned with the notion of ideology, with the distortion of knowledge which tended to conform with an inequitable social structure, the misuse of social power and the denial of human rights. When all is said and done, the philosophers developed, however sketchily, a theory of ideology as an important first step towards a sociology of knowledge.[5] The critical rationalism which was to feature so much in Marxian social theory was already prefigured in the Enlightenment's theory-sketch of ideology, a sketch which

> criticized the alienation of man's
> natural reason, and saw the prime
> source of that alienation in the
> propagation of superstitions about
> religion by a priestly class who
> used irrational beliefs to justify
> their own privileges and power.[6]

That sketch, however, was not fleshed out or given the necessary fillip until Marx confronted these, via his devastating critique of institutional life and of political economy as a whole.

The Marxian Sketch of the Sociology of Knowledge

The sociology of knowledge, as an outstanding problematic in social science, actually emerged with Marx, whose profoundly suggestive apercu and paradigmatic formulation went, as Mannheim puts it, "to the heart of the matter." Marx's formulation of the sociology of knowledge, as a concern with the intricate relationship between knowledge and social structure, remained central to his life's thinking, and there is some justification for saying that from his youthful 1844 Manuscripts through to the Grundrisse be battled with substantive sociology of knowledge issues. In castigating the classical political economists, for instance, and as he was to do later in settling his conscience with the Left Hegelians such as Feuerbach, he continually drew attention to their characteristic static one-sided ontology which thrived not on a total structural view, but on atomized, piecemeal conceptions of reality. The theorists of classical political economy, he argued, assumed as "given" what had to be explained, for example the dynamics of private property, exchange, division of labor, and, crucially, the theoretical rationalization of these social processes. Too often they were viewed as immutable laws of nature. Such views never fully grasped that the very ideas used to justify the going concern, were themselves inseparable from, and hence explicable in terms of, society as historically created structures of social relations.

As we pointed out above (Chapter 4) Marx's own profound insights into the relations between knowledge (or consciousness) and social structure are firmly grounded in a philosophical anthropology which hoists the ontological centrality of the labor process as the key to understanding history as it is made by humans. It is only in the critical analysis of this history as a history of material dialectics, can we expose the categorical imperatives of private property with its built-in alienating tendencies, the thingification of human activity, and the resultant partial understanding of the relationships between these factors. Someone like M. Proudhon, Marx points out in his polemical The Poverty of Philosophy, could not be expected to understand that men who produce their social relations in accordance with their material productivity also produce ideas, categories, "theories" and other abstract ideal expressions of these same relations. And the simple reason for this mental opacity was that Proudhon failed to regard social institutions as historical creations. In effect his "theory" was but a formal and distorted rationalization of bourgeois social arrangements. The truly decisive leap by Marx into a sociology of knowledge is detected, as we said in Chapter 4, in switching the subject and predicate in Feuerbach's anthropology, much like turning a glove inside-out, in order to demonstrate that it does make a vast difference if one starts one's analysis from "real premises," who in all of social history happen to be human beings, in dialectical interplay with nature. Throughout the whole of Marx's investigations into political economy he pressed home the point that at no time could knowledge or consciousness be fruitfully considered as epiphenomenal to social structure, or as disinterested.[7]

Marx's principal premise regarding a sociology of knowledge was that the dynamics of material activity (as a structure of social relations) strongly influenced thought or consciousness, from which he deduced that the realm of ideology had to be accounted for by reference to material praxis, and could not arise independently of man's existence. There are several places where Marx confronts this problem, but the crux is to be found in his nuclear proposition that "it is not the consciousness of men that determines their existence, but, on the contrary, their <u>social</u> existence determines their consciousness";[8] not consciousness in the abstract, but consciousness <u>about</u> the practice of human society. Consciousness is <u>always</u> consciousness of, or about, something. Whatever interpretation one wants to place on this idea, at the very least we should take it to be a complex empirical assertion about the geneses of ideational constructions of all kinds, and definitely including "theories," ideologies, myths and folk knowledge. It is the very hub of the Marxian sociology of knowledge.

The critique of knowledge did not begin with Marx. It must be recognized that such an intellectual tradition reaches back to Kant, Hegel and Fichte and the whole tradition of transcendental philosophy. But Marx's enduring accomplishment, surely, is that he infused his dialectical theory with an explicit historicality and gave it a contextual framework which ruptured the closed philosophical systems of his mentor Hegel, and of Feuerbach. Thus, in place of Hegel's philosophy of Absolute knowledge, Marx presented a phenomenological reconstruction of the genesis of human consciousness not as a "natural" product but as an <u>historical</u> product. In a word, the phenomenological reflection upon the formation of consciousness which Hegel made central to his philosophy but which was never taken to be problematic by Hegel, was unmistakably reiterated by Marx, whose insights showed the inseparability of human history and self-creating praxis. If we accept that human being's practical activity is part of the definition of <u>social</u> being, then it follows that the "life-process" of humankind is important in shaping the mode of life in any given epoch, including specific thought-patterns. It is thus that ideology, idea-systems and world-views are produced or generated - by structures of social relations, all of which led Marx to the conclusion that consciousness, insofar as it can be conceptualized, is from the beginning a social product, and remains so as long as men and women exist at all. <u>Society</u> then becomes something which is more than a structure of social relations; it is a <u>productive</u> system of social relations. Consciousness alters when men and women change their structures of social relations, and this is a problem into which the sociology of knowledge must always probe, first in order to understand the inevitability of social involvement; and second in order to interpret, at close quarters, the process whereby men and women work out ideas, plot world-views and organize themselves into institutions on a continuing basis, in order that life can go on, and history can be constructed.

We must fully understand that the Marxian materialism and sense of history is not deterministic in any crude mechanical sense. Marx argues for a dialectical relationship between existence and consciousness[9] and this standpoint is fully revealed in his criticisms of the materialistic dialectic of Feuerbach and others which we have already commented on above (see Chapter 4). He cryptically charged that Feuerbach was simply aware that material reality was a determinant of human activity, without analyzing the modification of the objective world by the subject, that is, by the activity of men and women. Feuerbach, for all his brilliant anthropological critique of philosophy and of religion, had not gone far enough, according to Marx, in concretizing the concepts of his model so that the double dialectic of human existence could be comprehended. In practical life, historical labor actively changes both nature and the human species. As Giddens points out, Marx criticized Feuerbach's approach as unhistorical, for in conceiving man as an abstract "man," prior to society, he reduces him to religious man, while forgetting that even "religious feeling" is itself a social product, and that the abstract individual he analyzes belongs to a particular form of society. Second, Feuerbach's (admittedly important) insight into a dialectic was to be faulted precisely because it remained at the "contemplative" level rather than at the level of material praxis.[10] Consequently, we are not taken far enough toward understanding that all bodies of thought from common sense, to ideology, to science can be given anchorage in definite social and cultural conditions. The focal issue for the Marxian sociology of knowledge is the understanding of the dialectical interplay between mind and society, knowledge and existence, subject and object. Fundamentally, Marx avers, in the course of history the dominant ideas tend to become detached from their social class locus, and are given what appears to be independent existence, and this highlights the problem of reification.

But the sociological problem still remains: how to grasp the connection between human beings' own activity and the products thereof; how, in short, to subjectivize the object. The problem of assigning subjectivity to social products is given articulation in Marx's discussion on the fetishism of commodities. It was in the German Ideology that he formulated the really penetrating analysis of the nexus between class relations and ideological hegemony: the key finding which we have already commented upon is that in real life "the dominant class is able to disseminate ideas which are the legitimations of its position of dominance";[11] hence the danger of taking an epoch at its own word, or of accepting as gospel the many fanciful ideologies of the ruling class. What does this all mean?

In her very important study of ideological perspectives on Canada, sociologist Patricia Marchak has provided some extremely lucid insights into this phenomenon in Canadian society. Abundant data on income, on private ownership, on statism, on the so-called law of supply and demand, are carefully analyzed by Marchak to dramatize the fact that the reigning liberal assumptions of equal opportunity, of free market, of equalization payments, are either not valid or are contradictory. They amount to gigantic myths. Similarly, the dominant liberal ideology, with its belief in "representative government," in individualism, the free market, simply does not explain the myriad puzzles of industrial Canada's growth patterns. In a word, the reigning explanations are partial, dehistoricized, even naive, and they obscure an accurate representation of the real situation and ignore the structural roots of such experiences as poverty, inequality and regional disparity. When the evidence is in, the liberal ideology fails miserably as an explanatory device. Yet it persists, and even seems to grow stronger because people take such an ideology at its word. As Marchak concludes, few people have seen any compelling reason to disbelieve what is matter-of-factly presented as public ideology.[12]

It may be true that the Marxian framework may not provide an explanation for some of the inequalities, injustices and other problems that are not necessarily class-problems, in Canadian society. But even if we accept this, the essence of the Marxian critique of ideology still stands out. That essence is couched in the metatheory offered for assessing the merits of competing explanations, and in cultivating a critical

consciousness when confronted with the claims of
entrenched dominant ideologies.

To take an epoch at its word concerning everything
that it imagines about itself was, for Marx, to leave
unnoticed the social circumstances in which activity
transpires, which circumstances effectively condition
the perception of the world. If in class societies the
ruling ideas of an epoch are the ideas of the ruling
class, then important questions must be raised about
claims to the legitimation of positions of power, and
about the very important mechanism facilitating or
hindering the communication of ideas. To ceremoniously
and uncritically take an epoch at its own word is to
engage in reification and to fetishize the social world,
in that we "forget," or are made to "forget," whence
the ideas arose, and in whose interests. Eventually,
such a perspective serves to disguise or deform the
precise historical character of society and its human
products. Where the sociology of knowledge takes these
problems as subject for serious empirical investigation,
it is likely to deepen our understanding of society and
history. The key is not the ideas per se but the
values they reflect and the interests they support.

In summary, Marx's pioneering work in recognizing
the importance of the social milieu in the production
of knowledge and ideas, makes him a key-note figure in
the sociology of knowledge. Like Mannheim, he
recognized that sociological analysis was called upon
to deal with existentially determined thinking and
knowledge, and he argued, in turn, that if the
construction of a corpus of knowledge is paradigmatically linked to the interests of those who produce it,
then knowledge as such is not disinterested. A
sociology of knowledge was possible through social
theory, and evidently a sociology which functions as a
critique of knowledge is necessarily a sociology
critical of the social construction of reality.
Specifically, knowledge of the socio-cultural world
could not be considered as external to science; nor
could it be considered apart from human praxis as the
ongoing historical process of doing, knowing and
thinking. This is one of the main thrusts of the
Frankfurt School's critique of positivism, and one
which is currently under much discussion in social
science circles. The many statements on critical
theory adumbrated by the Frankfurt School, congeal
around the fundamental principle that critical social

206

science seeks to be more than data-gathering in the conventional sense, and seeks total as opposed to fragmented understanding, seasoned with ruthless criticism of that which exist. In the words of Horkheimer, critical theory does not take the goals and tendencies in the existing society for granted once and for all, but investigates them critically, tries to see them in relation to society as a whole and the legitimations given for it, all this in the interest of a more rational order of human activity.[13] From this brief sketch of Marx's formulations let us turn next to the ideas offered by Mannheim.

Mannheim's Perspective on the Sociology of Knowledge

Karl Mannheim's ideas on the sociology of knowledge parallel Marx's, but only to a certain point. Like Marx, Mannheim's approach is structural, in the sense that ideas and Weltanschauung or "total ideologies" were to be interpreted not in isolation, but in contextual relation to definite groups of men[14] and their interests. On the premise that every point of view is particular to a certain definite situation,[15] Mannheim regarded the sociology of knowledge as specifically concerned with the study of the relationship between knowledge and existence.

Beyond this point, Mannheim does not agree that one can relate an intellectual standpoint directly to a social class. This certainly was the position he took in his early writings[16] when he argued that the best one could do was to find out the correlation between "styles of thought" underlying a given standpoint and the "intellectual motivation" of certain social groups.[17] Although he softened this position later on, Mannheim was still reluctant to conceptualize knowledge as class-based. Thus in Ideology and Utopia (1936) Mannheim resorted to what he regarded as one of the many bases of collective existence, namely, the existence of differently situated generations[18] and presented the idea of a "free floating intelligentsia." This stratum of intellectuals, presumably because of their unique education, would be capable of transcending the very stratum from which they came. The knowledge produced by these intellectuals would not be "class-bound" but free-floating and valid.[19] This is head-on confrontation with the problem of relativism and reductionism. Mannheim, recognizing the dilemma,

introduced the idea of _relationism_ as a sort of
epistemological basket capable of retaining the big
bits of truth while the fine and perhaps insignificant
pieces are allowed to escape - much as a fisherman uses
nets to strain different species of fish. This,
presumably, would simply mean closely examining a given
corpus of idea with a view to discriminating between
valid and erroneous claims to knowledge. One is very
tempted to pursue the analogy: the fisherman may
indeed catch many fish of a desired size, but given
such (important) factors as an overabundance of thorny
spines, or possible toxins in known species, etc., he
will be forced to discard some of his catch immediately,
or else risks some serious consequences.

In any event, the Mannheimian solution to the
"thorny" question of what constitutes valid knowledge
is elusive and questionable. By Mannheim's own
criteria, knowledge of the social and cultural world
could never be context-free or transcendentally neutral.
It becomes necessary, then, to entertain doubts
regarding his free-floating intelligentsia, who are
supposed to be the neutral bearers of a political
synthesis because of their excessive training. They
might have been thought capable of rising above
partisan or class squabbles, and of understanding view-
points other than that of their own, in neutral terms.
But they could not extricate themselves from their
stratum. Furthermore, the reality of European politics
of Mannheim's own day severely undermined his (and our)
optimism concerning such a group in modern society.
Therefore, the avowed solution to the problem of the
validity of existentially-determined knowledge is
contradictory and unacceptable. As a wholly social
product, knowledge phenomenologically reflects the
life-aspects of those who produce it. And by limiting
valid knowledge to a free-floating, classless, European
intellectual elite, Mannheim effectively brackets off
that corpus of "everyday" knowledge that is produced
and communicated by "non-intellectuals" as part of the
fund of workable knowledge in a society.

The epistemological impasse to which Mannheim's
theory takes us, is a key one in social sciences, and we
shall have to return to it later on. Suffice it to say
that no human individual, or group, which has been shaped
by the social process, can be completely independent of
that process, even if he moves from the generational
specificity to a more generalized set of interests or

cultural priorities. On the role of the sociology of knowledge, Mannheim is more explicit. He conceived of the sociology of knowledge as a perspective for solving the problem of the social conditioning of knowledge by boldly recognizing these relations and drawing them into the horizon of science itself and using them as checks on the conclusion of our research.[20] As a theory on the social or existential determination of actual thinking, and as a tool of social science practice, the sociology of knowledge does not criticize thought on the level of assertions themselves but examines them on the structural level.[21]

The conclusion which Mannheim arrived at was that the sociology of knowledge was both a theory and an historical-sociological method. As a theory, it takes two forms: in the first place it seeks to analyze the relationship between knowledge and existence; in this sense it is a purely empirical investigation through description and structural analysis of the ways in which social relationships influence thought, and vice versa. The dialectic is as relevant for the analysis of ideas as it is for the analysis of "concrete" labor, and other physical activities.

In the second place, it is an historical-sociological method, that is, an epistemological inquiry concerned with tracing the forms which this relationship has taken in the intellectual development of mankind. This latter facet inevitably hoists troublesome questions about the "validity" or truth-claims of a given body of knowledge. To some of those questions we now turn our attention.

Some Standard Criticisms of the Sociology of Knowledge

In a recent essay, Derek Phillips argued that scientists who ignore epistemological questions exclude questions pertaining to the social nature of science (including sociology) and that by neglecting such questions sociologists effectively cut themselves off from a concern with the issue of legitimate authority in Western society.[22]

It is obviously of immense interest to the sociology of knowledge that, as Norman Birnbaum has written, the primary ideological difficulty of many contemporary sociologists is that they are unwilling to face up to the implications of the problem of ideology for their own work. If sociologists are truly interested in the credibility and veracity of their own version of social reality, that burden of demonstrative credibility falls on them, and involves subjecting their own conceptions to the rigor and scrutiny they typically bring to bear on "commonsense" notions. To assume that the highly placed and elitist version of reality is necessarily superior to any other is to pose a deep problem in the sociology of knowledge. If, as Popper says, all our theories are conjectures, then the incorporation of ethnoscience into all our conjectures is a precondition of the search for knowledge writ large. This key observation has central relevance to the concern of this chapter, because, as we shall indicate below, without critically questioning the bases of one's own theories and findings, the door is wide open for "sociological finality," or, worse, the dogma of certainty. Any such dogma may easily serve, without question, the interests of despotic state bureaucracies or charismatic despotic political leaders, or unprincipled experts in government or politics.

The problem of the validity of knowledge that was in the first place situationally determined (as the sociology of knowledge itself must be), has of course, been the target of the major criticisms of the sociology of knowledge. The main point, is this: If as the sociology of knowledge asserts, all ideas are socially determined and are at the same time relative to a particular socio-cultural context, then the sociology of knowledge itself is a product of the socio-cultural forces operative at a particular time and is thus lacking in validity except in terms of the immediate situation.[23] In other words, the sociology of knowledge is itself a body of ideas that is either a social product or an exception to the rule that culturally standardized ideas such as myths, ideologies, and political doctrines are the products of social influences or determinants. If it is a social product, then there is no a priori reason to believe that it has any validity beyond an immediate situation, but is merely an ideological expression of the interests of a political movement, or of sociology itself. If, on the other hand, it is claimed to be an exception, then it suggests that there may be some bodies of ideas which have some autonomy with respect to the social structure and which may, in principle, act as causes of social change and not as consequences of them.[24]

There is no doubt that this is a powerful criticism. It is this complex epistemological issue which has led Berger and Luckmann to suggest that any attempt to apply the sociology of knowledge to sociology itself represents a case of trying to push the bus in which one is riding. Yet this seemingly boundless relativism to which the sociology of knowledge seems to take us, remains overly troublesome only if we insist upon defining truth in a narrow static way, and make categorical claim to the truth-content of ideas.[25] If, on the other hand, we accept the position that truth is a matter of social consensus, then we can view it as consisting essentially of the culturalized response to reality, as that reality is understood in a given epoch.

Mannheim eventually adopted a very Hegelian conception of truth, by suggesting that the truth attainable to humankind must be the truth expressing the essence of historical reality, rather than truth in some transcendental or universalistic sense.[26] In Hegel, the truth could only be derived from the historical process, more specifically, from historical struggles or "correct praxis," i.e., through the actualization of human potential inherent in given situations. For Marx, there was also some Hegelian content. As he says in his Thesis on Feuerbach, the question whether objective truth is an attribute of human thought, is not a theoretical but a practical question ... Man must prove the truth of his thinking in practice, otherwise the dispute over the reality or non-reality of thinking that is isolated from practice is a purely scholastic question. Insofar as purposive and intentional activity (praxis) helps men and women to organize the knowledge they obtain, praxis serves as one epistemological criterion for the historical validity of knowledge. In a word, theory is tested in historical struggles. And for Lukacs, later, truth could only achieve an "objectivity" relative to the standpoint of individual social classes and the objective realities corresponding to it. The truth about human history can thus be discovered by a rational insight into the unfolding of the historical process. This is also the position taken by most of the Frankfurt School theorists, who, despite their different styles, concede that historical considerations are far more crucial than purely epistemological ones in demarcating valid and true knowledge from false or distorted knowledge.

211

Against this background, the sociology of knowledge, as one body of ideas amongst many, is not an exception to any epistemological rule. Its own validity must be judged on the basis of the historico-philosophical awareness that it brings to the contextual evaluation of all ideas, including its own, and on the central importance that it places on the social nature of knowledge in society. Indeed, as Mills and others have pointed out, the fact that the sociology of knowledge operates from a perspective does not necessarily mean that the results of inquiry must be false; it merely means that its truth is always conditional, not absolute. This position does not, of course, cancel the utility of the sociology of knowledge to sociological theory. Instead, it dramatizes the importance of the metatheoretical under-currents of social theory, while recognizing the depths of the uncertainties that lay wait for those who seek to decipher the historical significance, and historical relativity of one's own order of values. In Stark's view, the challenge to the sociologist of having to sift through "many points of view of equal value and prestige," each showing the relativity of the other, forces on us, whether we like it or not, a question - the question of Pontius Pilate, as excruciating in our own circumstances as it was in his: what is truth? In other words, it not only stimulates us to develop a new branch of historico-hermeneutic learning, it also compels us to reconsider the epistemological reliability of much, perhaps all, that we have so far taken for granted.[27] In the final analysis, objectivity is unavoidably normative. This conclusion, however, creates anxieties among sociologists.

Theoretical Prospects for the Sociology of Knowledge

It remains for us to delineate that whilst the sociology of knowledge does not serve as a lodestone of truth per se, it nevertheless displays unmistakable potential as a referee of social science reasoning. As Colfax and Roach remarked, those who first developed the sociology of knowledge (especially Marx and Mannheim) conceived of it primarily as an attempt to get under the cloak of notions men have about them-selves and society.[28]

The first point to be made then is that it is mandatory that sociologists constantly be made aware of their own theoretical biases and methodological rationale and why a given experience or set of experiences are defined and responded to in certain ways. This bears on such basic questions as: the topic the sociologist selects for study, the assumptions he/she makes, the research strategy he/she adopts, and so on. The sociology of knowledge demands continuing self-analysis and self-criticism of all of these, in seeking to foster a deeper understanding of the effects of value premises on our research operations, and our eventual formulation of theory. As Stark so graphically puts it, for a sociologist of knowledge, it is impossible not to realize that there are other gardens and parklands beyond, which have their own greenness, their own flowers, and their own specific, and perhaps even unique, beauty. The challenge to scholarship lies precisely in utilizing the mind to penetrate the outer shell of appearances in order to understand the inner kernel of significance.[29]

This exposes a second prospect, namely, that the essential starting point of a sociology of knowledge is an explicit historicity in which it is assumed that every human event belongs to, and can be understood in, a total context which includes ideas as well as their social roots. The thrust of the Marxian and Mannheimian sociologies of knowledge is that the nature of the world had to be discovered by empirical and historical study. Historicism becomes for Mannheim the corner-stone of a "dynamic" sociology of knowledge;[30] and for both Marx and Mannheim ideas exist, not in the void, separated from the purposes and priorities of a culture, but rather as weapons used on behalf of a way of life, and in the struggles for its achievements. The task therefore becomes that of situating knowledge processes and idea-systems in the social matrix which produces them. From 1845 onwards (The German Ideology) Marx, for his part, took every opportunity to situate idea-systems directly within social structure, and, of course, dared where Mannheim feared to tread, in developing theories about society as a process historically shaped by social conditions such as the typical mode of production.

While the sociology of knowledge makes no claim to providing universalistic conceptions of truth (which it takes as problematic), it nevertheless sharpens our image of a given system of ideas, by permitting us to understand it as it is historically situated in a wider

213

context or social orbit. In this way we may come to
recognize the <u>social</u> and historical origins, and hence
the limitations and relativity, of our theories,
conceptions and paradigms. As Stark says, it is not
the least valuable service which the sociology of
knowledge has to render, that it can teach all men
humility and charity, both of which are not only
virtues of the heart, but potentially also virtues of
the intellect. For, as he argues further,

> it shows up the essential
> limitations of one's own knowledge
> and thereby inculcates humility;
> it shows up the rationality in the
> apparent irrationality of the next
> door neighbour's point of view and
> thereby indicates charity. In so
> far as the truth is the truth only
> <u>in its own proper sphere</u>, the
> sociology of knowledge contains a
> precious corrective of that most
> dangerous and objectionable form
> of error - error arising from
> abuse of the truth.[31]

Third, we believe that it is the business of the
sociology of knowledge (as opposed to sociology in
general) to undertake analyses of the structural forces
that in any epoch bring about and consolidate a world-
view, including ideas, dogmas and the whole thought-
process of a culture. This involves the historical
appraisal of the genesis and basis of social judgments
and social prescriptions as these are imbibed in a
culture and automatically transmitted from generation
to generation. In analyzing the mentality of a period
or of a given stratum in society with respect to any
claim to legitimacy, the sociology of knowledge
concerns itself with explaining phenomena not in an
isolated, self-contained manner, but <u>relationally</u>, that
is, in terms of the thing's wider connections and
relationships. As we reasoned above, it is relatively
easy, especially in class societies, for ideas and
interests to become dislodged from their human sources
and genesis over time, only to confront individuals and
groups as some "natural" unalterable, even divine order,
as opposed to what they really are: encrusted and
solidified <u>social</u> creations.

Fourth, as a perspective concerned with the

214

historical roots of ideas as cultural phenomena and with the "extrinsic interpretation of the world of ideas as such,"[32] the sociology of knowledge is as much concerned with the social roots of error as with the truth, that is, with the intellectual explanation of historical social life. We may wish we had a non-relative concept of truth; but where this is absent, we should at the very least be concerned to take the sphere of the social determination of knowledge as problematic rather than as a given.[33] The sociology of knowledge seeks explicitly to do this, and thus as far as possible tries to avoid reification; it does not assume as "given" that which has to be explained, reminiscent of an idea from Francis Bacon: Begin with certainties and we will likely end in doubts; begin with doubts and we will likely end in certainties. To pose the issue as highly problematic is to stimulate the mind to develop the historico-hermeneutic branch of learning and to review at every stage the epistemic relation of being and thought.

If we accept that men and women are the authors and definers of their own actions and social arrangements, then what they in fact define as reality can be understood only against the background of their particular existence in groups such as social classes. This assumption forces the sociologist of knowledge to look, where he or she perhaps normally would not, for an understanding of the various types of ideological rationalizations often made by individuals and cultures to protect and/or justify various sorts of interests, and to defend positions of power. The social process whereby beliefs and cultural definitions come to establish themselves as "independent givens" in society, and the ways in which they grow out of and reflect social conditions, are central problems of the sociology of knowledge. But equally as crucial as the social origins of ideas is the problem of validity or justification [34] of a given corpus of knowledge. The widely-held thesis that the problem of justification is solved by putting up ideas to the adjudication of the "scientific community" becomes suspicious when it is recognized that, as both Kuhn and C. Wright Mills, among others, have pointed out, paradigms rise and fall by virtue of political factors, quite apart from the intrinsic quality of the paradigm themselves.[35] This fundamental point about theory displacement seemed to have been missed by many sociologists who have freely used the concept of "paradigm" as discussed by Kuhn.

215

What Kuhn's work has done (and this is quite consistent with the positions of both Marx and Mannheim) is to pry open the thorny question of the social nature of science, and hence to restate the point that insofar as "the scientific community" is comprised of human beings, its intellectual viewpoints, facts, and judgmental verdicts are shaped by existential factors, and quite often ineluctable ideological ones as well.

There is no escape from social theory. As a special conceptual framework through which we view society and the world, it is important that it reflects reality as accurately as possible. And if our intent is to view the social world as it is shaped by human ideational virtuosity, then there is no justification in relegating the sociology of knowledge to the periphery of sociological theory, as is typically the case in conventional sociology texts. We have no basis for claiming that we have a sociological theory - a theory of human society - if at the same time we fail to recognize that humans are the producers of their own conceptions, ideas, and cultural world. In our period of the twentieth century when processed information is a key requirement for simply coping from day to day, it is imperative that the information being transmitted be scrutinized for its possible ideological ballast. We may or may not agree with what is being presented, but we would at least have a frame of reference for developing an informed critique. Whatever fragmentary understanding we have of the cultural process can be enhanced, too, if we distinguish between information per se as miscellaneous bits and pieces of stimuli, and knowledge, that is, a knowing based on a structural understanding of the socio-cultural world and of the men and women who struggle within it.

A sociology of knowledge ought to be central to any theory of society, for the intellectual creations of humankind are easily reified. It seeks explicitly to understand and interpret ideas, world-views, intellectual currents and thought-patterns against the background of certain existing social conditions. Thus, the sociology of knowledge would be interested in how the existential conditions determine what knowledge will be sought, how it will be interpreted, what problems will be investigated and how the investigation will be made.[36] In seeking always to probe into the structure of long-established idea-systems, and the styles of thought that underpin social relations, the

216

sociology of knowledge facilitates the kind of reflection upon the genesis of knowledge which is the beginning of critical self-awareness and self-reflective knowledge. Such awareness, in turn, can serve to challenge ideological assumptions as well as to reveal the limitations of our theories, methodological rationale, and justificatory systems.

A problem which sociologists are often called upon to address is why a given set of ideas or ideological formulae should be accepted by those who did not produce them? The traditional answer is that consensual validation guarantees the acceptance of ideas - they need not be given through charismatic leaders, or prophets. But this is an overly simplistic view. For what is so deceptive about the state of mind of the members of complex societies is precisely the "consensual validation" of their concepts. It is naively believed that the fact that the majority of people share certain ideas or feelings proves the validity of these ideas and feelings. Nothing could be further from the truth. Clearly, the notion of consensual validation (or what Birnbaum calls "consensual schizophrenia") as such, has no bearing whatever on reason or mental health. The fact that millions of people share the same vices does not make those vices virtues; the fact that they share so many myths or stereotypes, or other distortions of the actual situation, does not make the myths truthful or the stereotypes accurate. The fact that the majority of plantation-owners agreed that the slaves were "happy" did not make those slaves experience happiness, as that value was understood by the plantocracy. More importantly, the designation of "happy slaves" detract from the objectively undesirable status of being a slave. But the sociologist is still very much interested in these problems for s/he wants to know how, in the first place, people came to share myths, ideologies, and other cultural definitions, and whether they have a choice. The search for the roots of consensus should not cause us to overlook what Birnbaum has termed "compliance by routine." In other words,

> enmeshed in the immediate struggle
> for material existence, ordinary
> persons generally limit their
> politics to acts of compliance,
> indistinguishable from a pervasive
> acceptance of routine - routine

and compliance are the usual
sources of consensus.

Birnbaum continues:

> The control of access to information,
> the control of the main media of
> communication, the command of the
> system of education, allow those
> who dominate the political order to
> impose their ideological will upon
> an intellectually inert population.
> How often, in industrial societies,
> does one hear ordinary persons
> repeating as if they were their own,
> the most insipid, the crudest
> cliches derived from the channels
> of mass communication.[37]

It is precisely via these cliches, as they emerge
from the "knowledge industry" that the myths, the
dogmas, and what we call cultural definitions are
perpetuated, as Marchak and others have clearly shown
in the Canadian context. In presenting the world as it
is, or in presenting one ideological version of it, and
in suppressing the possibility of critical thought (a
suppression itself hardly conscious), the channels of
mass communication generally reinforce that political
compliance produced by routine. Industrial societies
such as modern Canada have been arenas for ideological
conflict and struggle. But this has been less a
struggle to convert populations to given beliefs and
more a struggle for command of the apparatus which
would ensure if not acceptance of certain beliefs at
least compliance with their institutional consequences.[38] What we should be careful to understand
then is the political process wherein the products of
human practice and the expressions of human interaction
with each other and with nature, become dislodged, as
it were, from their actual locus, and appear in
consciousness as autonomous independent phenomena. Any
careful study of the cultural process sharpens this
awareness, since knowledge as a socio-cultural
phenomenon is one of the most easily reified products
of human social and intellectual activity. Knowledge,
or all that passes for such, is a phenomenon wholly
social.

Finally, it will perhaps be useful to reflect

further, on the well-known, if little understood, process of socialization. What Berger and Luckmann (1966) call "recipe knowledge" consists of the categorized and communicable knowledge that members of a society must have for practical competence in routine performances. This kind of knowledge is irreducible in that it is the basic shared understanding of "the everyday." Recipe knowledge exists routinely in the everyday and forms a central element of the social stock of knowledge.[39] But even this mundane type of knowledge must be communicated, if its usefulness is to be realized. Even so, there seems to be a certain kind of ignorance amongst sociologists regarding (a) the nature and content of the whole corpus of available knowledge in society and (b) the way recipe knowledge is distilled from that corpus. Both facets constitute a significant problem in the sociology of knowledge.

The definition, construction and communication of social reality constitute important cultural processes. The boundaries of these processes, and hence of social relations, are negotiable and are always shifting as the giving and taking of meaning-structures undergo continuous subtle changes. In view of the relative efficiency of communicating meaning systems, it is worthwhile to inquire into the nature of the major principle that guarantees the communication of cultural definitions, namely, socialization. Close examination of this principle reveals that it is because it has an important power dimension, as well as being coercive perhaps even repressive, why it produces social men imbued with their culture and not merely individual personalities. Socialization is the primary means for the perpetuation of social forms. And this process itself is one of coercion. Thus "consensus" is derived from coercion. From toilet training to taxes and take-home pay, it is coercion which maintains society and its subdivisions.[40] On this count alone, the sociology of knowledge challenges sociologists to critically reflect upon, and examine their own structure of belief, their committed participation in cultural goings-on, as well as the whole complex process by which the "normative givens" are given legitimacy and "credibility."

The problem of legitimacy in liberal democracy is closely related to that of false consciousness and the actual indoctrination of dominant values. In an empirical study of social cohesion of the liberal democracies of Britain and the United States, it was discovered that the most common form of manipulative socialization by the liberal democratic state does not seek to change values, but rather to perpetuate values that do not aid the working class to interpret the reality it actually experiences. These values merely deny the existence of group and class conflict within the nation-state society and therefore, are demonstrably false.[41] Given this finding, perhaps, then, the key to a better understanding of the cultural process and the communication of definitions lies in a closer, more critical examination of the problem of manipulative socialization. The task of exploring how all forms of knowledge gets produced and distributed, and the theoretical specification of how knowledge and society interpenetrate are made the subject and concern of the sociology of knowledge. Much of social theory seems to have avoided any serious discussion of this particular problem. The central task which social theory faces comprises an analysis and understanding of the internalization and normalization of social reality. Only by detailed systematic analyses of socialization, as a <u>coercive</u> mechanism for converting the world of "the everyday" into "science," can we penetrate the reification of social roles to the subjective world of the individual. To some extent this promise has been taken up by the ethnomethodologists with their concern that social interaction (and hence society) can only be understood when we seek to determine how meanings are taken for granted, and often have to be re-negotiated.

Any inquiry into the precise ways in which the structure of a social system provides means of organizing the framework of available knowledge, or into the production of new knowledge, or into the communication of both old and new knowledge, is a worthwhile advance beyond orthodox sociology which takes these processes for granted, and the sociology of knowledge as redundant.

A related, final point, often overlooked by criminologists, is the habit of simply taking the value assumptions of authority structures and the powerful for granted, and devoting all energies to policy oriented research. This is clearly brought out in the work of criminologist Austin Turk, who in discussing the criminalization process in western society claims to be rejecting the consensus view of society; yet, in the same breath declared that his interest was never in understanding how authorities (from whom the rules defining criminality emanate) came to be authorities. That, he says was irrelevant; it was simply sufficient that a social structure built out of authority relations exists. Indeed, he feels that authority-subject relationships are accepted because most people feel that such is necessary to the preservation of the social order. This is a fairly conservative argument which perhaps could have been left alone as such.

But Turk has introduced another angle to this dispute. Thus, in a vain attempt to separate the values one studies from the values one possesses, he reasoned that ideology concerning what one considers should be, ought to be separated from one's study of what is.[42] His charge that critical criminological analysis is characterized by dogmatic theories whose validity is politically rather than scientifically determined, completely, and conveniently ignores the crucial fact that laws in class societies are ideological formations whose legal form unmistakably serve to consolidate ruling class economic interests. As such, the "legal order" in modern societies may be accepted by most people. But it still reflects the racist, sexist and other ideological concerns of the dominant class. Contrariwise, it conceals the reality of the social structure for the masses and subordinate classes.

This excursion into the sociology of knowledge was necessary, it will be recalled, in order to point out that sociologists are often, like any other human beings, blinded by their own preconceptions and assumptions. It is highly probable that the crucial issue of socio-cultural pluralism suffers from inadequate exposition because Canadian sociologists, by virtue of being in the midst of the problem, cannot see the total situation. The sociology of knowledge is in the critical spirit, for it seeks to question our comfortable answers, to dislodge our accepted wisdoms, as an impetus to self-understanding. To a large extent, this is uncomfortable. It is in the essence of the sociology of knowledge that at some stage of its inquiry it turns the searchlight on the inquirer himself/herself which could then reveal biases, blindness and deficiency in both conceptualization and explanation. But if all of this drives home the message that social theory is not epiphenomenal to socio-cultural arrangements, but is integrally rooted in them, the effort would have been well served.

Conclusion

This chapter has been purposefully progenitorial, and much of it has been schematic. There is no opportunity here to go into the many contributions offered by the heirs or critics of Marx and Mannheim, or into the original insights and extension to social theory which theorists such as Durkheim, Schutz, Mead, Merton, Horowitz, and others have given. Our intent has been to highlight and expose the revelatory path shaped by two well-known classical thinkers who sought to analyze the situational determination of knowledge and belief systems. In formulating this discussion, we have also demonstrated some of the inherent pitfalls and penetrating weaknesses of the sociology of knowledge, notably the problem of epistemological relativism, thus hoisting the sociology of knowledge on its own petard for full view, and for systematic utilization by social theory in general. But the sociology of knowledge does not consist simply of presenting the sociologist with a witch's cauldron of difficulties, and of stirring up the epistemological dust in the face of the sociologist. We have reason to be more optimistic about its prospects, even if, at times, we experience anxiety in having to face some very difficult philosophical questions.

It is easy enough to become entwined in the old debate, still very much alive today, as to whether from the perspective of the sociology of knowledge fragments of the truth can be found among the debris of social life.[43] Clearly, the perspective of the sociology of knowledge must seek to uncover the contours of the complex process whereby idea-systems and knowledge are articulated with social structure. The debate started by Marx and Mannheim has been revealing and heuristic; and in the case of Marx the dereifying thrust has served as an effective antidote and reminder to those who would conveniently forget the importance of values in all spheres of social life. The prospect of keeping open this key theoretical contention, perhaps sufficiently justifies reiteration of its centrality to social theory and critical understanding.

The import of this perspective for critical sociological analysis is amply demonstrated in Wallace Clement's book on the Canadian corporate elite. Given that dominant ideologies are promoted by and reflect the interests of particular groups in society (for example the media elites), and given that the dominant ideology often becomes instilled in the lower classes contrary to their existential position, the sociology of knowledge must constantly be called upon to examine the social basis of ideology. The ideology of consumerism for example, is fully recognized by critical social scientists as something which operates as a means of social control by the creation of artificial needs. This involves the dissemination of corporate propaganda, aimed at all society's members for goods and services beyond actual needs. Even the selective transformation of knowledge into "news" becomes bastardized, as news becomes a commodity which sells products and is itself a valuable commodity, treated as a means to attain an audience and the audience to sell products.[44] The triumph of advertizing in the culture industry is that consumers feel compelled to buy and use its products, even though they can, presumably, see the triviality of it all.

If nothing else, the sociology of knowledge sensitizes us to the fact that scientific activity always takes place within a framework of assumptions about the nature of the world and the kind of knowledge it is possible to acquire about that world. This set of assumptions, or conceptual framework, is ultimately established or rejected on the basis of value considerations. The history of science teaches us that the choice of assumptions and of methods as well as the choice of questions to be investigated are choices based on values. Since our values enter into our social prescriptions, we might as well attempt to come to grips with them, and do that consciously. Scientific knowledge will not do that for us. Science will tell us many things about what we can and cannot do; it may inform us of some of our possibilities and some of our limitations. It cannot, however, free us from the fundamental human task of making value choices.[45]

The foregoing brief notes on the sociology of knowledge are useful for shedding light on the theoretical analysis of cultural pluralism, economic inequality, theories of social protest and many other areas in sociology. As the kernel of reflective social science, the role of the sociology of knowledge is virtually assured, as that of badgering possible paralysis of the critical will. As far as the develop ment of social theory is concerned, our aim should be to unmask prevailing prejudices, or at least to enter- tain the critical awareness of how social, economic and historical contexts shape and color our cultural productions, such as social theory itself. It is interesting to note that the subject of pluralism raises one of the oldest concerns in the sociology of knowledge, namely, the problem of the diversity of history and cultures. And this raises the further key point of whether there are, as Kant supposed, a universal pattern of social organization, together with a supposed universal standard of reason. All social action is mediated by ordinary language and symbolic stimuli, and the riot of ideas incubate in social structure. But where the communication of ideas in society is given over to political elites or dominant classes, the likelihood of unnecessary fragmentation of thought and experience and the eventual elimination of subjectivity, is very real. We have not escaped this situation in Canadian society, as recent studies have clearly shown. In Canada, the media elites

> are organized primarily as
> corporations and as such seek
> profits, but they are more:
> they are also organizations whose
> major activity is the dissemination
> and reinforcement of ideologies and
> values.[46]

It is a known fact that some sociologists believe, and say, that if one is too critical, that makes it difficult to "get along" in society. It is not possible, in the scope of this book, to reply adequately to that sort of uneasiness. Suffice it to say that the freezing of critique accomplishes several objectives, whether or not they are fully recognized. Such a position would (a) provide implicit support for the status quo; (b) minimize the self-reflective stance of the sociology of knowledge, making it difficult to acknowledge our own structure of prejudice; (c) produce a version of distorted communication to the degree that outward appearances may be taken as coinciding with what is not revealed. Things are never usually what they appear to be; the sociology of knowledge is always mindful of that. Finally, to abstain from critique typifies intellectual default. But there is a choice.

"All social scientists, by the fact of their existence, are involved in the struggle between enlightenment and obscurantism." The choice is whether or not one faces this condition and makes up one's own mind, or whether one conceals it from oneself and from others and drifts morally.[47]

NOTES

1. Berger and Luckmann, 1966, p. 15; and Mannheim, 1936, p. 237 ff.

2. Curtis and Petras, 1970, p. 27; Merton, 1972, p. 9; and Horowitz, 1968, p. 65.

3. For further, important reading on the subject, see Curtis and Petras, 1970, a compendium comprising a wide selection of some of the major testaments in the field. The bibliography following the editors' "Introduction" is exceptionally rich with sources. Also, see Hamilton, 1974; Merton, 1972; Stark, 1958; and Horowitz, 1968.

4. Mannheim, 1936, p. 86; and Stark, 1958, p. 51.

5. Hamilton, 1974, pp. 2-3; also, see Swingewood, 1975, pp. 58-86.

6. Ibid., p. 11.

7. These points are vigorously expressed in Marx and Engels, 1974; Marx, 1963a.

8. Ibid.; and Marx, 1971c, p. 21.

9. See Giddens, 1971, pp. 20-23; 1976; and cf. Chapter 4 above.

10. Ibid. Note, also, Marx and Engels, 1947, p. 22; and Marx, 1964, p. 108, et passim.

11. Giddens, 1971, p. 41.

12. See, here, Marchak, 1981, pp. 135-137, et passim. In this connection Harris has written that "because the roots of ideology lie in the existence of a social group, not an individual, critique in terms of logic may be of relatively little relevance. What destroys the ideology is the destruction or transformation of the group or the disappearance of the purposes to which it was originally wedded" (1968, p. 39).

13. Horkheimer , 1972, pp. 188 ff. Developments in social theory such as ethnomethodology, have given added fuel to the debate centred on the social

nature of knowledge in society.

14. Mannheim, 1952, pp. 33-38:   'On the interpretation of weltanschauung.'

15. Mannheim, 1936, p. 80.

16. See, for example, Wolff, 1971.

17. Mannheim, 1952, p. 184, et. passim.

18. Ibid., pp. 276-320.

19. Mannheim, 1936, Chapter 2, esp. pp. 67-74, 158-160.

20. Ibid., pp. 237-39; 1952, p. 180.

21. Ibid.

22. Phillips, 1974, pp. 60, 78.

23. Curtis and Petras, 1970, p. 60.

24. Cohen, 1968, p. 200.

25. Mannheim, 1936, p. 262.

26. Ibid., p. 71; 1952, pp. 31, 262; Stark, 1958, pp. 152-65. For a discussion on the Hegelian conception of truth, see Marcuse, 1960, pp. 25-27, 258-61, 320-22.

27. Stark, op.cit., p. 154; cf. Rex, 1974, p. 232; and Mills, 1940, p. 24.

28. Colfax and Roach, 1971, pp. 104-105.

29. Stark, op.cit, pp. 156-57.

30. See Mannheim, 1952, pp. 84-133.

31. Stark, op.cit., p. 159, emphasis added.

32. Ibid., Chapter 5.

33. See Horowitz, 1968, pp. 22-23.

34. It used to be thought by one generation of philosophers of science, notably of the "logical

positivist" ilk, that one could easily make a clear demarcation between the context of discovery (or how one comes to have an hypothesis), and the context of justification (the claims one makes for justifying the validity of the hypothesis). It was thought that the former raised purely empirical issues, logically solvable; the latter raised logical issues, empirically solvable. It turns out, in all that we have learnt from the history of science, that the matter is not that simple, and that there is no sharp and absolute separation between these areas.

35. See, e.g., Mills, 1940; Ritzer, 1975a, pp. 156-157; and Kuhn, 1962.

36. Colfax and Roach, 1971, pp. 104-5. For a very important demonstration of what this means with respect to the very structure and practice of sociology trans-nationally, see the interesting analysis by Hiller who shows how different national contexts decisively mould the character of "national sociologies." In his words, "the relative importance of social problems, government policy, traditional conceptions of the nature and value of social science, national needs ... will affect the way sociology is institutionalized in a nation." In reasoning which is quite consistent with the claims of the sociology of knowledge, Hiller points out that wherever sociology is practiced, "national contexts give shape to the questions, problems, and methods the sociologist will choose to investigate social phenomena." See Harry H. Hiller, "Universality of Science and the Question of National Sociologies," The American Sociologist, Vol. 14 (August) 1979, pp. 124-35.

37. Birnbaum, 1969, pp. 66, 72. It should be remarked, in this context, that the Frankfurt School's work on culture and the "culture industry" is replete with insights into the ways in which the dominant ideology penetrates and occupies the consciousness and everyday conception of reality of the subordinate classes. Cf. also, Mann, Consciousness and Action Among the Western Working Class, op.cit.

38. Birnbaum, 1969, p. 70.

39. Berger and Luckmann, 1966, p. 56.

40. Adams, 1966, pp. 714-17.

41. Mann, 1970, p. 437; idem., Consciousness and Action ...

42. See Turk, 1969, and especially, idem., 1979, p. 459.

43. See, e.g., Martin Jay, "The Frankfurt School's critique of Karl Mannheim and the sociology of knowledge," Telos, Vol. 20, Summer, 1974, pp. 72-89; and James Schmidt, "Critical Theory and the sociology of knowledge: a response to Martin Jay," Telos, Vol. 21, 1974, pp. 168-180. In this connection, it is important to note that several of the theorists of the Frankfurt School have, at one time or another, attacked the sociology of knowledge, especially as expounded by Mannheim, with which they were never really at ease. Adorno, for instance, was careful to point out the "positivist mentality" in Mannheim; Walter Benjamin complained of the same "positivism," plus "inescapable and baffling contradiction" in Mannheim; and of course Habermas' famous inaugural lecture, in addition to spelling out the types of science, is also a stinging critique of knowledge and a view that science, as conceived by positivism in sociology, is ideological and produces anti-scientific sociologies of knowledge. See, for instance, Theodor Adorno, "The sociology of knowledge and its consciousness," Prism, 1967, pp. 37-49; Adorno, "The sociology of knowledge and its consciousness," in Arato and Gebhardt, 1978, pp. 452-65; Walter Benjamin, "The sociology of knowledge and the problem of objectivity," in Llewellyn Gross (ed.), Sociological Theory: Inquiries and Paradigms, New York: Harper and Row, 1967, pp. 335-357; Habermas, 1968b; Hamilton, 1974, esp. pp. 55-65.

44. Clement, 1975, pp. 270-86; and Horkheimer & Adorno, 1972, p. 167.

45. Margaret Osler, "Apocryphal knowledge: misuse of science," op.cit., pp. 278-286.

46. Clement, 1975, p. 270.

47. Mills, 1959, pp. 178, 179.

CHAPTER IX

DILEMMAS AND CONTRADICTIONS IN
MODERN SOCIAL THEORY

The Idea of Critical Theory

This final chapter attempts a double task: one,
to introduce the idea of critical theory; and two, to
illustrate some of the on-going dilemmas and contradictions in modern social theory. By critical theory,
we refer specifically to that body of anti-positivist
thought which extends from the Left-Hegelians through
Marx to the now renowned Frankfurt School associated
with the many and complex works of Max Horkheimer,
Theodor Adorno, Herbert Marcuse, Jurgen Habermas,
Friedrich Pollock, Erich Fromm and others less well
known in the English-speaking world. A number of
important elements within this tradition will be
pursued, in order to determine why critical theory is
deemed necessary in the first place, and what the
meaning of critique is, in this tradition. Secondly,
it will be important to identify the major assumptions
of critical theory, for they form the basis of critical
theory's argument against positivism. Thirdly, some
attempt will be made to identify the most salient
features and goals of critical theory, as well as the
nature of its major limitations.

Basically, critical theory conceives of itself as
the theory of late capitalism. Its primary aim remains
that of an historically oriented analysis of contemporary society with all its built-in crises and
cultural convulsions. Its significance for sociology
lies in its rigorous and patient use of dialectical
reason in forging a critique of late capitalist society.
Undoubtedly, there is an important sociological sense
in which being radical and critical means always to
expose the nature of such processes as domination, to
explain actual relationships as social arrangements, to
clarify that which has been needlessly confused and
mystified. To tackle one or all of these tasks is
often to run foul of the interests and acquired status
of the powerful groups in society. As Radnitzky
remarked,

> Critical sociology studies society
> as a totality and in its historical
> setting from the viewpoint of

> criticism and socio-political
> practice, i.e., with a view not
> only to making visible what happens
> anyhow, but rather to making us
> aware of and keeping us aware of
> what we must do, viz. the planning
> and shaping of the future which we
> cannot avoid being engaged in.[1]

Only critical theory within sociology constantly reasons that no social arrangement is inevitable or beyond question. Other perspectives, such as phenomenology and symbolic interactionism, tend toward the critical spirit, forcing us to look beyond the details of social life to the conditions that shape existence. But the concepts of critical theory are firmly grounded in the Marxian tradition of dialectics, which, as we have seen, focuses on totality. Penetrating outer form, in order to reveal inner meaning is a key objective, for, as Marx himself pointed out in Volume 3 of Capital, "all science would be superfluous if the outward appearance and the essence of things directly coincided."

The overall program of critical theory is many-sided, but the following distinct concerns can be identified within the School. First, critical theory is concerned with fully expounding the very idea of critique as that idea is rooted in Kant, Hegel and Marx. Secondly, it is part of critical theory's major project to develop and sustain a critique of positivism; thirdly, critical theory conceives of the need for a radical critique of modern industrial society and its dominative tendencies; fourthly, critical theory understands the importance of a critique of Marxism; and finally, it is one of the aims of critical theory to utilize insights from the psychoanalytic paradigm in constructing a critical theory of society. The implications of this last focus have already been dealt with in Chapter 2, and will not be pursued further here.

It is particularly important to note that whilst critical theory builds on humanist Marxism, the School nevertheless sees the need to subject Marxism to far-reaching criticisms, as radical a criticism perhaps as that directed at positivism, but of course for quite different reasons. The scholars of the Frankfurt School have consistently argued that the Marxian critique of political economy must either be supplemented or replaced by a critique of instrumental reason, and by an up-to-date analysis that would take sufficiently into account the strategic role of the modern state, the contemporary role of science and technology, the growth of cultural domination, and the mechanics of capitalism in the Third World.[2]

These, and other points pertaining to the Frankfurt School's concerns, will be taken up again later. For now, let us focus on the historical roots of critical theory

The Contextual Foundation of Critical Theory

It has already been suggested that critical theory is critical of the scientistic pretensions of positivism. Along with other anti-positivist schools of meta-science, critical theory is concerned about the dubious claims of positivism in social sciences. The theoretical and methodological assumptions of positivism have, in fact, sustained a permanent objection to, and critique of, sociology's obsession with natural science's styles. Several anti-positivist schools of meta-science can be identified in sociology: existentialism, phenomenology, and of course critical theory. All of them, singly or in combination, reason for a more humanistic approach to social phenomena, for a more philosophical definition of humankind, and for the possibility of interpretive categories in social explanation.[3] They also, in contrast to positivism, accept the concept of human subjectivity as germane for comprehending the constructed nature of the social world.

Of the anti-positivist schools of meta-science by far the most radical and synthetic is critical theory, associated with the Frankfurt School. The theorists in this tradition have long regarded the assumptions of positivism as misguided, and have forcefully reasoned that human behavior cannot be adequately described in sets of laws or understood by an appeal to an epistemology directly similar to natural science. In fact, the social sciences and the physical sciences are two different categories of knowledge and must therefore utilize different <u>logic of analysis</u> to account for their different results. Critical theory takes then as its point of departure the view that the natural and cultural sciences rest on fundamentally different

233

methodological and epistemological foundations.

In attempting to present the idea of a critical theory, it is important to be aware that the debate concerning the viability of critical theory has been going on in the social sciences for a very long time. The so-called "positivist debate" in German sociology involving such figures as Karl Popper, Hans Albert, Theodore Adorno, and lately Habermas, turns on the methods of knowing and the methods appropriate for knowing in the social as opposed to the natural sciences. The quarrels are multi-faceted, but in a nutshell they have to do with the key differences between an analytical as against a dialectical theory of science, as Habermas makes clear in his powerful argument against the transference of natural science modes into the social sciences, a debate into which we shall not enter in this short book.[4] However, we can say that at issue here is nothing less than the relation between types of knowledge and their sub-terranean interests. Habermas has reasoned all along that because we know hardly anything about an onto-logical correspondence between scientific categories and the structure of reality, critical theory doubts whether science, with its avowedly instrumental interests, can proceed toward the world produced by men and women just as indifferently as it does with such success in the exact natural sciences.[5] Against the "naturalism" of positivist social science, critical theory proposes a more philosophical, dialectical social theory, rooted in the social philosophy of Marxian humanism. Consequently, critical theory seeks to understand science, not as a body of objective interest-free canons, but as a system of discourse based on unrestricted and competent communication, i.e., that form of discourse in which no form of domination or compulsion exists. The notions of open discussion, uncurbed expression of opinions and non-distorted communication are central to the overall aims of critical theory, as is the Kantian idea of inquiring back into the source of all the formations of knowledge. In essence, critical theory is committed to the continuing refinement of the hermeneutic tradition.

The distinctions drawn out by Horkheimer in his book Critical Theory, between critical theory and what he calls traditional theory, reveal that a critical theory of society is anchored in Marxian dialectic and in the substantive critique of political economy and of culture. Horkheimer's portrayal sets out the basic but fundamental differences between a critical theory as an ongoing analysis of modern society, and traditional theory which is typified in "value-free" social science. Critical theory, unlike traditional theory, has strong but _explicit_ political convictions; secondly, it is committed to change, more precisely to the possibility that any human creation can ultimately be altered by them; thirdly, it has an unmasking, debunking function or potential; and, finally, it advances a clear concern for the abolition of all kinds of social injustice.6 In a nutshell, critical theory sets the goal of transforming society through radical critique and action. Critique is radical when it aims at the roots; action without a radical, hence critical understanding or theory of society was in danger of terminating in futility. As we shall see, some of the aims of critical theory have foundered dramatically, and have, therefore, disappointed neo-Marxists who have generally placed much emphasis on the ability of critical theory to liberate humanity from the bondage of ruling class ideology and state bureaucracy. William Leiss has expressed very clearly the orientation of critical theory when he says that nothing more clearly distinguishes critical theory from the predominant modes of social science research than this principle, namely, that the theoretical analysis of the social process and the concepts employed therein, as an integral part of that process, are "self-reflexive." In essence, the aim of critical theoretical analysis is to uncover and clarify the possibilities for transition to a just society.7 Leiss, and other modern day scholars, have done much to capture and preserve the kernel of critical theory as that analysis of society, rooted in a Marxian critique of political economy, which seeks to cultivate the spirit of oppositional thinking, as an activity of unveiling and/or debunking.8

It is in the Kantian notion of _reflection_ on the conditions of possible knowledge that the critical theory of society is anchored. As such, the critical theory of society strives to work out the nature of the intricate connections between the individual and society, and to expose the contradictions and inconsistencies of the whole. Critical theorists, in attempting to apply dialectical reason to social arrangements seek, as Horkheimer puts it, to show the underlying relations between persons, to "see the human bottom of non-human things." Finally, insofar as critical theory developed out of metatheoretical queries and concerns about the very nature, scope and possibility of radical social analysis that would confront actual social problems and conditions, it takes in its swath, at least in the formulations of the Frankfurt School, a critique of <u>culture</u>, including ideology and instrumental science, even "everyday" life.

The common belief that there are some tasks that people want to do, for which sociology would give them an intellectual foundation that they might otherwise lack, must at all times be countered by the observation that it is not every brand of sociology which seeks theoretical analysis of a distinctly revealing and hence potentially transformative nature. It is, in fact, along this dimension that critical theory stands out from the traditional, disinterested, scientific research posture of much of contemporary social science.

Some Assumptions and Distinguishing Features of Critical Theory

Several of the assumptions of critical theory are shared by other anti-positivist schools of meta-science from which critical theory derives some insights, for example, phenomenology and hermeneutics. First, critical theory assumes that <u>all</u> scientific knowledge about social reality carries <u>with</u> it either implicitly or explicitly certain ideological, political and evaluative convictions.[9] Second, there is the related assumption that there can be no objective knowledge in the social sciences, if that is taken to mean knowledge which is not inherent in the experience of human reality. Critical theory would perhaps go as far as to suggest that knowledge of the social and cultural world is not so much a "science" in the narrow positivistic sense, as it is a form of consciousness about the shifting boundaries of reality and the on-going distillation of meaning from social existence. The position subscribed to by critical theory can be taken, briefly, to mean that all knowledge in the social science is infused with unavoidable value premises and is therefore not "objective" in the positivist sense of being "value free." It is nevertheless meaningful. Third, critical theory rejects the Kantian duality between noumena and phenomena (see the discussion in Chapter 4 above). Fourth, it is a key assumption of critical theory that even the most apparently neutral methodology - the methodology of the natural sciences, when it is applied to the social world, becomes political in its findings and implications. Fifth, it is a fundamental assumption of critical theory that the interest in Reason can develop only through critique, and that the critical power of reason helps to reconstruct the built-in distortions that originate in social institutions and which permeate social relationships. In critical theory, Reason and Critique are by definition inseparable. Thus, Horkheimer in his Eclipse of Reason spells out the important distinction between instrumental reason and practical reason. His thesis is that over time instrumental reason with its emphasis on the practical control of humans and nature has "eclipsed" practical reason which, since the days of the Greek nation states, was concerned with the "good life" and how to achieve it.[10]

Among the several distinguishing features of critical theory, perhaps the dominant feature is the explicit recognition that social theory is inter-connected with social practice. It takes the connection between these two realms as one of its basic starting points, and attempts, always, to tie its knowledge claims to the satisfaction of human purposes and desires. Practice is the intentional activity which produces material and social life. In the task of tying knowledge to the satisfaction of human desires, critical theory makes the self-conscious integration of theory and practice its central core.[11] But this does not imply in any crude mechanistic way that the unity of theory and practice is a way of telling us how to change the world. A gap has always existed between the idea of critical theory and the concrete realization of the theory. As Marx himself was well aware, intellectual criticism of society and the world will not automatically lead to radical changes of material conditions. Critical theorists fully recognize the problematic nature of change in modern capitalist societies. This is why they are so insistent on a full-fledged critique of ideology, a critique that would demonstrate that the beliefs and attitudes which happen to be dominant, are not necessarily congruent with lived experiences. This realization has important consequences for social apathy and protest.

Realistically, changes in social structure and values could occur after discussion and testing in the marketplace of ideas. This makes sense, however, only if all participants in the discussion are rational, informed and free from indoctrination. But the recent experiences of various dissident groups in society clearly reveals that these conditions do not obtain. Radical dissent is often either co-opted or repressed, and innovative cultural themes used as simply a new opportunity for profit. This makes it all the more urgent and important for critical theory to attempt to explain, as Fay puts it, the ignorance people have, not only about their social order, but their needs and wants as well. Such a theory is necessarily rooted in the felt needs and suffering of humanity. It names the people to whom its insights are addressed, and openly admits that its understanding is to be utilized on behalf of the great mass of people[12] whose uncritical compliance-by-routine serves to challenge or transform, but to preserve contemporary society.

Increasingly, sociologists have come to take the critical position that sociology is a discipline whose insights and findings should contribute to the understanding of social and political problems. Often, however, the image given in the sociology of modern society is one in which the possibility of both understanding and of change seem unreachable. Sociology could greatly enhance both our understanding of the modern world and of the possibility for change if it were not itself involved in, what Rex terms a double mystification: The first is the mystification through ideological meanings; the second is the mystification which arises when sociology itself clouds instead of clarifies social reality.[13] Critical theorists have therefore come to regard much of what is given as sociological knowledge as a needless mystification of reality, devoid of that special clarity which sociology potentially can deliver. This failing in sociology makes it difficult for them to accept the given universe of facts as the final context of validation.[14]

This exposes, then, a second critical element in critical theory: the concept of Reason, understood in the sense of Hegel and classical German philosophy: as the critical faculty which reconciles knowledge with social change that further human fulfillment and freedom. In the conceptual framework of critical theory, Reason means, or generally implies, the ability to go beyond mere appearances of forms to deeper reality. In Reason and Revolution, Marcuse explains Hegel's position to have been that a truly decisive turn in Western history came when, with the French

Revolution, and the secular critique of religion and divine right, men and women first discovered reason's potential for challenging the status quo. In Marcuse's theory, Reason explicitly means the capacity of thought to understand the existing social reality, to criticize it, and to project alternatives.[15] It clearly then has the potential of challenging existing society.

As understood and used by the Frankfurt School, Reason has this classical meaning, and with the idea of praxis, form the two poles of critical theory.[16] Or as C. Wright Mills puts it "reason is the advance guard in any field of learning." For Mills, freedom is not an empty term: it means the chance to formulate the available choices, to argue over them - and then, the opportunity to choose between set alternatives. Reason and freedom are interlocking aspects of social life. If, as we have intimated, our reason has fallen somewhere by the way, perhaps fatally injured, then chances are that freedom is somewhere there with it. The Frankfurt School was always skeptical of what has passed for Reason in the modern world.

The works of Horkheimer and Marcuse can be interpreted as a gigantic critique of the type of reason on which modern industrial society is premised - instrumental reason, a type of reason which cannot penetrate beyond mere appearance to detect what history reveals about the nature of humankind. On the other hand, critical reason, which is central to Marxism, ceaselessly and without shame seeks to reflect on the human meaning of the historical struggle. Martin Jay points out in his important book that positivism has always denied the validity of the traditional idea of reason, which it dismissed as empty metaphysics. It is on this ground that so many of the writings of the Frankfurt School address the problem of "negative dialectics" to imply the negative possibility of a rational society, as opposed to the positivistic irrationality and denial of modern society.[17] Rationality without Reason is a rationality which is not commensurate with freedom, but the destroyer of it. On questions such as these Mills, Marcuse, Baran, and other critical theorists are agreed. In the many works of Marcuse runs the central theme that modern industrial society which operates under the auspices of "scientific rationality," has managed to dump the traditional conception of Reason which had a critical dimension, and in its place install an "instrumental" conception of reason. The latter conception leaves no room for public judgment; indeed, it becomes in due course the unquestioned justification and defense of the existing structures of inequality, privilege and domination, which are in turn taken to be a god-given order of "nature." Freedom is lost when for the majority of the population their political socialization constrains public debate and political communication about the interests that govern society.

Two further important ideas which serve to set critical theory apart from traditional theory should be mentioned specifically in the context of this discussion. The first is the philosophical emphasis. Unlike, say, structural-functionalism, which is almost hostile to philosophy and history (as C. Wright Mills and others have pointed out), critical theory rests on a philosophical and historical conception of human beings. This is a salient Marxian premise. The second feature, while closely related to the first, is stated differently. O'Neill calls this "historical remem- berance" an anti-reification position, which lays great importance on the concept of historical totality and the need to resist "social amnesia," as was discussed in a previous chapter. Critical theory does not fore- close future possibilities. In fact, critical theory can be said to stand or fall on its estimate of the possibility of social change. As Marcuse puts it, in the theoretical reconstruction of the social process, the critique of current conditions and the analysis of their tendencies necessarily include future-oriented components. The emphasis on the possibility of a transformed future forms critical theory's "utopian" dimension, an emphasis, nonetheless, which transcends the present limits of reality and which links philosophy with the real history of mankind. Praxis and Reason form two poles of critical theory, and these two ideas cannot be divorced from that of the task of understanding the possibility of a rational reorgani- zation of society.

Unlike the rigorous anti-speculative bias of American social science, critical theory stresses that only by speculating about and attempting to creat post- capitalist alternatives,[18] can people successfully begin to overcome, or at any rate understand, relations of subservience and authoritarianism in the context of their own lives. The term which seems to capture this speculation is <u>historical possibility</u>. At the level of theory, possibility means that any adequate study of present day society must be able to delineate and sharply focus on particular aspects of social reality; for example, the precise way in which the established set of institutions function; the present possibilities for a transition to a more rational set of institutions or social arrangements that would bring an end to war, poverty, injustice and oppression (critical theory defines itself as the theory explicitly focused on this task); and finally, the present possibilities for increased barbarism and the negation of humanity itself.[19]

It may in fact be objected that if, as a result of our analysis of society, we cannot know what the (present) historical possibilities are for changing society, then such a theoretical analysis is without much merit. Here the critical theorists recognize that the limitations of predicting the future are as much theoretical as they are methodological. Thus, Marx consistently refused to offer anything like a blueprint for post-capitalist society on good epistemological grounds. On the basis of his own philosophical anthropology which defines human beings as being in a process of self-creation, which cannot be described in advance, he reasoned that one could not say anything sensible about the future. One must first of all fully understand the nature of society. Marx kept clear of making categorical statements or predictions about the structure of future society. For one thing, the shape of such a society would depend largely on how newly liberated humans take their new freedoms; for another, its contour was contingent upon how fully we understand the present. It is here that a dialectical approach seeks a practical-critical orientation, that is, a method of critical thinking that reveals the essential limitations of the given, and the practical possibilities of overcoming them. This is why Marx criticized the "utopian socialists," not because they were utopians, but because they were "socialists." They tried to draw up blueprints of future communities in the mistaken notion that theory had a purely mechanistic projective function rather than a synthesizing role informing existential struggle. A critical theory of society demands some reference to utopian possibilities. But only if the theory systematically reveals the nature of the existing situation can it meaningfully formulate the conditions for transcending it.

In Marx's own analyses, he operated on the assumption that every social formation contained within itself the germs of a higher form of social organization. But whether these latent possibilities are utilized, depends upon historical circumstances which have to be investigated in their concreteness. Only when society was more rational would it be possible for social scientists to foretell the future. And yet, the realm of freedom and unalienated accomplishment could hardly be grasped by men and women who were still unfree, and who were smothered by multiple cultural distortions and reified consciousness, as we reasoned in Chapter 5. The pessimism of the critical theorists revolves around the realization that men and women do not exist as free subjects, or in situations in which they can reasonably avoid the more stultifying requirements of modern capitalism; they were not therefore performing radical deeds. If they were not engaged in self-creating activity they were incapable of expressing <u>negation</u>, and could not be expected to champion any specific alternative to that which is. They could not even, in these circumstances, use protest as a true political resource nor successfully present the problems of the oppressed. In critical theory, theoretical analysis of the social process effects change in the prevailing situation by uncovering and clarifying the <u>possibilities</u> for a transition to a qualitatively different society. As Marcuse was to put it, the new sensibility or experience provide a perception of the given, and the means for discovering new possibilities and capabilities. It is in the new sensibility that human freedom (that is, the potential for it) resides. This change simultaneously transforms the basis of the theoretical analysis itself by specifying more concretely the content of the concepts used.

In the theory of Marxist sociologists, a principal focus is how to integrate philosophy and social analysis to the degree where real possibilities of transforming social arrangements through human praxis and intentionality could be presented. As we have argued, Marx himself was most sensitive to the epistemological problems inherent in fancy utopian vision which was not thoroughly informed by a critical understanding of the present. In this context, the old debate as to whether Marx claimed that capitalism would inevitably disappear, or not, is somewhat pointless and ridiculous. He claimed that, given certain structural tendencies or laws of motion within capitalism, there was the real <u>historical possibility</u> that it would disappear. Capitalism had not always existed; it succeeded or replaced an earlier system of production and structure of social relations. It seems reasonable to think that by the same historical token, it, in turn, might be replaced. Whether that is something that is possible, determined, or inevitable, can only be grasped by a thoroughgoing structural analysis of the way human societies change and why. It was just such an analysis that consumed Marx's energies, and even after that he never made a concept such as the dictatorship of the proletariat central to his project. He nevertheless drew on his familiarity with working class history in the Europe of his day to sketch for that class a certain historical importance, which, given the right conditions, they might conceivably maximize and inaugurate a new, different society. Anyone, then, who has read Marx with any degree of seriousness can realize that the overworked charge that he was a determinist amounts to nonsense. In the words of Giddens, Marx refused to go into any detail about the society of the future on the grounds that such speculations degenerate into utopian socialism, since it is not possible to foresee the form of social organization that will characterize a society based on very different principles to the existing ones.[20] Even so, a classless society is an <u>historical</u> possibility.

In contrast to traditional theory, in which the social genesis of problems, and the real situations in which science is put to use, are regarded as external to itself, the critical theory of society has for its object men and women as producers of their own historical way of life in its totality. Critical theory tries to reveal and illuminate the history, conditions and significance of [the] "dialogue" which, according to hermeneutics, we "are" and which for hermeneutics must remain <u>qua</u> reflection on ultimate datum.[21] In these terms, critical theory seeks to fulfill its major role <u>as theory</u>.

To the degree that critical theory conceives of itself as a substantive structural critique of current conditions and a critique of knowledge, it is a penetrating metacritique. As such, Fay argues, it pursues two key interrelated tasks: first, the educative role; second, the emancipatory role. In the former role, it unashamedly seeks to raise the consciousness of those whose situation is studied. This is attempted in three ways: (a) by helping actors to see themselves in ways radically different from their own self-conception; (b) by showing how certain experiences can be overcome or changed only if they are conceptualized in a certain way; and (c) by enlightening actors as to the precise mechanisms which combine to frustrate them, but about which they have been ignorant. The emancipatory role follows from the first. By exhorting all humans to think critically about domination, about reification and "distorted communication" critical theory hopes to reveal to the relevant actors the possibilities for liberation and, possibly, engagement in unorthodox forms of struggle.[22] This is, of course, the heart of the problem. By critical theory's own admission, there is not an ideal situation of public discussion in modern society, that is, there is not an "ideal speech situation" characterized by freedom from coercion and constraint. Consequently, attempts to raise the level of consciousness are destined to much frustration, coupled with the feeling that the forces against which critical theory mounts its attack are not in principle amenable to intellectual or rational debate. Wellmer voices this stance where he pessimistically concedes that critical theory, like existential philosophy, conceives itself as a protest, but as a protest somewhat impotent in practice, against an apocalyptically self-obturating system of alienation and reification.[23]

The second major task which critical theory sets itself is equally significant. For the assumption that by enlightening actors as to the precise causal relationships which determines their situation, we will therefore stir them to emancipatory struggle, is a patently false one. No modern critical thinker can doubt the problematic character of human emancipation. The goals of enlightenment and emancipation which form a cornerstone of critical theory are not without their weaknesses. Prima facie, it sounds reasonable enough to say that by the same logic of self-preservation that brought men to involve themselves in the social-system-turned-external-authority (what he calls "this external destiny") they must also eventually liberate themselves from it.[24] Yet, Habermas and others have not sufficiently dramatized how problematic it is for populations in the modern world to think their way to liberation. As Giddens points out, the thesis that awareness of the conditions of human social life leads ipso facto to the achievement of control over them reveals the confusion involved in the discussions on the dissolution of reification.[25]

The essence of a critical theory of society is that it is not concerned only with the goals already imposed by existent ways of life, but with men and all their potentialities. It never aims simply at an increase of knowledge as such, but rather with man's emancipation from himself.[26] Consequently, critical theory lives by anticipation of a total social subject, the validity of its findings being bound up with the efficacy of a liberating interest in cognition.[27]

This idea is rooted in Habermas's metatheoretical scheme and his conception of types of science. According to Habermas the different kinds of theory can be distinguished according to their formative processes and their knowledge-constitutive interests. Thus, he argues, the empirical analytical sciences (or theory) take labor as their formative process or essential problematic; their interest, in turn, is in the instrumental and technical control of that process. On the other hand, the historical-hermeneutic theory's major problematic is interaction, and the chief knowledge-constitutive interest of such theory is understanding. Finally, critical theory differs from the preceding two traditions in that its "formative process" or problematic is domination - socio-culturally constructed forms of restrictive arrangements, including idea-systems. Critical theory's interest then is in emancipation from the domination of science and technology as ideaology, from illegitimate authority, and from distorted (partial) communications. The knowledge generated by critical theory, Habermas argues, is self-reflective, and is potentially capable of providing the subject with emancipatory insights aimed at realizing autonomy and freedom from distorted (dominant) forms of consciousness and practice.[28]

Habermas, who is the chief exponent of this interpretation of the modern world, suggests that it is the singular achievement of the ideology of science and technology to detach society's self-understanding from the frame of reference of communicative action and from the concepts of symbolic interaction, and to replace it with a "scientific" model. Accordingly, the culturally-defined self-understanding of social life-world (Husserl) is replaced by the self-reification of men and women under categories of purposive - <u>rational</u> action and adaptive behavior. Analytically, one can distinguish between Production Science, which is geared to profit maximization and for the accumulation of capital; and Social Control science, related to protection against potential external enemies and to the development of techniques for the pacification, manipulation and control of the indigenous population.[29]

Along the line of thinking about the "empirical analytical science" with its technical interest in manipulation, prediction, and control, Habermas presents another element of his position in social theory. It amounts to the thesis that in the modern period, technology and science have achieved a status which makes them the major source of wealth (and domination). Consequently, this is seen as a key development which renders inoperative the conditions for Marx's labor theory of value.[30] Habermas goes even further than that. <u>Legitimation Crisis</u> carries the critique of Marx resolutely along and moves beyond Marx by arguing that the crisis tendencies, as structurally inherent contradictions within capitalism, are no longer located immediately in the economic sphere, but in the socio-cultural. In other words, to the degree that politics and economics have become fused in the current period, there is a new requirement within capitalism: direct legitimation for political power which facilitates state intervention and <u>permanent</u> regulation of the economy. This development, which amounts to a repoliticization of the institutional framework and of issues, means that issues are increasingly defined in technical terms, requiring technical solutions by self-appointed experts and technicians. Politics thus appears to be increasingly a function of "objective" exigencies that <u>must</u> be obeyed, if the (assumed) needs of society <u>are</u> to be met. This development, it can be seen, is manifested in the plethora of <u>injunctions</u> in Canadian politics, as attempts are made to either discredit or suppress the power of the working class, in order to generate more surplus value out of them. It often seems that if they have any freedom, it is freedom to be exploited.

There are a number of problems with this inter-pretation. First, it seems that Habermas is very close to throwing out the baby with the bath-water. For in taking up the cultural dimension of Marxism (undoubtedly masterfully and creatively) and of

dialectical social theory, he may have dislodged, somewhat, the key link between a materialist critique and
the contemporary manifestation of cultural domination.
If emancipation from the modern versions of domination
is to come about, then that emancipation, it seems to
us, must be premised on both a materialist critique
which maintains the ontological centrality of labor,
and a critique of socio-cultural domination. A second
point is this: the actual structural conditions under
which work (or labor) transpires under capitalism have
changed drastically since Marx's time. But that in no
way suggests that critical theory must weaken its grasp
and critique of political economy. It is true that
critical theory fully accepts Marx's critique of
political economy, even though it severely diminishes
the role of the proletariat as a revolutionary force.
This aspect of critical theory became especially
problematic after the humiliating defeat of the German
working class by fascism, and the veritable integration
of western working classes into predatory capitalism.
But Marx, too, recognized that a theory, such as
critical theory, would conceivably face situations
where the people to whom the theory was directed either
reject or show indifference to its revelations, even
though such interpretations are rooted in their
existential self-understandings. This was why Marx
said that consciousness was a thing the proletariat
must acquire, even if they don't want to.[31] Even
against these eventualities, the role of critical
theory remains one of clarifying and demystifying the
actual existing situations. As such, it remains,
essentially, a de-reifying force, a pioneer and a
badger, an invertive revolutionary praxis.

      A final point concerns Marx's critique of culture.
It is easy to see that Marx did not develop a full-
fledged critique of culture. But this in no way
suggests that he was totally unmindful of the
tendencies toward the kind of cultural domination which
we experience today. His analysis of "use-value"
versus "exchange-value," for instance, contains the
distinct idea that cultural juggling would always seek
to make a "use-value" of everything. In other words,
in the long run anything, initially produced for its
exchange-value, would acquire a "use-value" however
short-lived or transitory that use may be. In today's
society, mass advertising and coaxing, and the manipulation of symbols serve to convert most, perhaps all,
commodities into having some use-value. The whole of

247

Marx's discussion pertaining to the "anarchy of production," "overproduction" and "exchange" point to the fact that the modus operandi of capitalism, coupled with the profit motive propel it towards the mass consumption of its commodities, even if that consumption must be forced on to a given population.

In Canada, as in the rest of the industrialized world, we have built massive (seemingly sacred) industries on advertizing alone. It is an industry in which the packages are so designed that everything in them is consumed, or else is infinitely consumable. What is more, the instrumental transformation of potentially norm-challenging themes and symbols (such as those created by the countercultural movement of the last two decades) into saleable product for the de-sensitized mass market, demonstrates the essentially parasitic, opportunistic side of instrumental rationality. Very few consumers, as far as is known in Canada, have bothered to query the ends of mass advertizing, never mind thinking that those ends may in fact diminish rather than enrich our cultural lives. It is important, then, for critical theory to include in its swath a sustained critique of science and culture. And in this sense Habermas is right in pointing out to us that "a critical theory of society can no longer be constructed in the exclusive form of a critique of political economy." For Marx, despite his brilliance, perhaps because of his emphasis on economic and political structures, under-estimated the socio-cultural aspects of capitalism. In the late stages of capitalism, the period in which we are now living, the symbolic communicative side of capitalist domination, and in particular the problem of distorted communica-tion, are not given the kind of analyses they demand, at least not by orthodox Marxists. Not only that, but the increase in state intervention which has come to characterize modern industrial society as a way to secure the system's stability, requires a rejuvenated critique.

The need for such a critique is seen as imperative. Thus Schroyer has carefully reasoned that we need a science that is capable of recognizing the ways in which existing structures exploit, alienate and repress human possibilities. Schroyer argues for critical science whose primary focus must be the critique of domination.[32] The basic argument for the development of this science is two-fold: first, because what he

calls "scientized civilization" with its one-sided
instrumental concept of reason, blocks our capacity to
recognize the socio-cultural significance of our acts,
and lowers our ability to act intelligently in novel
situations. Consequently, as a people we are becoming
less able to reformulate our identity and less capable
of recognizing the need for re-examination of our
values, actions, and institutions. But second, because
of Marx's oversight which we previously mentioned. The
avowed aim of Schroyer's The Critique of Domination
itself is to relate the political-economic and cultural
forms of critical theory, as well as to develop a
theory which can serve as a force and as a meaningful
structure of ideas that would foster the understanding
of domination, domination being "coerced control of
human behavior, the result of denying cultural soverei-
gnty and liberty to people to interpret their own
needs."[33] One key role of such a theory, is a
critique of ideology, or what Schroyer calls "those
belief systems which can maintain their legitimacy
despite the fact that they could not be validated if
subjected to rational discourse."[34]

        Schroyer, like other cultural Marxists, still
insists that the central task of critical theory is the
cultivation of a general enlightenment of the population in order that they may prosecute a struggle
against instrumental domination, and eventually
emancipate themselves from "repressive communication."
The scholars of the Frankfurt School, notably Marcuse
and Habermas, have systematically sketched a
communication theory of society. But there is still an
initial deficiency in Marx which has not been met,
which explains why "Marx was unable to really unite his
profound critique of capitalist development and his
theory of revolution."[35] Understandably, in assessing
the work of the Frankfurt School of critical theorists,
Schroyer gives the greatest credit to Habermas, for his
systematic study of distorted communication, for his
clarification of the categorical framework of a
critical materialism, and his reflexive comprehension
of the relation of knowledge to the cognitive interests
of the human species. While Schroyer does not spell
out what distorted communication is, Marxists have
understood it to mean the many forms of unnecessarily
restricted, and perhaps therefore prejudiced, communication that intrinsically inhibit a full public discussion of problems, issues, ideas and intellectual
currents. Distorted communication, as we discussed

249

above, is <u>manipulated</u> communication. Habermas's perspective is seen to derive from the transcendental philosophy of Kant, and from Hegel's phenomenological reflection upon the formation of consciousness. It is argued, further, that Habermas' dialectical theory amounts to a metatheory, a reconstruction of Marx's critical materialism which reveal two moments of material synthesis: one, the transhistorical evolution of human society through human productive praxis; and two, the reflexive self-formation of class struggle. Both mechanisms, constituted as active production and praxis, are essential to the emancipation of men and women. The innovative and lasting contribution of Habermas lies in his attempt to develop that component of critical theory which was neglected by Marx's critique of political economy, namely, a communication theory of society. Critical science, in contrast to positivism, is

> a historically generated and
> necessarily ongoing attempt to
> understand and transform the human
> world in accordance with the basic
> interest of human emancipation
> from domination.[36]

The Limits of Critical Theory

A theory may face severe limitations while at the same time will not be summarily without merit. This is the case with critical theory. We have already suggested that one of the limits of critical theory concerns the problem of translating "enlightenment" or structural knowledge into emancipatory action. Yet the fact that the theory insists that the concepts which it employs must embody a determinate <u>possibility</u> of a new social situation is to its merit. It certainly cannot guarantee that that possibility will be realized; any "proof" of its correctness can only be shown in the actual realization of the changes it advocates. As Schroyer aptly remarked: Theory can be used as a general interpretive scheme for the reconstruction of self-development processes that involve domination. But it cannot in itself "force" emancipation.[37] The role of critical theory has to be assessed in the light of its own structural locus. For, as we have reasoned throughout, the cultivation of a deep understanding of modern society does not happen automatically, and even where critical theorists seek to "educate" toward the objective possibility of transforming society, they have to compete with the thoroughly sophisticated tutelage of bourgeois ideology. The admission which critical theorists from Marx to Marcuse have made, is that critical theory does not propose to know the truth. The critical theory has limits, the same limits as any theory of social change: qua theory it is incapable of putting the results of its analysis into action, and must give way to praxis. As Marx put it, we do not come doctrinally forward with a new principle, saying: here is the truth, kneel down... We show them [the proletariat] only why they actually struggle.[38]

With acknowledgements like this, it is hardly surprising that many critical theorists have kept clear of formulating a truly revolutionary program commenserate with their theoretical ideas, and some of them (for example, Horkheimer and Adorno) were even rather distressed at the specific use or "application" of their theories made by the radical student rebellions of the 1960's. Their deep pessimism and their recognizable ambivalence are to be regarded as a "limitation" of their theory. Of course (and this is germane), such pessimism is thoroughly grounded in a structural understanding of modern society. Nevertheless it constitutes the second major limitation often cited. Let us dwell on this for a moment.

This pessimism must be understood against the broader historical canvas and experiences of the Frankfurt theorists. It is not unfounded pessimism, although one must admit that it weakens their overall thrust. From their exiled situation in America, the Frankfurt theorists observed, helplessly, the triumph of racism in Europe, and closer yet, in America, the exaltation of a mindless consumer society epitomized in such works as Galbraith's The Affluent Society, together with the de-stinging of any radical ideas that may have been latent in the American working class. Indeed, the unprecedented levels of State intervention into the affairs of the economy was proof positive that capitalism was not going to be left alone to dig its own grave. History would disavow Marx's insights into political economy through a process of "self-refuting prophecy," and not because Marxian concepts have become petrified or because class analysis is redundant within the structure of monopoly capitalism.

Against the background of a structural understanding of late capitalism, many critical theorists were bound to reason that the stability of the capitalist system in the West could no longer be shaken or seriously undermined, and Marcuse, at any rate, looked to the Third World for the impetus to transform the all-powerful system (see his "The obsolescence of Marxism"). Other observers, while wary of the instability of late capitalism, see no positive outcome at all, in view of the system's capacity to contort the consciousness of modern population. And all of this ambivalence seems to create what has been termed as unnecessary "historical pessimism,"[39] a stance which in the final analysis entertains the denial of the possibility of emancipatory struggle. Marcuse's position in his early works, notably One Dimensional Man, reveals the depth of such pessimism, even a defeatist posture, for his thesis clearly spelled out that advanced industrial society was capable of generating new and all-pervasive forms and instruments of cultural domination, the end result of which was the debasement of human beings to "one-dimensional," de-sensual, pseudo-beings. The worse of this situation, at least for Marcuse, was that the forms of social control and domination were linked to the very affluent character of modern society, and to the sophisticated and ubiquitous justificatory ideology of mass consumption, so much so that people come to "recognize themselves in their commodities: they find their soul in their automobile, hifi set, split level home, kitchen equipment." Critique is swallowed, extinguished.

It is frequently presented as a limitation of critical theory that since Marx's predictions concerning the developments within capitalism did not hold true, then in effect something must be radically amiss with the Marxian paradigm. It is argued, for instance, that it must be regarded as a limitation of critical theory the fact that the conceptions of the theory, especially in its formative years, did not fully comprehend the possibility that late capitalism could stabilize itself for an extended period of time.[40] And, if carried back to Marx, he underestimated the capacity of capitalism to manage economic fluctuations and contradictions within its structure, and, more seriously, underestimated the symbolic communicative side of capitalist domination, as we discussed above. Therefore, the charge goes, he did not take into account, sufficiently, the potential of the late stages of capitalism to utilize linguistic distortions and other cultural accoutrements as a legitimizing technique and as an effective instrument of domination. Clearly, the major problem which Marx encountered is the problem of the inherent tentativeness of all long-range social science forecasts: they will either be self-fulfilling or else they will be self-refuting. There is nothing in social science theory which requires that "accurate" and true predictions be made about future human thought and action. His critical theory was conceived during an early and transitional phase of capitalism. That he did not see all the possible permutations of its future development is not enough to destroy his otherwise critical and accurate analysis of society.

Furthermore, however, those who constantly proclaim that Marx's predictions are falsified by history and that that thereby demolishes his theory, have not fully understood his work or the society he was addressing. Given the traditional maximum misunderstanding of Marx's theory, and the cultivated indifference to his ideas in North American sociology, much of those positions attributable to ideological delirium, it is not surprising that so many have come to see Marxian analyses as outdated, and his predictions unconfirmed. Such claims notwithstanding, Marx's theory of capitalism is quite consistent with many of the modern manifestations of the capitalist economy. For instance, the overproduction of commodities (for exchange value); the periodic but "managed" crises as indices of the inherent irrationality of capitalism's structural dynamics; the tendential fall of the rate of profit; the dialectical creation of the "surplus class" as advanced capitalism jettisons labor from the productive process by "lay-offs" of productive labor; the obsession with continual expansion and the ecological costs and other social consequences of ruthless profit-seeking. In short, the phenomena of production, exchange, price, credit and the market being plagued with contradictions which make for crises, were clearly prefigured in Marx's own theory.[41] And all of these contradictions can be identified in the capitalist economy of today. The contradiction-in-process precipitate the crises; and the crises will not be eliminated, given the very way the economy works. The drive for surplus value and the concomitant ideology of growth and what Marx called the "entanglement of all peoples in the net of the world-market" must structurally lead to crises. To have foreseen these structural tendencies on the basis of his analysis of nineteenth century capitalism is undoubtedly one of his lasting accomplishments.

But there is room for the argument that Marx underestimated the extent to which the true believers in capitalism would go to ideologically defend and buttress its existence. Nor did he imagine how they would learn from maverick economists how to control recession and accept the permanence of twentieth century booms and busts, or even sacrifice the laissez-faire principle in order to save the structure as such. What the cultural Marxists from Lukacs to Habermas have done is to articulate that the very formation of rationalized subsystems destroys any objective image of the whole and promotes instead an internal incapacity to grasp these systems. In Schroyer's words:

> The index to crises is here the
> degree of blindness to the source
> of crises that permeates a
> rationalization process. For
> example, the great depression of
> the 1930s and the utter inability
> of businessmen or social scientists
> to objectify the crises is a case
> in point.[42]

If technology, as man's creation, has achieved a domination over nature and man, then a second self-creating praxis is needed in order to liberate free man from his own designs. In fact, however, to the extent that we have lost a critical, dialectical notion of reason we are left without meaningful and tangible guides for emancipatory activity. To the extent that the knowledge we have of how the total package functions, is in unconnected fragments, no real understanding is provided.

The cultural Marxists have simply demonstrated what was latent in Marx, who foresaw the possibility of production controlling human needs themselves. No one who has looked at The Grundrisse can doubt this. So Marcuse's central thesis in One Dimensional Man, minus the pessimism, is but a reformulation of Marx's model of capitalist society. What is important in Marcuse is that he

goes on to point out that the
productive forces of advanced
industrial society have become
so powerful that a qualitatively
different form of domination has
emerged... The difference
ushered in by the development of
a higher technological rationality
is not visible, but has been
mystified by the seeming
"rationality" of the whole.[43]

Marx's reflections come out clearly in the Grundrisse
where he notes that the possibility of proletarian
revolution is not a simple deduction from the labor
theory, but is rather contingent upon capitalism's
own contradictions-in-process. He therefore had an
insight into the tendency that will make for some
breakdown in capitalism (or contrariwise, increased
state intervention to mend and manage those break-
downs).[44]

A third limitation, pointed out by Hamilton, is
one that has frequently been suggested for other
theoretical systems besides critical theory. This is
the presumed "unscientific" nature of the theory. It
has been argued, for instance, that hermeneutical
reflection or interpretation as a "methodology" ought
not to be termed scientific, since such methods lack a
systematic means of verifying or testing hypotheses.
In the eyes of the analytic-empirical tradition, any
subjective interpretation of social life by a theory,
effectively disqualify it from inclusion in any but the
most general notion of "science."[45] This same objection has been raised against participant observation,
against ethnomethodology and against symbolic interactionism, and it is the capital issue raised by the
logical positivists against interpretive understanding
and its role as a verifiable source of "data." But the
germane issue, surely, is not whether or not the theory
conforms to the traditional (empiricist) conceptions of
science, but whether it provides the kind of deep
insight into previously ignored or culturally camouflaged social and historical processes.

Besides (and this is what must be grasped), the
fact that critical theory does not free-wheel into
"empirical research" in the traditional sense, carries
some profound implications. Principally, the crux of

the matter is that critical theory is not to be understood as [just] another sociological theory on the same
level as functionalism, symbolic interactionism and so
on. Rather, it is as Paul Piccone neatly puts it, a
Hegelian Marxism interested in the present as a part of
an historical process inextricably constituted by both
the past that provides the structure of the present,
and a future that determines its dynamic. The temporal
structure of this theoretical mediation is such that
its meaning cannot be captured in quantitative data
whose determinations fix reality in timeless abstrac-
tions thereby losing precisely what is most valuable:
becoming.[46] Critical theory is, nevertheless, informed
by evidence at every stage.

The key difference between the way it assesses
data and the way traditional theory interprets data is
simply that critical theory leans more toward the idea
that sociology (theory and practice) ought to make the
examination of its own rules a problematic topic for
analysis. This entails a reflexivity that permits open
admission of the ground rules for adopting interpretive
schemes. Traditional theory argues instead that there
is no possibility of epistemological self-reflection of
the sciences. For Habermas, it is precisely the
essence of positivism to deny and refuse reflection and
thereby to deny the critique of knowledge which is the
task of modern philosophical discussions; besides, a
critique of knowledge is possibly only in the form of
social theory. Habermas has probably infuriated more
sociologists than he has stimulated, and there is a
continuing debate in the current literature about the
merits and demerits of his excursion into metatheoretical investigations. We have, throughout the
preceding pages, shown what sorts of issues and topics
are of paramount interest to him, and we have also
shown that he is largely responsible for bringing into
focus some of the highly elusive and slippery ideas of
socio-political life. But he is not without his sharp
critics, and we shall have occasion to point to some of
the kinds of questions raised by recent critics against
his ideas. Before that, however, the fourth criticism
of critical theory in general.

It is a common charge of critical theory that in
its contemporary shape it has not been related
concretely to its social situation: Divorced from an
intense concern with the ongoing active forms of
opposition, critical theory loses its distinctive

characteristic and assumes a regular position within the Academic (and social) division of labor.47 It should be noted that the contention is that the isolation of the Frankfurt School from political practice is in part <u>responsible</u> for the pessimism and ever growing sense of impotence of critical theory. But is it that simple? As we have reasoned above, the pessimism is rooted in a profound and <u>deep understanding</u> of the current functioning of modern society, and would not therefore necessarily change even if the theorists became immersed in political practice. Indeed, it is quite possible that if they became so immersed they would lose most of their keen perception and critical grasp of political economy. This leaves the question unanswered, nevertheless, of where theory should meet practice. If it is utterly important that critical theory be applied to political and social life, it may very well be that the sociologist has to be a harbinger and catalyst of radical social change. In the case of the Frankfurt theorists, it is not enough to suggest that because the theorists have been huddled behind academic walls, they therefore chose to be incurable pessimists. Their own situation was a lot more complicated than that.

Because Habermas is (aside from Marcuse) the best known and certainly the most controversial figure of the Frankfurt School, we will state some of the major criticisms that have been levelled against his work, and, for convenience, take these to mean criticism against the School as such. Among the various criticisms made of Habermas's substantive ideas, as opposed to his style, is this many-dimensional one by Giddens: <u>first</u>, a failure to break radically enough with the <u>residue</u> of the <u>erklaren/verstehen</u> opposition with consequent difficulties for Habermas's treatment of the interconnections of the nomological and hermeneutic. <u>Second</u>, the unsatisfactory character of Habermas's fundamental distinction between labor and interaction, which has the effect that the latter becomes treated as equivalent to symbolic communicative action. <u>Third</u>, the persistence of a strongly marked Hegelian strain in the posited relations between "self-reflection" and autonomy, especially in Habermas's earlier works, such that the transformative capacity of human action is not adequately connected to rational understanding of conditions of action. <u>Fourth</u>, the associated reliance upon a psycho-analytic model of ideology critique which does not effectively illuminate the conjunction of differentials of power and asymmetries of material interests between groups in society. Fifth, the dearth of a theory of reference which would tie in Habermas's more recent discussions of truth as the redemption of validity claims in theoretical discourse to the themes of his preceding treatment of self-reflection.[48]

On the other hand, it has recently been argued that Habermas's criticisms of nineteenth and twentieth century philosophy - especially scientism and hermeneutics - offer original interpretations along with radically new proposals for epistemology. Besides that, his theories of knowledge-constitutive interests and a communicative competence rank as bold achievements in philosophy and his review of the philosophy of science provides one of the most systematic and coherent accounts of the field. Finally, his explication of the scientization of politics and his reworking of crises theory... is a novel framework for posing basic questions about past and contemporary society.[49] In sum, it must be remembered that the criticisms are voiced in the same breath which suggests that Habermas ranks as "one of the most pre-eminent of contemporary social philosophers who has done more than any other to bridge the chasm between Continental and Anglo-Saxon philosophies," and that critical theory, for all its weaknesses, "constitutes one of the major sources for contemporary social and political thought," and "makes one of the major sources of stimulus in twentieth century philosophical and social thought."[50]

Finally, critical theory's contention that modern industrial society is unmistakably dominative and irrational has been seen by some to represent a clear case of "overkill." Quinton, for instance, argues that if the charge means that society can be improved and that many institutions do not serve the purposes that men want them to, or do so only at extravagant cost, then the charge is quite acceptable. However, if the claim is that modern society is uniquely and hyperbolically dominative, then the charge cannot be accepted.[51] This criticism fails to recognize the pervasive nature of the domination that concerns critical theorists - from the ubiquitous fast-talking television salesperson ("commercial break") to the highly sophisticated and eager cash registers at coldly impersonal supermarkets that print out "thanks" for cash received. Enough evidence has been meticulously

258

amassed by critical theorists to dramatize and to confirm beyond all doubt that modern science as it is anchored to technological rationality, even if not inherently dominative or repressive is infinitely debilitating.

It may well be, as Meyer has argued, that in the final analysis critical theory's limits are also perhaps its chief virtues. For the breadth of its vision, coupled with its esoteric language are not in themselves without merit. As he put it, the language may serve more as a barrier to understanding than as a communications medium. However, the language is esoteric not only because it serves to convey exceedingly complex ideas and relationships, but also, in part, because it originated in continental rather than Anglo-American philosophy.[52] It is, then, the theoretical seriousness of these theorists which, to some extent, has prevented the wholesale carnage of their views and has preserved for us the sharpness of the profile of modern industrial society, and of the various sciences and claims to knowledge. This way we can at least recognize just what it is that, as sociologists, we seek to understand, and to engage in research about. It is not true that critical theory has been divorced from the ongoing concerns of everyday life or that it has assumed the regular just-another-theory posture within the university set up. Rather, it daily struggles to secure a serious audience, and to be allowed the opportunity to present its case. And here is where it confronts its true political test. For, as Ritzer has pointed out,

> One paradigm wins out over another because its supporters have more power than those who support competing paradigms and not necessarily because their paradigm is "better" than its competitors. For example, the paradigms whose supporters control the most important journals in a field and thereby determine what will be published are more likely to gain preeminence than paradigms whose adherents lack access to prestigious outlets for their work.[53]

All of this throws into sharp relief the fundamental

259

importance of the linkage between interests and knowledge in society, and sheds much light on the ways in which people undertake the social construction and the social destruction of reality. All of this leaves critical theory, as the most radical of all the anti-positivist schools of meta-science, partly to the whims and wishes of a supposed free market-place of ideas. The trouble is, the ideas contained in critical theory seek to challenge the very legitimacy and pretentions of this same market-place; critical theory challenges, in fact, a good deal of what passes for sociology, not least because so much of conventional sociology deletes the specific ontological assumptions about humankind.

All in all, the literature pertaining to critical theory reveals a wide range of criticisms directed at Habermas or at the school as a whole. When they focus directly on Habermas they invariably include reference to his style, which, Rex claims, lends toward the mystification of social reality. We have already raised some queries about the supposed congruence of knowledge and emancipation, and about the modelling of social theory on the psychoanalytic paradigm. But perhaps the most telling criticism as far as the tone of this book is concerned is the one which charges critical theory with the "tendency to lapse into ... and encourage a complete 'politicization' of scholarly inquiry and of the university as a whole."[54] It is on account of such criticisms that critical theory exists in a state of perpetual tension within the still firmly entrenched tradition of "value-free" social science and the liberal university.

It might now be incontestably clear that, as we said at the beginning, to add yet another book to the legion already existing in the field of "theory" is to encourage the cynicism of sociologists. And some might well now ask: Is there anything to this book that hasn't already been said "hundreds of times." On the other hand, it is hoped that the very tone in which certain ideas are presented here will serve to dislodge whatever collusion of mediocrity there might be between students and teachers in the articulation of social theory. We have wished that the polemical thrust of this small project would stimulate and even disturb sedimentary thought, reactivate certain questions and revive certain arguments in the continuing effort to understand and explain modern society.

This idiosyncratic encounter with social theory has reaffirmed the importance of critical structural analyses as the prerequisite for grasping the limitations and possibilities of our period of the twentieth century. There was no intention here to "force" critical theory on the reader. But to the extent that an encounter with this perspective creates its own uncertainties, tensions and doubts, it may perhaps serve to forge a macro-diagnosis of modern industrial society. To engage in theoretical thinking often seems to leave more questions than answers, and such difficulties have not been overcome by critical theory. As Held has argued, while the critical theorists have convincingly exposed some of the major flaws of certain traditional and conventional approaches to philosophy and social investigation, they have not adequately demonstrated that critical theory has a special theoretical status; that is, they have not resolved a whole series of epistemological and methodological issues they intended to settle or render redundant. Yet, as a theory which seeks deliberately to foster critical understanding, the Frankfurt scholars have "contributed extensively to the debates and disputes over what constitutes the 'scientific' and what does not."[55] Finally, they have forged an urgent project for "uncovering and exposing the factors which currently make positive claims about the possibility of revolutionary change in the West appear a mere fantasy."[56]

If, as it is often claimed, a science advances by being always alert to its own uncertainties and doubts, then the ambivalences, tentativeness and doubts of the Frankfurt theorists are not to be seen in purely negative terms. No one who has sifted their ideas can doubt that they have delivered some profound insights into the workings of modern society: from the growth of state intervention, to the entrenchment of technological "reason," to the diminshed opportunities for negotiated consensus in society. They have alerted us to implications of a shift of crises from the economic to the political sphere with all the intellectual and ideological consequences that that shift entails. And they have shown the Welfare State to be politically and ideologically repressive, by necessity; that is, since statism does not fundamentally affect (or intend to affect) the essential features of the capitalist system, it is bound to be repressive if it is to assure capitalism's continuing extraction of surplus value from an increasingly depoliticized, inert,

261

working class. Moving us far beyond any account available in conventional liberal theories, the critical theorists have sharpened our awareness of the pervasive nature of domination in modern society, in all its various forms and in the different spheres of life. This searchlight has also contributed to our grasp of the complex factors which prevent modern populations from developing a structural sense of understanding of a world which, nevertheless, they have made and are continually helping to make.

It is possible, in light of even this brief introduction to the ideas of critical theory, to conclude that there is a lasting appeal to the theories offered concerning modern society and its sophisticated relations. The cutting edge of the theories of the School is an immanent critique, one which systematically evaluates modern society by calling into question the abdication of what that society promised, at its inauguration, to achieve or what it historically could do. Critical theory's raison d'être, in contrast to other types of critiques, is to situate critique within the very internality of society as it is.

Eventually, the basic questions for this and all other theories of society must be: (a) how much should we expect from a theory?; and (b) what do we expect a theory to do? The position taken in this book is that the critical tradition has immeasurably deepened our understanding of the ontological tension between humankind and their struggle with nature and society. Critical theory, more than any other paradigm in sociology has uncovered the double dialectic of life: that between human beings and society; and that between human beings and nature. In the process, this paradigm has also sharpened our historical sense of human possibilities. The clear, unfettered understanding of these processes is what we most need to achieve as a result of studies in social theory.

Dilemmas and Contradictions in Modern Social Theory

One of the persistent themes that runs through sociology as a discipline is the acknowledged absence of any general consensus on how to "do" sociology. The discipline is fragmented by a variety of perspectives and conceptual frameworks, each seeking to provide an "adequate" explanation of the world around us. In particular, sociology is plagued with serious disagreements about (a) what is and is not an appropriate problem; (b) what is and is not "adequate" or "good" evidence; (c) the definition, aims and purposes of theory; (d) what are proper techniques for investigating a particular problem. These are basic, yet rather devastating problems and they show, amongst other things, that sociology is not nearly as sure-footed as many sociologists seem to think. It is therefore appropriate, in this final section of the book, to reflect upon some of the more important issues and ingrained debility which mark contemporary sociology.

Given the lack of clear specification of something so basic as what constitutes a good problem, doing sociology is an enterprize fraught with dilemmas and contradictions. It seems that where we may be right, we are not original; and where we are original, we are not right, since, as we have already remarked, some say we have not discovered anything new since the great masters propounded their theories. Others claim that perhaps we have enough theory, and all that we need now are fresh insights into already existing situations so that we can interpret anew our own historical period. But then, when sociologists seek to add something new to the literature and to the existing body of knowledge, or seek simply to generate fresh insights, there is the grave risk that they will be accused of doing nothing new and different, and nothing truly original. Originality or heuristic innovations are key conditions for   ideas taken seriously, according to the standard ethos in social science.

Yet this posture is highly hypocritical, and is definitely at variance with the historical evidence relating to novel ideas in sociology. The case of ethnomethodology can be cited to illustrate this point. When Harold Garfinkel published his highly innovative and novel approach to social life (Ethnomethodology), sociologists were, to judge from their public outcry, almost ashamed of it. For some (and one suspects a small minority) ethnomethodology was a qualitative advance beyond conventional sociology, at least in some very important ways. For many others it was: "old sociology in new clothes"; "what sociologists have been doing for years"; "basically well-trodden ground"; "sociology without society"; "a new name for old practices"; "the new conservatives"; "sociology of the absurd"; and so on.[57] Lewis Coser, as President of the American Sociological Association, attacked ethno-methodology as "trivia" and as an "orgy of subjectivism and a self-indulgent enterprize" which he claimed was

> a massive cop-out, a determined
> refusal to undertake research that
> would indicate the extent to which
> our lives are affected by the socio-
> economic context in which they are
> embedded.[58]

In essence, a fresh and decidedly innovative re-interpretation of the taken-for-granted rules that govern our lives and actions, was seen as not nearly enough. But why?

The answer is that the great bulk of North American sociologists see themselves as engaged in the building of a science (whether or not they clearly understand what science is) or the fundamental implications of the sociology of science. However, this means, further, that first and foremost most sociologists accept and argue for the appropriateness of the natural science model for the development of contemporary sociology and for the study of social phenomena. Form this point of view, sociology seeks to be a science of the same type as biology or physics, where the goal of investigation is to construct laws or law-like generalizations, so that human conduct, like nature, can be explained and predicted.[59] This search for some underlying "scientific law" in society and the striving for a "social physics" goes back to the titular founder of sociology, Auguste Comte, and has always taken centre-stage in the development of sociology since then with a number of attendant contradictions and dilemmas. Among the results of this orientation has been the leading of sociology away from the understanding of the intersubjective behavior and interpretive competence of ordinary persons. As well, this viewpoint claims for science a superior status, as the unique, even pure, body of knowledge.

According to Karl Popper (whose view of science is highly respected in the current period) science is separated from other forms of traditions insofar as its findings and theories are, in principle, capable of being exposed to empirical testing and therefore to potential falsification. In the Popperian view, scientific method is distinctive in that the scientist aims to provide theoretical conjectures that are falsifiable, and the scientist is then enjoined to actually try to falsify his own theoretical conjectures - hence the title of his well-known book: Conjectures and Refutations.[60] When the scientist succeeds in falsifying his conjectures, this should be viewed, according to Popper, as a success, and he should then go on to propose a hypothesis of greater empirical content which should in turn be subjected to falsification, and so on. Such seems to be the ideal of the practice of science; the content of science is quite another matter.

Now, while this view of science seems at first to be foolproof and beyond reproach, it is important to recognize that the structure which Popper proposes is based on what he (and other members of his discipline perhaps) holds to be proper.[61] Sociologically, this is crucial, for it straightaway highlights the inescapable normative quality of science as human praxis. Several key points may be noted here: first, science is that intellectual enterprize or instrument of understanding concerned with elaborating and systematizing all forms of knowledge, including processes and relationships in the social world. But it is nevertheless one amongst others and must be comprehended epistemologically as one category of possible knowledge. Second, science as a distinctly human enterprize cannot completely escape the normative ingredient, and this, perhaps, explains why there have been many criteria used to distinguish science from other intellectual concerns, making it difficult to find a simple normative criterion that applies to all times and places. Clearly, there are and always have been, alternative ideologies of what science is or ought to be; that is, there are always alternative norms attempting to define what is scientific and what is not scientific. Thus, we cannot say, loosely, that science is simply knowledge-seeking, for that does not differentiate it from other kinds of intellectual pursuits, such as literature. And we may well ask: is the novel then science? Or is demography, or meteorology? Third, however, science is a cultural affair, distilled, preserved and "transmitted from one generation to the next, partly because it is valued in its own right, and partly because of its wide techno-logical applications."[62] It is a value, and like all values, is systematically contested. Finally, we owe to Thomas Kuhn the significant analysis concerning the social quality of science. In Kuhn's works we are reminded that there can be no universal criteria of truth (that which science claims to seek) nor indeed any transhistorical truth, since truth is a constructed consensus of a scientific community, liable to change from one time period to the next. Therefore, what ends up as truth, or what counts socially as science, is deeply dependent upon the consensus of the membership of the scientific community on its conception of what should pass for science, how science should be done, and eventually what criteria to accept. It is very difficult to see how we can have a totally non-normative natural science, let alone non-normative social science.63 As Habermas has shown, definite constitutive interests hide behind all knowledge claims.

Precisely because of its ability to yield coherently structured knowledge, science is inescapably grounded in specific socio-historical circumstances, for as the sociologists of knowledge constantly point out knowledge is a social/cultural product. Any attempt to elevate science to a universal epistemology misses this point. Science done within a particular social order reflects the norms and ideology of that social order, so that if we assume that norms change over time, scientific thought must also change and shift according to and in line with new historical periods and unfolding needs. A sociological paradigm which ignores this historical fact is ignoring a very important dimension of science. Popper himself reminds us that science never starts from scratch; it can never be described as free from assumptions, for at every moment it presupposes a horizon of expectations. Thus, today's science is built upon yesterday's science; and yesterday's science in turn, is based on the science of the day before. And the oldest scientific theories are built on pre-scientific myths, and these, in turn, on still older expectations.64 If there is a lesson in this view, it is that we cannot simply proceed on the assumption that the social world exists as some independent, lifeless phenomenon, and all that we have to do is to close in, like a predator on its prey, and apply the natural science model to the antics of the social world. In this remote fashion, some of Popper's ideas parallel the perspective of ethnomethodology. But by and large, conventional sociology subscribes to a model fundamentally at odds with the one advanced by ethnomethodology.

The theoretical perspective in sociology which closely follows a natural-science model is normally termed "positivist" or "neo-positivist" (traditional theory for Horkheimer). The modern-day sociologists who have gravitated to this perspective have used as their defense the simple argument that the social science can and ought to conform to the enviable standards set by the natural sciences. The standard view seems to be that any sociological work (theory and research) which does not meet the criteria of natural science is unworthy of serious consideration as a potential contributor to knowledge. Such work may, in fact, be dismissed off-hand on an a priori basis as "unscientific," "ideological," or worse, the implication being that science proper is somehow purified of ideology, values and interests. This brings us back to Garfinkel and ethnomethodology. If indeed science proceeds by challenging the seemingly obvious and well established thought patterns, styles of intellectual work and pet ideas, the ethno-methodoligical approach is radical, for instead of assuming a natural science paradigm with a "given" world of phenomena, ethnomethodology hoists the very nature of the social world as itself highly problematic.

It is clear that Garfinkel's study, for all its importance in helping us interpret and make intelligible the social world, did not comply with the natural-science model. Not only was it regarded then as unscientific, but there were strong hints that perhaps some ideology operated to help provide the final outcome, which in turn served to shield the work from its weaknesses and shortcomings. Yet the demarcation between science and ideology is not as clear cut as Althusser and others have tended to suggest. Some philosophers of science see ideologies in fact as attempts, like science, or religion, or myths, to make the world meaningful to specific sections of given societies. As such, the problem of ideology is both sociological and epistemological. Very often ideology and science not only compete; they are joined to provide a version of reality which may or may not reveal the world in the precise way in which multitudes of human beings experience it. When this happens inspite of sociology's efforts we can certainly speak of dilemmas and contradictions in the scheme of explanation. But "scientizing" that scheme, whether in sociology, or economics or politics does not ensure that we will automatically thereby explain more, or explain absolutely, beyond question. Social reality, and by extension science, does not rest, as Popper puts it, "upon solid bedrock." Ethnomethodologists are very conscious of this fact, and approach the social with the implications clearly in focus.

The human factor is what gives social theory its substantialism. That factor cannot be deleted, or if it is, we could not then speak so much of theory as of ideology. As Hamilton's very apt comment on economics reminds us, as an ideology, bourgeois economics is not straightforwardly either wrong or untrue, it is rather a systematically distorted cognitive structuring of reality in which the vital historical dimension of that reality is left completely out of account.[65]

The requirement of ethnomethodology to suspend belief in the existence of a pre-constructed social reality in order to be able to make the process of reality-construction itself an object of investigation, is a crucial one. In this requirement is an embryonic philosophical anthropology as well as an epistemological challenge. Sociologists frequently argue that they do not wish or want to get involved in epistemological disputes, but at the same time they claim that their own field - social science - rests upon a specific epistemological position, namely, the scientific one. This kind of dilemma and contradiction obscures the fact that the theory about the nature and scope of knowledge (epistemology) is central in deciding the "truth" or "falsity" of theoretical statements. Thus, no sociologist can work without an epistemology, or, for that matter, without taking a position on the ontological status of social reality.

Phenomenological sociologies, such as ethnomethodology have established sufficiently clearly that sociology stands in a more complex relation to its subject matter than the natural sciences do, and cannot therefore claim to rest on the same methodological or epistemological foundation. The natural world does not depend upon human recognition for its existence - the social world does. Natural phenomena are inherently meaningless; the social world is pre-eminently meaningful. Social events, unlike natural ones, do not simply occur; they are produced. Theories in the natural sciences are typically deductive, taking the form of universal statements from which certain connections are drawn - descriptions are potentially context-free; whereas the descriptions of a social scientist are not empty of meanings and consequently do not allow for the <u>same</u> deductive logic as that used in the natural sciences. Finally, the observer/researcher in the social sciences is already a member of the social world and cannot remove himself/herself from it. This is because the social world is an existential product of human praxis, created, sustained and changed through the human agent. It is an inter-subjective world, and in it the social scientist, in doing his work, faces a problem of double-hermeneutics where the natural scientist does not. In short, sociology is inescapably different from the natural sciences because its findings have consequences for human value-judgmental behavior.

As a critical reflection upon society, social theory will often appear to restate ideas of an earlier period or group of thinkers. But this is because, in social science, the ways of knowing and what is known are always in a process of change concomitantly with the dialectical change that characterizes human social development. It is not always the case that social theorists do no more than rehash old ideas and trample well-known ground; rather, they continually seek to reinterpret the on-going drama of human beings caught up in their own historical nets of social arrangements, and we have not satisfactorily understood or explained how, in the modern period, these arrangements tend to become our masters and means of domination. The anxiety amongst sociologists concerning the breaking of new ground lingers on for the same reason that anxiety obtains with respect to the "scientific status" of sociology: the majority of sociologists feel that only by continuous path-breaking "discoveries" can we accumulate knowledge about society, and only if such knowledge is derived via the model utilized in natural sciences are we likely to gain the respectability and status as professionals. But the concepts, findings and application of social theory remain, always, contested and self-consciously unfinished. And this is precisely why the <u>meta</u> aspect of sociology is so important. There <u>is a</u> strong and persistent tendency on the part of most sociologists to view <u>meta</u> as indicative of a prescientific state of a <u>discipline</u>, and as such ought to be quickly left behind. In fact, the position taken in this book is that <u>meta</u> designates the theoretically postulated aspects of <u>a science</u> or discipline. So designated, meta-sociological issues deal with the ontological and epistemological postulates necessary to render the theory and method of the discipline intelligible. In our haste to become "scientific" it would be tragic if we somehow manage to by-pass the meta-aspects of sociology just so that we can claim that whilst we have wandered away from sociology we are nevertheless accelerating full speed ahead.

Conclusion

It is the nature of sociological problems that they are never completely solved and laid to rest so that the sociologist can embark upon untrodden or unexplored areas. Rather, they typically subside in relative importance only to return to the sociological consciousness as the shifting boundaries of reality are sharpened or blurred from time to time. Given that the meaning, practice, and ideological importance of science are old, but far from being settled issues; and given that it is still being debated as to whether social research can be "disinterested," using "neutral techniques" to discover "good quality data," and so on, it is necessary to keep these debates alive in order to guard against the premature closure of inquiry. The dilemma which many sociologists find they must confront is a dilemma which poses human beings as social-relational beings in process, which means that their reality (like modern cities) is fundamentally unfinished, and undergoes a metamorphosis as a function of the historically evolved material conditions in which they find themselves. This does not mean that it is impossible to understand humankind. But it does mean that such understanding must be flavored with an historical understanding of human experience and with a reflectiveness (Kantian transcendentalism) which inquires back into the source of all the formations of knowledge. To a large degree, positivism closes off these dimensions; ethnomethodology wants them open.

All social theory is necessarily rooted in socio-historical situations, which means that objective social reality cannot be assumed to exist independently of the knowing, teleological human subject. The steady development of increasingly mathematically-sophisticated techniques for the explicit purpose of generating laws, has eclipsed conceptualization in sociology at the same time as it has failed to

historically situate humans <u>as subjects</u>, as being
intersubjectively in charge <u>of their</u> relations and
experiences in the production and reproduction of
everyday life. The social meaning of explanation in
sociology requires that sociology ground itself at the
level of intentionality, and inquire into and build on
the social meanings out of which humans construct their
actions. This is the promise of ethnomethodology. It
may very well be that the attempt to apply natural-
scientific modes of investigation to the social world
has taken us further and further away from the understanding of the problem of <u>meaning</u> and intentionality.
If that is the case, or even just a real possibility,
then a cardinal message in ethnomethodology, is worth
remembering, namely that the more "objective" our
observation or other methods become in social science,
the further we are removed from what we want to know.
The ongoing dilemma of ethnomethodology is that while
it presents a valid sociology of everyday life, it has
not succeeded in sharpening a critique of positivist
epistemology and presenting instead an adequate
epistemology which would itself be a social theory.

NOTES

1. G. Radnitzky, Contemporary Schools of Metascience, 1970, cited Israel, 1971, p. 346.

2. See, in this connection, Marcuse, 1962, 1964; Habermas, 1968a, 1968b, 1974; Horkheimer, 1974; Horkheimer & Adorno, 1972.

3. Unfortunately, the standard fare in conventional books on "sociological theory" never quite seem to grasp the fact that the majority of the theories discussed are responses to positivism and, in sociology, the leading positivist school: structural functionalism. It is no wonder that many students fail to see the point to it all. Somehow, the connection between positivism and its multiple critics tends to remain obscure. For a clear and systematic tracing of the entire anti-positivist tradition in social science, see Giddens, 1976a and 1977. Cf. also, Fay, 1975; and Filmer et.al., 1972. And for up-to-date excellent, thorough treatment of the entire Critical School tradition, see Jay, 1973; McCarthy, 1978; Arato and Gebhardt, 1978; and Held, 1980. An important, brief statement on the philosophical argument of Critical Theory is to be found in Garbis Kortian, Meta-critique: The Philosophical Argument of Jurgen Habermas, London: Cambridge University Press, 1980.

4. For Habermas's conception of critical social theory, and his key distinction between types of science, see Habermas, 1968b, pp. 214-272, 306-17; and 1969. On the distinction between "traditional" and critical theory see Horkheimer, 1972; Wellmer, 1971. For details of the nature of the bitter debate that occurred in German sociology, see Adorno, et.al., 1969; Connerton, 1976; and Giddens, 1977. Arato and Gebhardt (p. ix) point out that it is a myth to conceive of the School as comprising a single, unified critical theory of society.

5. Habermas, 1969, p. 133.

6. Horkheimer, 1972, esp. pp. 213-20, 242.

7. Leiss, 1972, p. 82.

8. Connerton, 1976, pp. 16-17; Hamilton, 1974, p. 62; Leiss, 1972, p. 76; Arato and Gebhardt, 1978, pp. xi-xxii; and Schroyer, 1973.

9. Farganis, 1975, p. 483; see, also, Gouldner, 1976, especially chapter 2.

10. The foregoing set of assumptions derive from Farganis' important article, 1975, p. 483.

11. See, e.g., Habermas, 1974; 1968b; and Fay, 1975, p. 109.

12. Fay, 1975, p. 109; Held, 1980, p. 245; cf. Marcuse, 1964, p. 120.

13. See, especially, Horkheimer, 1972, pp. 213-15, 242; Marcuse, 1964; and Habermas, 1968a; cf. Rex, 1974, pp. 10ff; Becker and Horowitz, 1972, pp. 52-53; Colfax & Roach, 1971, p. 16; and Taylor et.al., 1973.

14. Marcuse, 1964, pp. x-xi; Habermas, 1968b; and Adorno, et.al., 1969.

15. See Marcuse, 1968, pp. 134ff; and 1960, pp. 6ff.

16. Jay, 1973, pp. 61, 64.

17. Ibid.; see, also, Mills, 1959, pp. 170, 174, 205.

18. Ibid., p. 39. It was in response to both the historical naivety and anti-philosophical orientation in North American sociology that Mills made his barbed remarks at the end of the 1950s. In pointing out that young scholars lacked what he called a "genuine intellectual puzzlement" Mills continued: "They have taken up social research as a career; they have come early to an extreme specialization, and they have acquired an indifference or a contempt for 'social philosophy' - which means to them 'writing books out of other books' or 'merely speculating.' Listening to their conversations, trying to gauge the quality of their curiosity, one finds a deadly limitation of mind. The social worlds about which so many scholars feel ignorant do not puzzle them." (1959, p. 105).

19. See, e.g., Marcuse, 1964, p. 252; Leiss, 1972, pp. 79-80 et passim; also Leiss, 1974a. These articles contain some of the most illuminating ideas on critical theory currently available. They are indispensable for anyone wishing to acquire a grasp, at a glance, of the strengths and limitations of critical thought.

20. Giddens, 1976a, p. 102.

21. Horkheimer, 1972, pp. 211-244; and Wellmer, 1971, pp. 49-50.

22. Fay, 1975, p. 103-105.

23. Wellmer, 1971, p. 52.

24. Ibid., p. 130.

25. Giddens, 1976a, p. 126.

26. Horkheimer, 1972, pp. 245-46.

27. Wellmer, 1971, pp. 133, 35.

28. Habermas, 1968b, pp. 306-17.

29. Rose and Rose, 1976, chapter 2, from whom the idea of Production Science and Social Control Science derives.

30. Habermas, 1968a, pp. 92-106.

31. See Howard, 1970, p. 233; and cf. Fay, 1975.

32. Schroyer, 1973, p. 27.

33. Ibid., p. 22.

34. Ibid., p. 163.

35. Ibid., p. 133.

36. Ibid., p. 130.

37. Ibid., p. 247; and Leiss, 1972, p. 85.

38. Cited in Howard, 1970, p. 233.

39. See, e.g., Agger, 1977, p. 3 et passim; and
    Wellmer, 1971, p. 52. For further discussions on
    the limitations of critical theory, as well as
    constructive criticisms of it, see Held, 1980, pp.
    353-407; Keat, 1981, pp. 12-65.

40. Leiss, L972, pp. 91-92.

41. See, again, Marx, n.d., esp. chps. 24-26, and 32;
    1973, pp. 699-712. On the historical tendency of
    capitalist accumulation and the movement toward
    monopoly operations Marx gave us the following
    vivid picture: "One capitalist always kills many.
    Hand in hand with this centralization, or this
    expropriation of many capitalists by few, develop,
    on an ever-extending scale... the conscious
    technical application of science... the
    entanglement of all peoples in the net of the
    world-market, and with this, the international
    character of the capitalist regime... The
    monopoly of capital becomes a fetter upon the mode
    of production, which has sprung up and flourished
    along with, and under it. Centralization of the
    means of production and socialization of labor at
    last reach a point where they become incompatible
    with their capitalist integument..." (n.d., pp.
    714-15).

42. Schroyer, 1973, p. 203; and see the relevant
    essays in Birnbaum, 1977, esp. Supek's.

43. Ibid., p. 211.

44. See Marx, 1973, pp. 705-706.

45. Hamilton, 1974, p. 61. This view is also shared
    by Tar who speaks disparagingly of critical theory
    as neither "scientific" nor "Marxist." Zoltan Tar,
    The Frankfurt School: The Critical Theories of
    Max Horkheimer and Theodor W. Adorno, New York:
    Wiley, 1977. One of the big myths which has long
    been held by traditional theorists about the
    Frankfurt theorists is that the latter were anti-
    scientific. That that myth has now been
    thoroughly banished is clearly demonstrated in the
    recent works on the School. See, especially, "A
    Critique of Methodology" in Arato and Gebhardt,
    1978, pp. 371-406.

46. Paul Piccone, Review of Martin Jay's The Dialectical Imagination, Telos, Vol. 16, Summer, 1973, p. 147.

47. Leiss, 1972, p. 93; and Perry Anderson, Considerations on Western Marxism, London: New Left Books, 1976, especially p. 53.

48. Giddens, 1977, pp. 163-164.

49. Held, 1980, p. 364.

50. Giddens, 1977; and Held, 1980, pp. 353, 364. But for a completely different, and extraordinarily negative, dismissive assessment, see Axel van den Berg. "Critical Theory: Is There Still Hope?" American Journal of Sociology, Vol. 86, #3 (November) 1980. He concludes: ..."For all their moral commitments, the critical theorists have contributed absolutely nothing to any of these debates [concerning the substance of reason; about the possibilities of greater democratic participation; about the causes and possible reduction of inequalities of all kinds; etc.]. Instead, they have chosen the comfortable heights of philosophical abstraction and obscurity, far away from the daily concerns of the rabble. To expect any public support for a philosophy whose only distinction is its sheer obscurity, for a notion of reason lacking all substances, for a utopia without any indication of its features or feasibility has absolutely nothing to do with emancipation of any kind." To drive home the point, van den Berg ex cathedra cites one of his teachers who, in 1972, apparently revelled that the "pathologies of current radicalism is distinctly anti-emancipatory."

The most that one can say of this article is that it is mis-titled. There is more to "critical theory" than a "second generation led by Habermas." After all, up to his death in 1979, Marcuse was very much a contributor to the flow of ideas pointedly relevant to the content of the discussion pursued by van den Berg. It is therefore very interesting to note the omission of a single reference to any of the works of Marcuse.

51. See Quinton, 1974, p. 53; and cf. Held, 1980,

p. 366.

52. Meyer, 1975, p. 213.

53. Ritzer, 1975a, pp. 156-7.

54. Dallmayr, 1972b, p. 219; 1972a, p. 93.

55. Held, 1980, p. 359-60, 363, 399.

56. Ibid.

57. See, e.g., McNall and Johnson, 1975; Gidlow, 1972; Mayrl, 1973; and Lyman and Scott, 1970. These are only some of the more hostile responses of sociologists in the 1970s. Cf. footnote 58 below.

58. Coser, 1975, esp. pp. 696, 698. This remarkable address by the then President of the American Sociological Association sparked off a long and bitter debate in the sociology journals. See, for instance, the several articles that took issue with Coser's narrow interpretation, and Coser's reply in The American Sociologist, Vol. 11 (Feb.) 1976, pp. 4-38; and Giddens, 1976b; Bauman, 1973.

59. In this connection can be found old and new exponents. Amongst the older versions, see Lundberg, 1963, esp. pp. 33-72 and idem., 1955, pp. 191-202; also Zetterberg, 1965, esp. pp. 81-85; idem., 1962; Catton, 1966, esp. pp. 40-58. For some very recent renditions see Babbie, 1979; and Papineau, 1978. It can easily be seen that the standpoint of the modern-day positivists is somewhat dogmatic and anti-philosophical. Papineau, for instance, claims for his book no less than that it is a "defense of the view that the social sciences can and ought to conform to the standards set by the natural sciences"; while Babbie says that "human social behavior can be subjected to scientific study as legitimately as can atoms, cells, and so forth." These views can be taken to represent a very common, hard-nosed mode toward sociological issues and styles of operation.

60. Popper has never really deviated from this position over the years, inspite of works such as Kuhn's which seem to offer some serious and substantive challenges to Popper's own version of

science. Cf. Popper, 1965, 1972, pp. 285-89.

61. The intransigence of caricatural presentation in the disputes between competing paradigms or ideological positions is well demonstrated in Popper's own works. Thus, even as a scholar of great accomplishment, he has developed a particular notoriety for using his status and omnibus publications to denounce, discredit and dismiss any theory with which he does not agree, and surprisingly usually only after superficial misreading of those theories. He did that in The Open Society volumes, where he (erroneously) accused Marx and Engels of providing the blueprint for fascist tyranny and authoritarianism. A generation later, after only a brief and cursory encounter with critical theory, he dismissed the Frankfurt School theorists as trivial and mistaken. All in all, Popper has used his influence to build up what one author has termed a "shocking compendium of misrepresentations." For Popper's ideas so utilized, see his The Open Society...; and "Reason or Revolution?" in Adorno et.al., 1969. For a good rebuttal to Popper, see Cornforth, 1968.

62. Joseph Ben-David and Teresa Sullivan, "Sociology of Science," Annual Review of Sociology, Vol. 1, 1975, p. 203.

63. See Kuhn, 1962; and Ritzer, 1975a; 1975b. The vexed question of value-free versus normative science is, of course, a hotly debated issue in contemporary sociology, and one which shows no sign of abating in the near future. For more interesting discussions and exchanges, see Rose and Rose, 1976 and the companion volume edited by them, The Radicalization of Science, London: Macmillan, 1976; Marsha P. Hansen, et al., eds. Science, Pseudo-Science and Society, op.cit., Rita Arditti, et al., Science and Liberation, Black Rose Books, 1980; Michael Mulkay, Science and the Sociology of Knowledge, London: George Allen and Unwin, 1979; Russell Keat and J. Urry, Social Theory as Science, London: Routledge & Kegan Paul, 1975.

64. Popper, 1972, pp. 346-47.

65.   Hamilton, 1974, p. 33.

Adorno, Theodor W., et al.
1969   The Positivist Dispute in German Sociology
        (translated by Glyn Adey and David Frisby,
        1976). London: Heinemann.
Adam, Heribert
1971   Racial Discrimination. Berkeley: University
        of California Press.
Adams, Bert
1966   'Coercion and Consensus Theories: Some
        Unresolved Issues,' American Journal of
        Sociology, 71 (May): 714-17.
Agger, Ben
1977   'Dialectical Sensibility I: Critical Theory,
        Scientism and Empiricism,' Canadian Journal
        of Political and Social Theory, Vol. 1, #1
        (Winter): 1-34; and II, Vol. 1, #2 (Spring):
        47-57.
1975   'Science as Domination,' in Domination, (ed.)
        Alkis Kontos. Toronto: University of Toronto
        Press: 187-200.
Allen, V.L.
1975   Social Analysis: A Marxist Critique and
        Alternative. London: Longman.
Althusser, Louis
1969   For Marx. New York: Pantheon Books.
Anderson, Charles
1974   The Political Economy of Social Class.
        Englewood Cliffs, New Jersey: Prentice-Hall,
        Inc.
1971   Toward a New Sociology: A Critical View.
        Homewood, Ill.: The Dorsey Press.
Andreski, Stanislav
1964   Elements of Comparative Sociology. London:
        Weidenfeld and Nicolson.
Arato, Andrew and Eike Gebhardt
1978   The Essential Frankfurt School Reader. New
        York: Urizen Books.
Armistead, Nigel
1974   Reconstructing Social Psychology.
        Harmondsworth: Penguin.
Avineri, S.
1968   The Social and Political Thought of Karl Marx.
        Cambridge: At the University Press.
Babbie, Earl
1975   The Practice of Social Research (2nd ed.).
        Belmont, Calif.: Wadsworth Pub. Co. Inc.

Baker, Donald G.
  1977   'Ethnicity, Development and Power: Canada and
            Comparative Perspective,' in Wsevolod Isajiw,
            Identities. Toronto: Peter Martin, 109-131.
Baran, Paul
  1969   The Longer View: Essays Toward a Critique of
            Political Economy. New York: Monthly Review
            Press.
Bauman, Z.
  1973   'On the Philosophical Status of Ethno-
            methodology,' Sociological Review, Vol. 21,
            #1: 5-23.
Becker, Howard and I.L. Horowitz
  1972   'Radical Politics in Sociological Research:
            Observations on Methodology and Ideology,'
            American Journal of Sociology, Vol. 78 (July):
            48-66.
Becker, James
  1977   Marxian Political Economy: An Outline.
            London: Cambridge University Press.
Bendix, R.
  1960   Max Weber: An Intellectual Portrait.   New
            York: Doubleday and Co., Inc.
Berger, Peter and T. Luckmann
  1966   The Social Construction of Reality: A
            Treatise in the Sociology of Knowledge.   New
            York: Doubleday.
Berger, Peter and Stanley Pullberg
  1965   'Reification and the Sociological Critique of
            Consciousness,' History and Theory, Vol. 4,
            #2: 196-211.
Birnbaum, Norman
  1969   Crisis in Industrial Society. London: Oxford
            University Press.
  1977   Beyond the Crisis.   London: Oxford University
  (ed)   Press.
Blackburn, Robin
  1972   Ideology in Social Science: Readings in
            Critical Social Theory. London: Fontana.
Blau, Peter
  1975   Dynamics of Bureaucracy. Chicago: University
            of Chicago Press.
  1956   Bureaucracy in Modern Society. New York:
            Random House.
Blau, Peter and R. Scott
  1962   Formal Organizations. San Francisco:
            Chandler Press.

Blishen, Bernard
1971   Canadian Society: Sociological Perspectives
        (3rd ed.). Toronto: MacMillan of Canada.
Bottomore, Tom and Patrick Goode (eds. and trans.)
1978   Austro Marxism. London: Oxford University
        Press.
Bottomore, Tom and M. Rubel
1961   Karl Marx: Selected Writings in Sociology and
        Social Philosophy. Harmondsworth: Penguin
        Books Ltd.
Bredemeier, Harry C.
1973   'On the Complimentarity of "Partisan and
        Objective" Research,' American Behavioral
        Scientist, 17, #1 (Sept./Oct.): 125-141.
Breines, Paul (ed.)
1970   Critical Interruptions. New York: Herder and
        Herder.
Breton, Raymond
1974   'Ethnic Pluralism and Social Equality,' Human
        Relations, 14, 22 (December): 6-11. Toronto.
Broom, Leonard
1960   'Urbanization and the Plural Society,' Annals
        of the New York Academy of Sciences, 83, 5
        (January): 880-886.
Bruyn, Severyn
1966   The Human Perspective: The Methodology of
        Participant Observation. Englewood Cliffs,
        N.J.: Prentice-Hall, Inc.
Buckley, Walter
1967   Sociology and Modern Systems Theory.
        Englewood Cliffs, N.J.: Prentice-Hall, Inc.
Caplan, Gerald
1963   'The Failure of Canadian Socialism: The
        Ontario Experience, 1932-1945,' Canadian
        Historical Review, Vol. 44, #2 (June): 93-121.
Card, B.Y.
1968   Trends and Change in Canadian Society.
        Toronto: MacMillan of Canada.
Catton, William
1966   From Animism to Naturalistic Sociology. New
        York: McGraw-Hill Co.
Chamblis, William
1973   Sociological Readings in the Conflict
        Perspective Reading. Mass.: Addison-Wesley
        Publishing Co.
Ciccotti, Giovanni; Marcello Cini and Michelangelo de
Maria
1976   'The Production of Science in Advanced
        Capitalist Society,' in Rose and Rose, The

Political Economy of Science. London:
            MacMillan.
Clairmont, Donald and Dennis Magill
    1970   Nova Scotia Blacks: An Historical and
            Structural Overview. Halifax: Institute of
            Public Affairs.
Clark, S.D.
    1973   'The American Take Over of Canadian Sociology:
            Myth or Reality,' Dalhousie Review, (Summer):
            205-218.
    1962   The Developing Canadian Community. Toronto:
    (1968) University of Toronto Press.
Clement, Wallace
    1975   The Canadian Corporate Elite. Toronto:
            McClelland and Stewart.
Cohen, Percy
    1968   Modern Social Theory. London: Heinemann
            Books.
Cole, Robert
    1966   'Structural Functional Theory, the Dialectic
            and Social Change,' The Sociological
            Quarterly, Vol. 7, #1 (Winter): 39-57.
Colfax, J. David
    1971   'Varieties and Prospects of Radical
            Scholarship,' in J. David Colfax and Jack L.
            Roach (eds.), Radical Sociology. New York
            and London: Basic Books Inc.: 81-92.
Colfax, J. David and Jack Roach (eds.)
    1971   Radical Sociology. New York: Basic Books,
            Inc.
Connerton, Paul (ed.)
    1976   Critical Sociology. Harmondsworth: Penguin
            Books.
Cornforth, Maurice
    1968   The Open Philosophy and the Open Society.
            New York: International Publishers Co.
Coser, Lewis
    1975   'Presidential Address: Two Methods in Search
            of a Substance,' American Sociological Review,
            Vol. 40, #6 (Dec.): 691-700.
Cox, Oliver C.
    1971   'The Question of Pluralism,' Race, 12, #4
            (April): 385-400.
Cross, Malcolm
    1971   'On Conflict, Race, and the Theory of Plural
            Society,' Race, 12, #4 (April): 477-494.

1968   'Cultural Pluralism and Sociological Theory:
           a Critique and Re-evaluation,' Social and
           Economic Studies, 17, 4 (Dec.): 381-397.
Curtis, James E. and John Petras (eds.)
1970   The Sociology of Knowledge: A Reader.   New
           York: Praeger Publishers.
Curtis, James and William Scott (eds.)
1973   Social Stratification: Canada.   Toronto:
           Prentice-Hall of Canada.
Dahl, Robert
1967   Pluralist Democracy in the United States.
           Chicago: Rand McNally.
Dahrendorf, Ralf
1958   'Out of Utopia: Toward a Reorientation of
           Sociological Analysis,' American Journal of
           Sociology, (Sept.): 115-127.
Dallmayr, Fred
1972a   'Reason and Emancipation: Notes on Habermas,'
           Man and World, Vol. 5 (February): 79-109.
1972b   'Critical Theory Criticized: Habermas's
           Knowledge and Human Interests and its
           Aftermath,' Philosophy of Social Science,
           Vol. 2: 211-229.
Despres, Leo
1975   Ethnicity and Resource Competition in Plural
           Societies.   The Hague: Mouton Publishers.
1969   'Protest and Change in Plural Societies,'
           Montreal: McGill University Center for
           Developing Area Studies.
1967   Cultural Pluralism and Nationalist Politics
           in British Guiana.   Chicago: Rand McNally.
1964   'The Implications of Nationalist Politics in
           British Guiana for the Development of
           Cultural Theory,' American Anthropologist,
           Vol. 66, #3 (October): 1051-1077.
Deutsch, Steven and John Howard (eds.)
1970   Where It's At: Radical Perspectives in
           Sociology.   New York: Harper and Row.
Driedger, Leo (ed.)
1978   The Canadian Mosaic: A Quest for Identity.
           Toronto: McClelland and Stewart.
Drietzel, Hans
1972   'Social Science and the Problems of
           Rationality: Notes on the Sociology of
           Technocrats,' Politics and Society, Vol. 2,
           #2: 165-182.
Durkheim, Emile
1951   Suicide.   New York: The Free Press

1960   The Elementary Forms of the Religious Life. New York: The Free Press.

Eisenstadt, S.N.
1966   Modernization, Protest and Change. Englewood Cliffs, N.J.: Prentice-Hall.

Elliott, Jean E. (eds.)
1971   Native Peoples. Toronto: Prentice-Hall of Canada.

Emmett, Dorothy and Alasdair MacIntyre (eds.)
1970   Sociological Theory and Philosophical Analysis. New York: The MacMillan Co.

Engels, F.
1972   Anti-Duhring. New York: International Publishers Co.

1968   Socialism: Utopian and Scientific. New York: International Publishers Co.

1940   Dialectics of Nature. New York: International Publishers Co.

Farganis, James
1975   'A Preface to Critical Theory,' Theory and Society. Vol. 2, #4: 483-508.

Fay, Brian
1975   Social Theory and Political Practice. London: George Allan and Unwin Ltd.

Filmer, Paul; Michael Phillipson; David Silverman and David Walsh
1972   New Directions in Sociological Theory. Cambridge, Mass.: MIT Press.

Fischer, George (ed.)
1971   The Revival of American Socialism: Selected Papers of the Socialist Scholars Conference. New York: Oxford University Press.

Frank, Andre Gunder
1966   'Functionalism, Dialectics and Synthetics,' Science and Society, Vol. 30 (Spring).

Friedrich, Robert
1972   'Dialectical Sociology: Toward a Resolution of the Current "Crisis" in Western Sociology,' British Journal of Sociology, Vol. 23: 263-374.

Furfey, Paul H.
1959   'Sociological Science and the Problem of Values,' in L. Gross (ed.), Symposium on Sociological Theory. Evanston: Row Petersen & Co.: 509-530.

Furnivall, J.S.
1948   Colonial Theory and Practice. New York: University Press.

1946   'Political Education in the Far East,'
            Political Quarterly, Vol. 17: 123-32.
Giddens, Anthony
    1977   Studies in Social and Political Theory.
            Cambridge: The University Press.
    1976a   New Rules of Sociological Method. Hutchinson
            University Library.
    1976b   'Hermeneutics, Ethnomethodology, and Problems
            of Interpretive Analysis,' in Lewis Coser and
            Otto Larsen (eds.), The Uses of Controversy
            in Sociology. New York: The Free Press.
    1971   Capitalism and Modern Social Theory.
            Cambridge: The University Press.
Gidlow, Bob
    1972   'Ethnomethodology - a New Name for Old
            Practices,' The British Journal of Sociology,
            Vol. 23, #4: 395-405.
Gitlin, Todd
    1965   'Local Pluralism as Theory and Ideology,'
            Studies on the Left, Vol. 5, #3: 21-45.
Glazer, Nathan and D. Moynihan
    1975   Ethnicity: Theory and Experience. Cambridge,
            Mass.: Harvard University Press.
Goddard, David
    1972   'Anthropology: the Limits of Functionalism,'
            in Robin Blackburn (ed.), Ideology in Social
            Science. London: Fontana: 61-75.
Gonick, Cy
    1975   Inflation or Depression: The Continuing
            Crisis of the Canadian Economy. Toronto:
            James Lorimer and Co.
Gouldner, Alvin
    1976   The Dialectic of Ideology and Technology: the
            Origins, Grammar, and Future of Ideology.
            New York: The Seabury Press.
    1968   'The Sociologist as Partisan: Sociology and
            the Welfare State,' The American Sociologist,
            Vol. 3 (May): 103-116.
    1962   'Anti-monitaur: the Myth of Value-Free
            Sociology,' Social Problems, Vol. 9 (Winter):
            199-213.
Gray, David
    1968   'Value-Free Sociology: a Doctrine of Hypocrisy
            and Irresponsibility,' Sociological Quarterly,
            Vol. 9 (Spring): 179-185.
Habermas, Jurgen
    1974   Theory and Practice. London: Heinemann.

1969   'The Analytical Theory of Science and Dialectics,' in T. Adorno, et al., The Positivist Dispute in German Sociology. London: Heinemann.

1968a   Toward a Rational Society: Student Protest, Science and Politics. London: Heinemann.

1968b   Knowledge and Human Interests. Boston: Beacon Press.

Hackler, James
1968   'Predictors of Deviant Behavior: Norms vs. the Perceived Anticipation of Others,' Canadian Review of Sociology and Anthropology, Vol. 5 (May): 92-106.

Halle, Louis
1965   'Marx's Religious Drama,' Encounter, Vol. 25, #4 (Oct.): 29-37.

Hansen, Marsha P.; Margaret J. Osler and Robert G. Weyant (eds.)
1980   Science, Pseudo-Science and Society (published under the auspices of the Calgary Institute for the Humanities). Waterloo, Ont.: Wilfrid Laurier University Press.

Hamilton, Peter
1974   Knowledge and Social Structure: An Introduction to the Classical Argument in the Sociology of Knowledge. London: Routledge and Kegan Paul.

Harp, John and John Hofley
1971   Poverty in Canada. Toronto: Prentice-Hall of Canada.

Harris, Nigel
1968   Beliefs in Society: The Problem of Ideology. London: C.A. Watts.

Heap, James
1974   Everybody's Canada: The Vertical Mosaic Reviewed and Re-Examined. Toronto: Burns and MacEachern Ltd.

Heilbroner, Robert
1975   'Marxism, Psychoanalysis, and the Problem of a Unified Theory of Behavior,' Social Research, Vol. 42, #3 (Autumn): 414-432.

Held, David
1980   Introduction to Critical Theory. Los Angeles and Berkeley: University of California Press.

Henry, Frances
1973   Forgotten Canadians: The Blacks of Nova Scotia. Toronto: Longman Canada Ltd.

Hiller, Harry H.
1976   Canadian Society: A Sociological Analysis.
        Toronto: Prentice-Hall of Canada.
Hobsbawn, E.J.
1959   Primitive Rebels: Studies in Archaic Forms of
        Social Movement in the 19th and 20th
        Centuries. Manchester: University of
        Manchester Press.
Hofley, John R.
1971   'Problems and Perspectives in the Study of
        Poverty,' in John Harp and John R. Hofley
        (eds.), Poverty in Canada. Scarborough, Ont.:
        Prentice-Hall of Canada Ltd.: 101-115.
Homans, George
1967   The Nature of Social Science. New York:
        Harcourt Brace and World.
Horkheimer, Max
1974   Eclipse of Reason. New York: Seabury Press.
1972   Critical Theory. New York: Herder and Herder.
Horkheimer, Mas and T. Adorno
1972   Dialectic of Enlightenment. New York: Herder
        and Herder.
Horton, John
1966   'Order and Conflict Theories of Social
        Problems,' American Journal of Sociology,
        Vol. 71 (May): 701-713.
Horowitz, Irving L.
1968   'Social Science Objectivity and Value
        Neutrality: Historical Problems and
        Projections,' in I.L. Horowitz, Professing
        Sociology: Studies in the Life Cycle of
        Social Science. Chicago: Aldine Publishing
        Co.: 30-45.
Howard, Dick
1970   'On Marx's Critical Theory,' Telos, Vol. 6
        (Fall): 224-233.
Howard, John
1970   'Notes on the Radical Perspective in
        Sociology,' in Steven C. Deutsch and John
        Howard, Where It's At: Radical Perspectives
        in Sociology. New York: Harper and Row: 1-19.
Hyman, Richard
1971   Marxism and the Sociology of Trade Unionism.
        London: Pluto Press.
Ingleby, David
1972   'Ideology and the Human Sciences: Some
        Comments on the Role of Reification in
        Psychology and Psychiatry,' in Trevor Pateman
        (ed.), Counter Course. Harmondsworth: Penguin.

Israel, Joachim
 1971   Alienation: From Marx to Modern Sociology.
         Boston: Allyn and Bacon, Inc.
Jackson, John D.
 1966   'A Study of French-English Relations in an
         Ontario Community Towards a Conflict Model
         for the Analysis of Ethnic Relations,' Canada
         Review of Sociology and Anthropology, 3
         (August): 117-131.
Jacoby, Russell
 1975   Social Amnesia: A Critique of Contemporary
         Psychology from Adler to Laing. Boston:
         Beacon Press.
Jay, Martin
 1973   The Dialectical Imagination. Boston: Little
         Brown and Co.
Jones, Frank
 1971   'Some Social Consequences of Immigration for
         Canada,' in Bernard Blishen, et al., Canadian
         Society: Sociological Perspectives,: 426-432.
Katznelson, Ira
 1971   'Comparative Studies of Race and Ethnicity,'
         Comparative Politics, 5, #1 (Oct.): 135-54.
Keane, John
 1978   'The Legacy of Political Economy: Thinking
         With and Against Claus Offe,' Canadian
         Journal of Political and Social Theory, Vol.
         2, #3 (Fall): 49-92.
 1975a   'On Belaboring the Theory of Economic Crisis:
         A Reply to Laska,' New German Critique, Vol.
         4 (Winter): 125-130.
 1975b   'On Tools and Language: Habermas on Work and
         Interaction,' New German Critique, Vol. 6
         (Fall): 82-100.
Keat, Russell
 1981   The Politics of Social Theory: Habermas,
         Freud and the Critique of Positivism.
         Chicago: Chicago University Press.
Kline, Stephen and William Leiss
 1978   'Advertising, Needs and Commodity Fetishism,'
         Canadian Journal of Political and Social
         Theory, Vol. 2, #1 (Winter): 5-30.
Kolko, Gabriel
 1959   'A Critique of Max Weber's Philosophy of
         History,' Ethics, Vol. 70, #1: 21-36.
Kornberg, Allen and Alan Tharp
 1972   'The American Impact on Canadian Political
         Science and Sociology,' in Richard A. Preston
         (ed.), The Influence of the United States on

on Canadian Development: Eleven Case Studies.
Durham: Duke University Press.

Kornhauser, William
  1959   The Politics of Mass Society. New York: The
          Free Press.

Kovel, Joel
  1976   'Marx's View of Man and Psychoanalysis,'
          Social Research, Vol. 43, #2 (Summer): 220-
          245.

Krauter, Joseph F. and Morris Davis
  1978   Minority Canadians: Ethnic Groups. Toronto:
          Methuen.

Kuhn, Thomas
  1962   The Structure of Scientific Revolutions.
          Chicago: University of Chicago Press.

Kuper, Leo
  1971   'Political Change in Plural Societies:
          Problems in Racial Pluralism,' International
          Social Science Journal, Vol. 23, #4: 594-607.
  1969a   'Plural Societies Perspectives Problems,' in
          Kuper and Smith, Pluralism in Africa.
          Berkeley: University of California Press.
  1969b   'Ethnic and Rural Pluralism: Some Aspects of
          Polarization and Depluralization,' in Kuper
          and Smith, Pluralism in Africa. Berkeley:
          University of California Press.

Kuper, Leo and M.G. Smith
  1969   Pluralism in Africa. Berkeley: University of
          California Press.

Lefebvre, Henri
  1969   The Sociology of Marx. New York: Vintage
          Books.

Leiss, William
  1974a   'Critical Theory and its Future,' Political
          Theory, Vol. 2, #3 (August): 330-349.
  1974b   The Domination of Nature. Boston: Beacon
          Press.
  1972   'The Critical Theory of Society: Present
          Situation and Future Task,' in Paul Breines
          (ed.), Critical Interruptions. New York:
          Herder and Herder: 74-100.

Lichtheim, George
  1974   From Marx to Hegel. New York: Seabury Press.
  1961   Marxism. London: Routledge and Kegan Paul.

Lipset, Seymour M.
  1963   Political Man. Garden City, N.Y.: Doubleday.
  1959   Agrarian Socialism. Berkeley: University of
          California Press.

Loewith, Karl
  1970   'Weber's Interpretation of the Bourgeois-
           Capitalist World in Terms of the Guiding
           Principle of "Rationalization",' in Dennis
           Wrong (ed.), Max Weber. Englewood Cliffs,
           N.J.: Prentice-Hall.

Lukács, Georg
  1971   History and Class Consciousness. Cambridge,
           Mass.: MIT Press.

Lundberg, George
  1963   'The Postulates of Science and Their
           Implications for Sociology,' in Maurice
           Nathanson (ed.), Philosophy of the Social
           Sciences. New York: Random House.
  1955   'The Natural Science Trend in Sociology,'
           American Journal of Sociology, Vol. 61, #3:
           191-202.

Lyman, Stanford and Marvin B. Scott
  1970   A Sociology of the Absurd. New York:
           Appleton-Century-Crofts.

Lynd, Robert
  1939   Knowledge for What? Princeton: Princeton
           University Press.

Mack, Raymond
  1965   'The Components of Social Conflict,' Social
           Problems, 12 (Spring): 388-95.

MacPherson, C.B.
  1953   Democracy in Alberta. Toronto: University of
           Toronto Press.

Mann, Michael
  1970   'The Social Cohesion of Liberal Democracies,'
           American Sociological Review, Vol. 35, #3
           (June): 423-39.

Mann, W.E.
  1971a   Canada: A Sociological Profile. Toronto:
           Copp Clark.
  1971b   Social Deviance in Canada. Toronto: Copp
           Clark.
  1970a   Social and Cultural Change in Canada, 2 Vols.
           Toronto: Copp Clark.
  1970b   Poverty and Social Policy in Canada. Toronto:
           Copp Clark.

Mannheim, Karl
  1952   Essays in the Sociology of Knowledge, edited
           by Paul Kecskemeti. London: Routledge and
           Kegan Paul.

1936   Ideology and Utopia: An Introduction to the
Sociology of Knowledge. London: Routledge
and Kegan Paul.

Marchak, M. Patricia
1981   Ideological Perspectives on Canada. Toronto:
McGraw-Hill Ryerson.

Marcuse, Herbert
1970   Five Lectures. Boston: Beacon Press.
1969   An Essay on Liberation. Boston: Beacon Press.
1968   Negations: Essays in Critical Theory. Boston:
Beacon Press.
1964   One Dimensional Man: Studies in the Ideology
of Advanced Industrial Society. Boston:
Beacon Press.
1962   Eros and Civilization. Boston: Beacon Press.
1960   Reason and Revolution: Hegel and the Rise of
Social Theory. Boston: Beacon Press.

Marx, Karl
n.d.   Capital, Vol. I. Moscow: Progress Publishers.
1973   The Grundrisse, translated with a foreword by
Martin Nicolaus. Harmondsworth: Penguin
Books.
1971a   Capital, Vol. II. Moscow: Progress
Publishers.
1971b   Capital, Vol. III. Moscow: Progress
Publishers.
1971c   A Contribution to the Critique of Political
(1904)   Economy. London: Lawrence and Wishart.
1964   The Economic and Philosophical Manuscripts of
1844. New York: International Publishers.
1963a   The Poverty of Philosophy. New York: International Publishers Co. Inc.
1963b   The Eighteenth Brumaire of Louis Bonaparte.
New York: International Publishers Co. Inc.

Marx, Karl and F. Engels
1965   Selected Correspondence, 2nd ed. Moscow:
Progress Publishers.
1956   The Holy Family or Critique of Critical
Criticism. Moscow: Progress Publishers.
1947   The German Ideology. New York: International
Publishers Co. Inc.

Marković, Mahailo
1974   The Contemporary Marx. Nottingham: Spokesman
Books.
1972   'The Problem of Reification and the Verstehen-
erklären Controversy,' Acta Sociologica, Vol.
15: 27-38.

Mayrl, William
    1973   'Ethnomethodology: Sociology Without Society,'
            Catalyst, Vol. 7: 15-28.
McCarthy, Thomas
    1978   The Critical Theory of Jurgen Habermas.
            Cambridge, Mass.: MIT Press.
McKinney, J. and E. Tiryakian
    1970   Theoretical Sociology. New York: Appleton-
            Century Crofts.
McNall, Scott
    1978   'On Contemporary Social Theory,' The American
            Sociologist, Vol. 13 (Feb.): 2-6.
McNall, Scott and James C.M. Johnson
    1975   'The New Conservatives: Ethnomethodologists,
            Phenomenologists and Symbolic Interactionists,'
            The Insurgent Sociologist, Vol. 5; #4 (Summer):
            49-65.
Mehan, Hugh and Houston Wood
    1975   'The Morality of Ethnomethodology,' Theory &
            Society, Vol. 2, #4 (Winter): 509-530.
Merton, Robert
    1972   'Insiders and Outsiders,' a chapter in the
            Sociology of Knowledge, American Journal of
            Sociology, Vol. 78 (July): 9-47.
Mészáros, Istvan
    1972   'Ideology and Social Science,' The Socialist
            Register, ed. R. Miliband and J. Saville.
            London: Merlin Press: 35-81.
Meyer, Alfred
    1976   'The Aufhebung of Marxism,' Social Research,
            Vol. 43, #2 (Summer): 199-219.
Mills, C. Wright
    1959   The Sociological Imagination. New York:
            Oxford University Press.
    1958   The Causes of World War Three. New York:
            Ballantine Books.
    1943   'The Professional Ideology of Social
            Pathologists,' American Journal of Sociology,
            49 (September): 165-180.
    1940   'The Methodological Consequences of the
            Sociology of Knowledge,' American Journal of
            Sociology, Vol. 46, #3: 316-330.
Mueller, Claus
    1973   The Politics of Communication: A Study in the
            Political Sociology of Language,
            Socialization, and Legitimation. London:
            Oxford University Press.

Myrdal, Gunnar
1969   Objectivity in Social Research. New York:
        Patheon Books.
1944   An American Dilemma. New York: Harper & Row.
Newman, William
1973   American Pluralism: A Study of Minority
        Groups and Social Theory. New York: Harper
        and Row.
Nicolaus, Martin
1972   'The Unknown Marx,' in Robin Blackburn (ed.),
        Ideology in Social Science: Readings in
        Critical Social Theory. London: Fontana/
        Collins: 306-333.
1971   'The Crisis of Late Capitalism,' in George
        Fischer (ed.), The Revival of American
        Socialism. New York: Oxford University Press.
1967   'Proletariat and Middle Class in Marx:
        Hegelian Choreography and the Capitalist
        Dialectic,' Studies on the Left, Vol. 1,
        (Jan.-Feb.): 23-49.
Offe, Claus
1976   Industry and Inequality. London: Edward
        Arnold.
O'Neill, John
n.d.   'On Theory and Criticism in Marx,' in Paul
        Walton and Stuart Hall (eds.), Situating Marx:
        Evaluations and Departures. London: Human
        Context Books: 72-97.
1976   On Critical Theory. New York: Seabury Press.
(ed)
Ossenberg, Richard
1971   Canadian Society: Pluralism, Change, and
        Conflict. Toronto: Prentice-Hall.
1967   'The Conquest Revisited: Another Look at
        Canadian Dualism,' Canadian Review of
        Sociology and Anthropology, Vol. 4, #4: 201-
        208.
Papineau, David
1978   For Science in the Social Sciences. London:
        MacMillan.
Pareto, Vilfredo
1935   The Mind and Society. New York: Harcourt
        Brace and Co.
Parsons, Talcott
1967   Sociological Theory and Modern Society. New
        York: The Free Press.
1951   The Social System. New York: The Free Press.
1937   The Structure of Social Action. New York:
        The Free Press.

Phillips, Derek
  1974   'Epistemology and the Sociology of Knowledge,'
           Theory and Society, Vol. 1: 59-88.
Piccone, Paul
  1976   'From Tragedy to Farce: The Return of
           Critical Theory,' New German Critique, Vol. 7:
           91-104.
Pinard, Maurice
  1970   'Working Class Politics: An Interpretation of
           the Quebec Case,' Canadian Review of
           Sociology and Anthropology, Vol. 7, #2 (May):
           87-109.
Plamenatz, John
  1970   Ideology. London: MacMillan.
Polsby, Nelson
  1963   Community Power and Political Theory. New
           Haven: Yale University Press.
Porter, John
  1975a   'Foreword,' in Wallace Clement, Canadian
           Corporate Elite.
  1975b   'Ethnic Pluralism in Canada,' in Nathan
           Glazer and Daniel P. Moynihan (eds.),
           Ethnicity: Theory and Experience. Cambridge,
           Mass.: Harvard University Press: 267-304.
  1972   'Dilemmas and Contradictions of a Multi-
           Ethnic Society,' Transaction of the Royal
           Society of Canada, Series 4, Vol. 10: 193-204.
  1965   The Vertical Mosaic: An Analysis of Social
           Class and Power in Canada. Toronto:
           University of Toronto Press.
Popper, Karl
  1972   Objective Knowledge: An Evolutionary Approach.
           London: Oxford University Press.
  1965   The Logic of Scientific Discovery. New York:
           Harper & Row.
  1963   Conjectures and Refutations. London:
           Routledge and Kegan Paul.
  1961   The Poverty of Historicism. London:
           Routledge and Kegan Paul.
  1945   The Open Society and its Enemies, Vol. II.
           London: Routledge and Kegan Paul.
Presthus, Robert
  1964   Men at the Top: A Study of Community Power.
           New York: Oxford University Press.
Preston, Richard (ed.)
  1972   The Influence of the United States on
           Canadian Development: Eleven Case Studies.
           Durham: Duke University Press.

Quinton, Anthony
  1974   'Critical Theory: On the Frankfurt School,'
            Encounter, Vol. 43 (Oct.): 43-53.
Rex, John
  1974   Sociology and the Demystification of the
            Modern World. London: Routledge and Kegan
            Paul.
  1973a   Discovering Sociology. London: Routledge and
            Kegan Paul.
  1973b   Race, Colonialism and the City. London:
            Routledge and Kegan Paul.
  1970   Race Relations in Sociological Theory.
            London: Weidenfield and Nicolson.
Richmond, Anthony
  1969   'Immigration and Pluralism in Canada,'
            International Migration Review, Vol. 4, #1
            (Fall): 5-24.
Ritzer, George
  1975a   'Sociology: A Multiple Paradigm Science,' The
            American Sociologist, Vol. 10 (August): 156-
            167.
  1975b   Sociology: A Multiple Paradigm Science.
            Boston: Allyn and Bacon.
Rose, Arnold
  1956   'Sociology and the Study of Values,' British
            Journal of Sociology, 9 (March): 1-18.
Rose, Hilary and Steven Rose
  1976   The Political Economy of Science. London:
            MacMillan.
Rossides, Daniel
  1968   Society as a Functional Process: An
            Introduction to Sociology. Toronto: McGraw-
            Hill Co.
Rytina, Joan H. and Charles P. Loomis
  1970   'Marxist Dialectic and Pragmatism: Power as
            Knowledge,' American Sociological Review, 35,
            #2 (April): 312.
Saran, A.K.
  1963   'The Marxian Model of Social Change,' Inquiry,
            6: 70-128.
Sallach, David
  1973   'Critical Theory and Critical Sociology: The
            Second Synthesis,' Sociological Inquiry, 43,
            #2: 131-40.
Schermerhorn, Richard
  1970   Comparative Ethnic Relations: A Framework for
            Theory and Research. New York: Random House.

Schroyer, Trent
   1973   The Critique of Domination: The Origins and
            Development of Critical Theory. New York:
            George Braziller.
   1970   'Toward a Critical Theory for Advanced
            Industrial Society,' in Hans Peter Dreitzel
            (ed.), Recent Sociology, #2. London:
            MacMillan Ltd.
Seeley, John R.; Alexander Sim and Elizabeth W. Loosley
   1956   Crestwood Height: A Study of the Culture of
            Suburban Life. Toronto: University of
            Toronto Press.
Selznick, Philip
   1943   'An Approach to a Theory of Bureaucracy,'
            American Sociological Review, 8: 47-54.
Shapiro, Jeremy
   1974   'The Critical Theory of Frankfurt,' The Times
            Literary Supplement. London (Oct.): 4.
   1970   'One Dimensionality: The Universal Semiotic
            of Technological Experience,' in Paul Breines
            (ed.), Critical Interruptions. New York:
            Herder and Herder: 136-186.
Shils, Edward
   1956   The Torment of Secrecy. London: Heinemann.
Sills, David
   1957   The Volunteers. New York: Free Press.
Silverman, David
   1972   'Introductory Comments,' in Paul Filmer, et
            al., New Directions in Sociological Theory.
            Cambridge, Mass.: MIT Press: 1-12.
Soloman, Albert
   1934   'Max Weber's Methodology,' Social Research,
            Vol. 1.
Smith, M.G.
   1969   'Institutional and Political Conditions of
            Pluralism,' in Kuper and Smith (eds.),
            Pluralism in Africa. Berkeley: University of
            California Press.
   1965   The Plural Society in the British West Indies.
            Berkeley: University of California Press.
   1960   'Social and Cultural Pluralism,' in Annals of
            the New York Academy of Science, Vol. 83
            (Jan.): 763-777.
Smith, R.T.
   1962   British Guiana. London: Oxford University
            Press.
Stark, Werner
   1958   The Sociology of Knowledge. London:
            Routledge and Kegan Paul.

Supek, Rudi
1977   'The Visible Hand and the Degradation of
        Individuality,' in Norman Birnbaum (ed.),
        Beyond the Crisis: 49-80.
Swingewood, Alan
1975   Marx and Modern Social Theory. London:
        Macmillan.
Szymanski, Albert
1971   'Toward a Radical Sociology,' in J. David
        Colfax and Jack L. Roach (eds.), Radical
        Sociology. New York: Basic Books Inc.: 93-
        107.
Taylor, Ian; Paul Walton and Jock Young
1973   The New Criminology: For a Social Theory of
        Deviance. London: Routledge and Kegan Paul.
Teeple, Gary
1972   Capitalism and the National Question in
        Canada. Toronto: University of Toronto Press.
Tiryakian, Edward
1970   'Structural Sociology,' in J. McKinney and E.
        Tiryakian (eds.), Theoretical Sociology. New
        York: Appleton-Century Crofts: 111-135.
1962   Sociologism and Existentialism. Englewood
        Cliffs, N.J.: Prentice-Hall.
Turk, Austin T.
1979   'Analyzing Official Deviance for Nonpartisan
        Conflict Analyses in Criminology,'
        Criminology, Vol. 16 (February): 459-476.
1969   Criminality and Legal Order. Chicago: Rand
        McNally.
Vallee, Frank and Donald R. Whyte
1971   'Canadian Society, Trends and Perspectives,'
        in B. Blishen, et al., Canadian Society:
        Sociological Perspectives. Toronto:
        MacMillan of Canada: 556-575.
van den Berghe, Pierre
1976   'The African Diaspora in Mexico, Brazil and
        the United States,' Social Forces, Vol. 54,
        #3 (March): 330-45.
1973   'Pluralism,' in J.J. Honigman (ed.), Handbook
        of Social and Cultural Anthropology. Chicago:
        Rand McNally: 959-977.
1967a   Race and Racism: A Comparative Perspective.
        New York: Wiley.
1967b   South Africa: A Study in Conflict. Berkeley:
        University of California Press.
1964   'Toward a Sociology of Africa,' Social Forces,
        43, #1 (Oct.): 11-18.

1963   'Dialectic and Functionalism: Toward a Theoretical Synthesis,' American Sociological Review, Vol. 28 (Oct.): 695-705.

Walsh, David
   1972a   'Sociology and the Social World,' in Paul Filmer, et al., New Directions in Sociological Theory. Cambridge, Mass.: MIT Press: 15-35.

   1972b   'Varieties of Positivism,' in Paul Filmer, et al., New Directions in Sociological Theory. Cambridge, Mass.: MIT Press: 37-55.

   1972c   'Functionalism and Systems Theory,' in Paul Filmer, et al., New Directions in Sociological Theory. Cambridge, Mass.: MIT Press: 57-74.

Walton, Paul
   1970   'Philosophical Anthropology in Marxism,' Social Research, Vol. 37, #2 (Summer): 259-274.

Walton, Paul and S. Hall (eds.)
   n.d.   Situating Marx: Evaluations and Departures. London: Human Context Books.

Watson, G. Llewellyn
   1975   'The Sociological Relevance of the Concept of Half-Caste in British Society,' Phylon, Vol. 36, #3 (Sept.): 309-320.

   1973   'Social Structure and Social Movements: The Black Muslims of the U.S.A. and the Ras-Tafarians in Jamaica,' British Journal of Sociology, 24 (June): 88-204.

Weber, Max
   1954   Law in Economy and Society. Cambridge, Mass.: Harvard University Press.

   1948   From Max Weber: Essays in Sociology. London: Routledge and Kegan Paul.

   1947   The Theory of Social and Economic Organization, trans. by A.M. Henderson and Talcott Parsons. New York: The Free Press.

   1930   The Protestant Ethic and the Spirit of Capitalism. London: Unwin University Books.

   1927   General Economic History. New York: Greenberg.

Wellmer, Albrecht
   1976   'Communication and Emancipation: Reflections on the Linguistic Turn in Critical Theory,' in O'Neill (ed.), On Critical Theory. New York: Seabury Press: 231-263.

   1971   Critical Theory of Society. New York: Seabury Press.

Westhues, Kenneth
1972   Society's Shadow: Studies in the Sociology of
        Counter Cultures. Toronto: McGraw-Hill
        Ryerson Ltd.
Wheatcroft, Les
1971   'Something's Happening Here: Trends and
        Counter-Trends in Canadian Society,' in W.
        Mann (ed.), Canada: A Sociological Profile.
        Toronto: Copp Clark: 545-558.
Whyte, Donald
1965   'Sociological Aspects of Poverty: A
        Conceptual Analysis,' Canadian Review of
        Sociology and Anthropology, 2 (Nov.): 175-189,
        reprinted in Harp & Hofley.
Wilson, H.T.
1976   'Science, Critique and Criticism,' in John
        O'Neill (ed.), On Critical Theory. New York:
        Seabury Press: 205-230.
Winch, Peter
1958   The Idea of Social Science and its Relation
        to Philosophy. London: Routledge and Kegan
        Paul.
Wolf, C.P.
1970   'Foreword,' in James Coleman, Amitai Etzioni
        and John Porter, Macrosociology: Research and
        Theory. Boston: Allyn and Bacon: xi-xx.
Wolff, Kurt (ed.)
1971   From Karl Mannheim. New York: Oxford
        University Press.
Worsley, Peter
1968   The Trumpet Shall Sound: A Study of "Cargo"
        Cults in Melanesia. New York: Schocken.
Wrong, Dennis
1964   'Social Inequality Without Stratification,'
        Canadian Review of Sociology and Anthropology,
        1 (Feb.): 5-16.
Zetterberg, Hans
1965   On Theory and Verification in Sociology.
        Totowa: Bedminster Press.
1962   Social Theory and Social Practice. Totowa:
        Bedminster Press.
Zijderveld, Anton
1970   The Abstract Society: A Cultural Analysis of
        Our Time. New York: Doubleday.

304

Ideology, counter-, 8; dominant, 3, 8, 9, 30, 154, 205, 223; end of, 95; failure of, 205; of growth, 253-4; liberal, 5, 6, 9, 10, 82, 126, 141, 152; (of free enterprize), 145; Mannheim's conception of, 7, 8; Marxian critique of, 204-206; and mystification, 3, 4; para-, 158; ruling class, 113, 156, 157, 205, 223; and science, 1, 7, 10
Inflation, psychology of, 156
Integration, in plural societies, 174, 188-9
Intellectuals, role of, 7, 10
Intelligentsia, Mannheimian, 12, 207, 208
Irrationality, of capitalism, 141, 143

Knowledge: critique of, 203, 256; and existence, 7, 8, 209; fragmentation of, 152, 159, 224; industry, 3, 218; recipe-, 219; situational determinants of, 201-209, 222; sociology of, 2, 12, 19, 46, 47, 50, 113, 178, 186-87, 190, 191, 197-229; and truth, 11, 12, 211

Labor (human): 81, 83; alienated, 83-84; (power) as a commodity, 79-80, 91, 102, 110; cheap in the Third World, 149; dialectics of, 77-82; ontological centrality of, 14, 78-87, 202; as a source of wealth, 148, 149
Labor-process, Marx on, 25, 78-82, 84
Labor-theory, of value, 26-27, 148, 255
Legitimacy, in liberal

democracy, 219-20
Legitimation, crises of, 143, 147, 246

Marx, K., against Feuerbach, 76, 91, 98; against Hegel, 76, 78, 85-87, 98; against Proudhon, 98
Marxism (Marxian analysis), 13-18, 29, 131
Marxists, cultural, 2, 249, 254
Materialism, monistic, 71; critical, 113
Minority, sociological conception of, 175

Negativity, 68, 86, 96, 141-142; in Hegel's theory (see contradiction)
Neutrality, in politics, 161
Noumenal realm (Kantian), 72, 236

Ombudsman, Canadian Broadcasting Corporation, 157-158
Ontology, xv-xvi; Feuerbach's static, 77; of labor, 83; Marxian, 84, 90, 93-95; one-sided, of Left-Hegelians, 201
Ontological assumptions, in Marx, 94; of Marx and Freud, 29; social theory, 260
Opportunity, equality of, 184, 185
Optimism, in Marcuse, 117, 118
Overproduction (in capitalism), 141, 142, 248, 253

Paradigms, and political factors, 4, 215, 259
Pessimism, of critical theorists, 117, 242, 244, 251, 252, 257; in Weber, 124-125
Phenomenal realm (Kantian), 72, 236

309

Phenomenology of work,
Marxian, 81, 99
Philosophical, view of human
(Marxian), 84, 89, 90;
anti-, orientation of
North American sociology,
273n
Philosophy, and sociology,
xv-xvi, xvii, 10, 40, 41
Pluralism, xix; and
comparative sociology,
171; two conceptions of,
172-177; defined, 172;
as "indirect rule," 184;
social/cultural, 173;
local, 176, 177; socio-
cultural, 60, 171-191
Pluralists, political, 175-76
Polemics, intellectual, xiii-
xiv
Political economy, classical
theorists of, 80-81, 201;
critique of, 38, 90, 166,
247; and critical theory,
234-5, 247
Politics, scientization of,
132, 161, 164, 165, 258
Poverty, and stratification
in Canada, 43
Powerlessness, institutionalization of, 155
Praxis, Hegelian idea of, 67,
73, 86, 202; and
reflexivity, 67; as self-
creating process, 203;
transformative, in Marx,
103, 113
Production, anarchy of, 85,
86, 142; rationalized
form of, 142, 143
Profit, rate of, 145;
surplus, 146; and
working class rebellion,
145, 146
Proletariat, as universal
class, 146, 150
Protest, as a political
resource, 153; absorbed
by instrumental

rationality, 248; used for
profit, 238
Psychoanalytic paradigm, 27, 30,
257, 258; Habermas's interpretation of, 27, 28;
Marcuse's view of, 26, 27;
major objections to, 30 ff.

Rationalism, Cartesian, 72;
critical, 201
Rationality: bureaucratic, 161;
computational, 118-120;
economic, 118, 121;
exchange, 159; formal, 100,
107-111, 141, 162;
inevitability of, 122;
instrumental, 114-117, 125,
130, 134, 159, 248;
procedural, 160; scientific,
239; substantive, 100, 107-
110, 160-162; technological,
120, 161, 255
Rationalization: Habermas's
objection to, 114-115;
Marcuse's objection to, 114-
115; of the modern world,
108, 110, 111; in Weber,
107-111, 162
Reality, problematic nature of,
40, 41, 47, 270
Reason, 7, 14; in critical
theory, 120, 237, 239, 240,
254; instrumental, 121, 130
Reification, xviii, 102, 109,
113, 117, 124, 125-134, 162,
164, 166, 244; and
alienation, 54; and sociology of knowledge, 204
Relativism (relationalism), 207-
208

Science: aim of, 49; and
domination, 246; and
explanation, 44; and ideology, 10, 267; instru-
mental use of, 115, 118-120,
234; normal, xviii, 69;
normative quality of, 265,
266; sociology of, 264-266;

310

ABOUT THE AUTHOR

G. Llewellyn Watson took degrees in social
sciences and sociology at the Universities of York,
England, and Guelph. He also studied at the University
of Alberta, Edmonton. His research interests include
social theory and modern society; social movements; and
minority and ethnic relations, and he has published
several articles in these fields. He is currently
Associate Professor of Sociology at the University of
Prince Edward Island, Canada.